THE COLLECTED LETTERS OF
JOHN MILLINGTON SYNGE

VOLUME TWO

1907–1909

Already published
THE COLLECTED LETTERS OF JOHN MILLINGTON SYNGE
Volume One: 1871-1907

THE COLLECTED
LETTERS OF
JOHN MILLINGTON
SYNGE

EDITED BY

ANN SADDLEMYER

VOLUME TWO

1907–1909

CLARENDON PRESS · OXFORD

1984

Oxford University Press, Walton Street, Oxford OX2 6DP

London New York Toronto
Delhi Bombay Calcutta Madras Karachi
Kuala Lumpur Singapore Hong Kong Tokyo
Nairobi Dar es Salaam Cape Town
Melbourne Auckland

and associated companies in
Beirut Berlin Ibadan Mexico City Nicosia

Oxford is a trade mark of Oxford University Press

Published in the United States
by Oxford University Press, New York

British Library Cataloguing in Publication Data
Synge, J. M.
The collected letters of John Millington
Synge.
Vol. 2: 1907–1909
1. Synge, J. M. — Biography   2. Dramatists,
English — 19th century — Biography
I. Title   II. Saddlemyer, Ann
822'.912   PR5535
ISBN 0-19-812689-1

Typeset by Hope Services, Abingdon
and printed in Great Britain
at the Alden Press, Oxford

To Joan

CONTENTS

ILLUSTRATIONS
in the text

INTRODUCTION

THE last twenty-one months of Synge's life, while marking a slow decline into an early death, provide ample proof of Yeats's later image of him as 'the best labourer . . . And all the sheaves to bind'.[1] In these letters, from 1 July 1907 to 19 February 1909, just five weeks before his death at thirty-eight, we see Synge as director of plays, business manager, art critic, and literary man-about-town. Confident in his own powers, with the rows over *The Playboy of the Western World* behind him and a world reputation steadily increasing, his life revolved more and more around the theatre and the work he and Molly Allgood shared.

Although the first letters in this volume are written from the Wicklow retreat where he and Molly idyllically planned an autumn wedding, they are appropriately to Lady Gregory on theatre business, reporting on the cast that would figure so prominently in the next crises at the Abbey: Miss Horniman, Frank and Willie Fay, the theatre's secretary W. A. Henderson. Sounding also, though still distantly, is the contrapuntal theme which will eventually take over: 'I have play ideas at the back of my mind but I'm not doing anything yet, as I want to get well first' (12 July 1907). The struggle towards health necessitated an operation at Elpis Nursing Home in September, for removal at last of the swollen glands in his neck; a recuperative visit to Kerry was cut short by an asthma attack. Back in Dublin he plunged into Abbey affairs: Willie Fay's stormy relationship with his employers on the one hand, and with the players on the other, erupted with greater force than anyone expected, and Synge, the only director on the spot, bore the brunt of intercession. Standing as he did between his fellow directors and the company, he was a sensitive recorder of individual reactions, and although the results of his mediation may not always have been satisfactory to Yeats and Lady Gregory, he evidently enjoyed the role and commanded respect. Finally, when the Fays departed from the Abbey in early January 1908, he took up the threads of his personal life, moving in to Rathmines in preparation for marriage, seething with the excitement of creating his new play, *Deirdre of the Sorrows*, tinkering with essays for a book on Wicklow and Kerry, writing poetry. But playwriting and theatre business — he

---

1 'To a Child Dancing in the Wind' (1912).

shared the administrative tasks with Yeats and the stage management with Sara Allgood — were cut short once again by ill health,
'queer pains in my inside'. After an exploratory operation on 5 May,
again at Elpis, the letters sound a darker tone as he struggles once
more with plans for work and marriage, neither he nor Molly aware
that the doctors had discovered an inoperable tumour.

The months of convalescence at his sister's home, wearied further
because he and Molly had even less privacy, were shadowed by
reports of Mrs Synge's ill health as she spent the summer in County
Wicklow; when he left for Koblenz in October 1908 to recover at
the home of his old friends the von Eicken sisters, he did not realize
that his mother was on the point of death. She died on 26 October,
and the winter months in Glendalough House after his sad return
were all the more poignant for her loss and the brooding presence
of the furnishings he and Molly had so happily gathered in antici-
pation of making a home together. Finally, on 2 February, he re-
entered Elpis, taking with him the unfinished manuscript of *Deirdre
of the Sorrows*; he died there at 5.30 a.m. on 24 March 1909.

Synge's concentration on Dublin and the Abbey Theatre in these
last years inevitably brought a realignment of friendships. This
second volume contains fewer letters recalling the friendships of
earlier years: remaining are the von Eickens alone in Germany;
only Stephen MacKenna and Synge's cousin Edward Synge from the
Paris years; John Masefield and Jack Yeats in England; Florence
Ross steadfast alongside his mother within the family circle; the
Aran Islanders only in anecdote. Europe now means translators
(Karel Mušek and Max Meyerfeld); critical support the enthusiastic,
demanding idolatry of Henri Lebeau, the Australian journalist Leon
Brodzky, the American poet and critic Louis Untermeyer. Other
friendships are with fellow artists — John Martin Harvey, James
Paterson, Charles Ricketts, Robert Gregory — and that heavyweight
patron, John Quinn. In Dublin Synge enjoys the comradeship of
Richard Best, W. K. Magee, Hugh Lane, and most of all John Butler
Yeats, while earlier supporters — Maud Gonne, D. J. O'Donoghue,
Padraic Colum — are banished to the camp of the enemy. Most
important, as the bond with Molly strengthens, his relationship
with his family weakens.

Watchful and concerned as always, Mrs Synge wrote to her oldest
son Robert on 16 March 1908, six weeks after Synge's move to
Rathmines:

Johnnie has not been to see me since so I wrote to him, I advised him not to
marry in a hurry but to wait until he had some more certain income. He writes
to me, received today, to say that he feels his situation very difficult in regard

to money but he thinks he will marry soon, as he cannot go on walking with Mollie and having her to see him much longer or people would talk scandal which is indeed quite true. I know you feel kindly towards poor J so I tell you this, but I wont tell Ned [her second son, Edward]or Annie [her daughter, Mrs Harry Stephens]. She is very hard in her way of speaking of him . . . . She does not sympathise as she used . . . . Ned is kind and sympathetic but he knows Johnnie very little, and has never tried to be brotherly to him, such a pity, I have always deplored it . . . . I am very lonely, feeling that Johnnie is gone, who I have had so long to look after.   (TCD)

Finally, reconciled to the inevitable, she wrote again to Robert on 14 April,

Johnnie said he thought they would be married in St. Mary's Parish Church as she lives in the parish. I was very glad to hear that as it is much nicer than the Registry and I hope it may be a good sign that his mind has become more enlightened. I asked no questions but I gave him some information and advice — he has been so busy with the theatre work he has left himself very little time to make any arrangements. The company has a few days holiday at Easter so he wants to avail himself of that but I doubt very much that he can manage it so quickly, because he did not begin in time. Annie has no sympathy in the matter so I don't talk to her. The boys [Annie's sons] are kind and sympathetic — Ned is kind but he has such a horror of Johnnie marrying on such small means I am afraid to say anything to him.   (TCD)

Ironically, Mrs Synge's death and her son's final illness brought the family closer together again. Two letters exist from Annie Stephens to 'Miss Allgood' on tour in Manchester, 17 and 19 February 1909 (TCD), reporting on her brother's condition and family visits to Elpis; she wrote again after Synge's death, 'My dear Molly', urging her to visit Silchester House (TCD). Predictably Robert Synge's correspondence is warmer; on 27 March 1909 he replied to Molly's letter of sympathy, at the same time arranging to meet over the will: 'During the past terrible weeks I have often thought of what you must have suffered. It has nearly broken my heart to see him failing day by day, our sorrow is indeed great, but yours is heavier still.' (TCD)

Synge's final illness also brought a change in the attitudes of Yeats and Lady Gregory. Yeats's entries in his private journal — all the more moving because during February 1909 Lady Gregory too was seriously ill — rail as always against his colleague's 'long, bitter misunderstanding with the wreckage of Young Irelandism'; but in addition, perhaps for the first time, Yeats acknowledged Molly's role: 'Poor Molly is going through her work as always; perhaps that is best for her. I feel Synge's coming death less now than when he first became ill. I am used to the thought of it and I do not find I pity him. I pity her.'[2]

2 *Memoirs: Autobiography and Journal*, ed. Denis Donoghue (1972), 154 ff.

Lady Gregory — at first most intransigent about Synge's liaison with Molly — seems to have relented even earlier: a letter to Molly, apparently written during his earlier confinement at Elpis in 1908, speaks reassuringly of an encounter with Dr Parsons: 'He says the patient is much more comfortable, & quite cheerful. My mind was rather anxious this morning.' (TCD) And after his death, both Yeats and Lady Gregory relied upon Molly for assistance with his manuscripts and further insight into their lost helper.

'One never had to re-arrange one's mind to talk to him,' Lady Gregory wrote to Yeats after Synge's death (25 March 1909, Berg). The direct and forthright response, so characteristic of the man who could not ever tolerate 'the modish lie',[3] is evident throughout his correspondence, as is the charm of his conversation and personality which could captivate even the nurses who tended him. But in the letters to his fellow directors, to John Quinn, and most of all to Molly, we can trace also the steady evolution of his theories both of art and of life. To Quinn he was forced to defend his contrapuntal method of play construction, explain the new experiment of tackling a saga play, expound his own political stance. To Yeats and Lady Gregory he counselled caution in dealing with individual players or rushing headlong into sweeping administrative changes, and offered wise criticism of play submissions. To Molly he spoke of acting techniques, the excitement and responsibility of creativity, above all the need to 'make personal' one's art. We learn also in his advice to his headstrong young fiancée the secret of his own seemingly elusive personality: 'do try and keep cool and quiet it is not worth while to make yourself ill or uneasy for anything our friends may say. There is nothing like keeping a check on one's self then no one can gain a point anywhere.' (3 December 1907) But especially in his letters from Germany can be seen how deeply his love of nature and his sense of the transient had become interwoven with a universe in which she belonged and had taught him to see through her eyes also. And throughout, where he feels most trusting yet vulnerable, secure yet highly emotional, runs the thread of self-mockery and irony that surfaces in his poems and plays.

It is significant that, as illness continued to plague him, Synge should have turned more and more to the personal art of writing poetry. He had always written verse privately, but now he was prepared to publish his most intimate thoughts and feelings, unprotected by the mask of drama or journalism. During the months recorded in these letters, although *The Tinker's Wedding*, unproduced, is added to his canon of published work for the theatre,

---

[3] Stephen MacKenna, letter to the Editor, *Irish Statesman*, 3 Nov 1928, 170.

Deirdre of the Sorrows never made its painful way to completion, nor did his volume of essays on Wicklow and Kerry (planned to follow *The Aran Islands*), and he published only four articles. Instead, most of his creative energy was devoted to *Poems and Translations*, the subject of his last letter. The book did not include a poem dated 25 September 1908:

> I've thirty months, and that's my pride,
> Before my age's a double score,
> Though many lively men have died
> At twenty-nine or little more.
>
> I've left a long and famous set
> Behind some seven years or three,
> But there are millions I'd forget
> Will have their laugh at passing me.[4]

As with the first volume of Synge's letters, I have been greatly assisted by access to the Synge papers in the possession of the Stephens family and in Trinity College, Dublin, Library, especially Mrs Kathleen Synge's letters to her son Robert and the complete text of Edward Stephens's 'Life'; the complete Joseph Holloway diaries and the W. A. Henderson scrapbooks, as well as other relevant manuscript collections in the National Library of Ireland, have also been of inestimable use. Andrew Carpenter's edition of Stephens's 'Life' (*My Uncle John*, 1974), Samuel Synge's *Letters to my Daughter* (Dublin, 1934), and the first four volumes of *The Modern Irish Drama* documentary histories compiled by Robert Hogan and associates (Dublin, 1975–9) have been of great assistance.

All letters have been transcribed from the originals where these still exist; where copies also exist in other collections these have been compared. (The originals of certain letters of which photographic copies are now in the National Library of Ireland are in the possession of Patrick Synge-Hutchinson.) Grammatical and spelling errors have been reproduced, with editorial emendations and additions provided only where absolutely necessary, in square brackets ([ ]). Where it has been possible to decipher passages struck out either by Synge or by MacKenna, these have been incorporated within angle brackets (⟨ ⟩). Synge's underlining is rendered as follows: a word underlined once is set in italics; twice, in small capitals; more than twice, in small capitals underlined, with the number of underlinings recorded in a note.

Individuals fully identified in the notes to volume I are given a

4 *Poems*, 59

cursory identification here, with a cross-reference to the previous volume.

Ann Saddlemyer

Victoria College
University of Toronto
August 1983

ACKNOWLEDGEMENTS

IN addition to those donors listed below under Manuscript sources, the members of the Synge family continue to deserve my gratitude for the assistance and encouragement they have given me over more than twenty years. It is impossible to thank them enough, or to acknowledge adequately the assistance I have been given by many other scholars, colleagues, and friends on two continents. In particular, John Bell, who initiated this edition many years ago and never lost faith through many silences, and Catherine Carver who has so ably shepherded me through the last rites towards completion, have earned a very special vote of thanks. My gratitude also to the following for sharing time, energy, and knowledge in many different ways: Professor William Benzie, Professor Andrew Carpenter, Professor Joan Coldwell, Mr John Doyle, Miss Rose Dunne, Mr Howard Gerwing (Special Collections Librarian, University of Victoria), Messrs Peter and Eric Gill, Dr Nicholas Grene, Professor A. Norman Jeffares, Mr Stephen B. Johnson, Professor Dan Laurence, Mrs Joan Lawrence, Professor R. G. Lawrence, Professor J. B. Lyons (Royal College of Surgeons in Ireland), Mr Alf MacLochlainn (former Director, National Library of Ireland), Dr Colin Meier, Dr Peggy Miller, Mr Robert W. Mills (The Library of the Royal College of Physicians of Ireland), Professor William Murphy, Mr William O'Sullivan (former Curator of Manuscripts, Trinity College Library), Miss Hilary Pyle, Professor Joseph Ronsley, Mr Anthony Rota, Professor Alan G. Sandison, Professor Peter L. Smith, Mr Colin Smythe, Professor Henry Summerfield, Dr Lola Szladits (Curator of the Berg Collection, New York Public Library), Mr John Wilson, Mr D. J. Wright (Librarian of the Nuffield Library, British Medical Association). A collective acknowledgement is due the staffs of the National Library of Ireland and the Library of Trinity College, Dublin, for serving with patience, courtesy, and cheerfulness for so many years. And, finally, my fond gratitude to Professor Kevin B. Nowlan, with whose assistance and in whose Dublin home the final touches were put on both volumes.

A.S.

LIST OF ABBREVIATIONS
AND MANUSCRIPT SOURCES

JMS = J. M. Synge

The following abbreviations and short forms are used in the description and provenance given at the foot of each letter, together with a record of its previous publication:

MS	autograph original or copy
TS	typescript original
copy	transcribed by another hand; original unavailable
draft	rough draft retained by JMS among his papers
photo	transcribed from photostatic copy

MANUSCRIPT SOURCES

Institutions

Berg	The Henry W. and Albert A. Berg Collection of the New York Public Library, Astor, Lenox and Tilden Foundations
Blackwell	B. H. Blackwell Ltd., Oxford
Lilly	Lilly Library, Indiana University
Lockwood	Lockwood Memorial Library, State University of New York at Buffalo
NLI	The National Library of Ireland
NYPL	Manuscript Division, New York Public Library, Astor, Lenox and Tilden Foundations
TCD	Manuscripts Division, Trinity College Library, University of Dublin
Texas	Humanities Research Center, the University of Texas at Austin

Private owners

AS	Ann Saddlemyer
Coxhead	the late Elizabeth Coxhead, Gerrards Cross, Bucks.
Gilvarry	Mr James Gilvarry, New York
Gregory	the late Major Richard Gregory, Budleigh Salterton, Devon
Healy	the late Mr James Healy, New York
Kain	Professor Richard M. Kain, Louisville, Kentucky
Langmuir	Mr Robert Langmuir, The Book Mark, Philadelphia
Ray	Professor Gordon N. Ray, New York
Synge	the late Dr Patrick H. Synge, Petworth, Sussex
Synge estate	the Bank of Ireland and Mr Denis Stephens QC
Yeats	Miss Anne B. Yeats, Dalkey, Co. Dublin

SOURCES OF PREVIOUS PUBLICATION

LM   *Letters to Molly*, ed. Ann Saddlemyer (Cambridge, Mass.: Harvard
        University Press, 1971)

TB   *Theatre Business. The Correspondence of the first Abbey Theatre
        Directors: W. B. Yeats, Lady Gregory and J. M. Synge*, ed. Ann
        Saddlemyer (Gerrards Cross: Colin Smythe/University Park, Pa.:
        Pennsylvania State University Press, 1982)

Other abbreviations and short forms used in the annotation:

Plays   J. M. Synge, *Plays* Book I and Book II (vols. III and IV of the
        Collected Works), ed. Ann Saddlemyer (1968, repr. 1983)

Poems   J. M. Synge, *Poems* (vol. I of the *Collected Works*), ed. Robin
        Skelton (1962, repr. 1983)

Prose   J. M. Synge, *Prose* (vol. II of the *Collected Works*), ed. Alan Price
        (1966, repr. 1983)

Stephens
MS   E. M. Stephens's unpublished MS, 'The Life of J. M. Synge', in the
        Library, Trinity College, Dublin

The place of publication for all sources cited is London unless otherwise indicated.

PART ONE

July–December

1907

*

Theatre Business, Marriage Delays

To LADY GREGORY[1]

Glendalough House | Kingstown
July 1st/07

Dear Lady Gregory

I am sorry there has been a little delay in sending you back Miss Hornimans' letter.[2] I have been away in Wicklow since Friday and only got your letter on my return this afternoon. I have read the Manifesto carefully, but I do not think there is any comment that I need make. You and Yeats can reply suitably, and include me. The political ⟨issue⟩ threat is ominous I am afraid. By this arrangement does she still pay part of our lighting and heating in addition to the subsidy? I suppose she does, but there have been so many changes I forget for the moment how we work at present in this matter.

I am overjoyed that we are to be free from her in future — ⟨and that⟩ Our *self-respect* I think, will gain by the freedom. It may be a hard fight to get on, but I feel hopeful.

I meant to write and thank you for your letter before you left London, but I was always expecting some new development that would make a letter necessary so the time slipped away. F. J. Fay has been walking long walks with Henderson and is in fairly good spirits I think.[3] I go back into Wicklow tomorrow, to a mountain cottage I have found that is ⟨fairly⟩ very high up, and fairly civilized so I may be there for some weeks it is suits me. It has become rather important to get rid of this influenza cough that I have had now for five months If I do not [get] better where I am going I may go abroad in August, I am begining to long for a place where it is not always raining. I do not at all know how long I shall stay in Wicklow so please write here as before.

I think your suggestion about Yeats writing an acting version in prose is excellent.[4] It might be of use to him also as he could then make the alterations he thought necessary in the prose version without the worry of continualy re-writing the verse.

⟨I must add this afterthought.⟩

Does Yeats know at all ⟨the⟩ whether Miss H. has any particular phase of political ill-doing ⟨on⟩ in her mind?

I suppose we may go on playing Kathleen and the Rising of the Moon![5]

Yours sincerely
J. M. Synge

MS, Berg. *TB*, 229

1 Augusta, Lady Gregory (1852–1932), co-founder with W. B. Yeats (see below, p. 109) of the Abbey Theatre and one of JMS's fellow directors; see I. 48.

2 Annie E. F. Horniman (1860–1937), owner of the Abbey Theatre and patron of the company (see I. 89), had written on 28 June 1907 to Yeats, lamenting the failure of Ben Iden Payne's tenure as manager (see below, p. 7). Adding that her letter could be shown to JMS, she wrote: 'In future I will pay the wages for staff (both before and behind) when the theatre is let . . . . . It must never be forgotten that if the theatre be used politically I am free to close it at once and to stop the subsidy.' (Berg) She added that she would have nothing directly to do with the theatre in future.

3 Francis (Frank) J. Fay (1870–1931; see I. 79) was one of the founding actors of the company, and W. A. Henderson (see below, p. 138) its business manager.

4 When sending on Miss Horniman's letter, Lady Gregory had written to JMS on 29 June 1907, 'I am only sad about Yeats not getting his work done as he likes but we may beat out a way. I want him to do his next play in prose for acting, & put it into verse afterwards.' (TCD)

5 *Kathleen ni Houlihan* (Yeats) and *The Rising of the Moon* (Gregory) were both popular with the nationalists attending the Abbey Theatre.

To LADY GREGORY

c/o Mrs. McGuirk | Lough Bray Cottage[1]
Enniskerry | Co Wicklow
July 4th/07

Dear Lady Gregory

As I am up here I am afraid I cant see Henderson for the moment, so I return his letter which Yeats had probably better answer in a quite amicable spirit. He is technically right about the book-keeping as he read me Yeats' letter going through all his duties and book-keeping was not mentioned. I would give him the three months notice — or equivalent — that he asks for,[2] or keep him on if possible as I suggested to Yeats and as you suggest as a sort of Master of the Ceremonies at the Abbey if he would come for a small salary. He says that he had been talking of giving up his post for nine years but that he would never have done so unless we had offered him our post, so that we are now responsible for his change of carreer. A funny argument!

It is much better to keep him in good humour, he has worked very hard, in his own way, at our audiences and we are unpopular enough. Perhaps it would be best if you would write instead of Yeats as his (Henderson's) letter is rather agressive. I hope the Theatre will shake into form now. I do not quite see that Yeats has much cause for dissa[tisfac]tion with his London shows. I thought his plays were better done than the 'Playboy' but still I believe our people on the whole do it better than any other company could do it.

I am still shaky in health I am sorry to say, but I am afraid, thanks, that Coole would not be quite the place for me now, as the Doctor says I want a dry bracing place. This is bracing enough but not of course dry; so if I do not get better this month I think it will mean going abroad in August.

Yours sincerely

J. M. Synge

P.S. By the way I found the letters Yeats wrote to me last year before I saw Henderson. There were several and Henderson was to have come to see me but didn't come. Then Yeats wrote definitely "Henderson has accepted and will probably call on you".[3] So I understood, as Henderson did, that he was then engaged.   J.M.S.

MS, Berg. *TB*, 231

1 A 1905 photograph of the McGuirks' cottage, nestled among a grove of larches overlooking both Lough Bray and the mountain-ringed valley of Glencree, is reproduced in Weston St. John Synge, *The Neighbourhood of Dublin* (Dublin, 1939), 376. Mr McGuirk was gamekeeper for the Guinness estate.

2 With Miss Horniman's decision not to give further financial assistance beyond the agreed subsidy, the directors had decided to economize by eliminating the position of business manager; see I. 372-3.

3 See *TB*, 144 ff. for the correspondence between Yeats and JMS over hiring Henderson in August 1906.

To MOLLY ALLGOOD[1]

c/o Mrs McGuirk | Lough Bray Cottage | Enniskerry

July ? [11]/07

Dearest Life

F.J.F[ay] overtook me today before I got back. I streeled along after I left you and lay in the heather here and there feeling very 'lonesome', and then when I was on the long stretch of road where we used to sit in the evening I saw F.J.F's little figure appearing on the sky-line and I recognised his walk at once. We went down then to Mrs Dunne's and he arranged to stay there tonight,[2] then we came on and had tea here. After that we walked off the whole way to Sally Gap and didn't get back till ten.[3] I wish I could have taken you out there but it might have been rather far for you at present. It would have been a good deal further than any of the walks we took. I wonder how you feel tonight, little love, entertaining F.J. kept me from being as lonesome as I expected to be; still it felt hard not to have you with me out on these wonderful hills. F.J. talks of coming back here next week for a few days. I told him he will have to amuse himself part of the time as I am going to fish and cycle a good deal next week. I will be glad if he comes, I think, it is wholesome to have someone to talk to, and he was very pleasant this evening.

We you and I have had a good little time and we know each other better than ever, take good care of yourself now[4] and I hope we'll soon be together for always, little sweetheart. I am tired now and cant write

Your old Tramp.

I am sending you one of my Wicklow articles with your song.[5] Please keep it safe for me. Tell me what you think of the other.

MS, TCD. *LM*, 158

1 Molly Allgood ('Maire O'Neill', 1887-1952), JMS's fiancée; see I, 166.
2 Fay had apparently walked the ten miles from the tram terminus in Rathfarnham over the Featherbed Bog. Mrs Dunne's cottage, where Molly and her sister Sally had stayed from 28 June, was about a mile below Mrs McGuirk's.
3 The climb by the Military Road from Lough Bray past the source of the river Liffey to the Sally Gap, the highest crossroads in Ireland, is one of the steepest grades in Wicklow, but commands an impressive view of the valley.
4 The onset of Molly's menstrual period had caused her to return to Dublin, in case medical attention was necessary.
5 Probably 'At a Wicklow Fair', first published in the *Manchester Guardian*, 9 May 1907, just before Molly went on tour; the only other article by JMS on Wicklow that includes a song is 'The Vagrants of Wicklow', published in *The Shanachie* in December 1906.

To MOLLY ALLGOOD

[Lough Bray Cottage]
Friday [12 July 1907]

Dearest

I haven't got my post yet as McGuirk hasn't been down and I couldn't get away from F.J.F. So I am still looking out for your letter.

I have been up at the upper lake this morning with F.J.F lying in the heather, it was beautifully warm and summery, it is the world and all of a pity that you aren't here still. F.J.F. is going back now 1 o'clock after his dinner so I wont see him till he comes out again.

I am writing in rather a hurry as I have to write my mother and Lady G. also before the post hour. I am going down on my bicycle today down past the school-house where we saw the girl climbing the tree and then back by our 'nook' road. I wish to —— —— you were here with me my dear love it's poor game to be alone up here

My poor dear love be happy and cheerful and take good care of yourself for my sake

Your old Tramp

MS, TCD. *LM*, 158

To LADY GREGORY

c/o Mrs. McGuirk | Lough Bray Cottage
Enniskerry | Co. Wicklow
Friday [12 July 1907]

Dear Lady Gregory

Thanks for your letter and enclosures which I return. Hendersons are amusing but I am glad he is in fairly good humour with us. Payne's letter is fair enough.[1] He could make nothing of our people with their accents and voices that were strange to him, and he has the grace to see that it was an impossible situation. F.J.F. turned up here last night and slept at a cottage lower down the glen. He seems quieter and better than I have seen him for some time. I hear there is difficulty with the city architect, or his staff, over the new dressing rooms. I suppose that is Holloways business not ours.[2] I am getting on pretty well thanks and if the weather keeps fine I hope I'll get all right.

I have play ideas at the back of my mind but I'm not doing anything yet, as I want to get well first.

Yours sincerely
J. M. Synge

MS, Berg. *TB*, 232

[1] Ben Iden Payne (1881-1976; see I. 299) had written the directors, at their request, a formal letter of resignation (Berg); see *TB*, 214 ff. for the full comedy of his appointment, which he took up in mid-February 1907, as manager of the Abbey company. The other enclosures are missing.

[2] Miss Horniman had made arrangements in late January 1907 to purchase a stable beyond the theatre annexe for extra dressing rooms; as architect responsible to her for the theatre, Joseph Holloway (1861-1944; see I. 117) was in charge of the arrangements. The annexe was finally in use the following spring.

To MOLLY ALLGOOD

c/o Mrs McGuirk | Lough Bray Cottage | Enniskerry
Saturday [13th][1] July 1907

My dearest Pet

I got your poor little note yesterday and it melted my heart inside me. I'm so sorry for you but we have to face what cant be got out of.

Only for your health, of course, I'd have kept you on here as long as I am staying but, as it is, you have to be in Dublin now, so cheer up and think what a good time we've had.

When I was going to the post yesterday after dinner I found my bicycle was punctured so I had a long job putting it right, and I had to send my letters down by McGuirk. I hope they were in time. After that I rode round where we were last Saturday — you remember the little lane — and on to the road where we had our wet walk before the tour. Then I crossed the river and came home by the 'nook' road. It was a heavy pull home and I got tired and out of spirit. In the evening I walked up again towards Sally Gap — about as far as we went — and then came in about nine. Today it is blowing a gale and is raining very hard every few minutes so you haven't missed much of the fine weather! It is a nuisance, I am so anxious to get well. I dont suppose F.J. will come out again if this sort of thing goes on. I wonder if you have sent me the envelopes! If you haven't you'll have to wait for your next letter — *for this letter*, unless I can borrow one from Mrs McG. — so I hope you've thought of it, little madcap! I'm going to write an article on that back road to Sally Gap — or rather a chapter for my book,[2] it would hardly have enough matter for a regular article.

I think F.J.F. seems better than usually. It is pathetic what a high idea he has of Sally,[3] and her wonderful *nobility* of character. If he only knew how she speaks of him. I suppose that is the fate of many of us!

I dreamt about you a lot last night but only harum-skarum dreams that I do not remember. Yes though! I remember we had taken a little house two doors down from the man who wrote me the curious letter from Manchester.[4] Tell me what you think of my Wicklow article. Poor old pet I wish you were here to make coffee for me and cheer me up today. The wind is howling in the trees of Jerusalem,[5] and the stream is roaring with the rain, God help us. You ought to go to Kingstown on top of the tram when it is fine and take a turn on the pier — you know the pier near my place — if you are *still quite well* write me long letters that I can *answer*.

Ever your old Tramp.

MS, TCD. *LM*, 159

    1 Misdated 12 July.

    2 JMS was planning a book on Wicklow and Kerry as a companion volume to *The Aran Islands*; but a few fragments only of his description of Glencree were preserved (*Prose*, 234-6).

    3 Sara Allgood (1883-1950), Molly's older sister and leading actress with the company; see I. 95.

    4 Perhaps the author of a fragment preserved by JMS which pleaded, 'Please

do not say such unkind things about "the descendants of the poor Irish people who have drifted away" . . . . Please do not make it any harder for us, how would you like to live in Manchester, after dear old Ireland since the 2nd Henry.' (TCD)

5 His name for the few wind-twisted laurel trees at the back of Mrs McGuirk's cottage, still standing.

To MOLLY ALLGOOD

[Lough Bray Cottage]
Saturday later [13 July 1907].

My dearest Love

I have got your second letter. Yes I felt nearly ready to cry — big ass that I am — when I turned away from you there on the road. It is very hard indeed to be pulled asunder so often, I did not say much of what I felt in my other letter as *we must be satisfied*.[1] I do NOT think it would be a good plan to meet you tomorrow. You will certainly be unwell soon and it would be the worst thing in the world for you to be standing and streeling about all day or even sitting about in the wet. Remember it will only make our marriage more difficult if you keep up this delicacy and perhaps have to give up some of your parts in the theatre or Heaven knows what. Do for my sake — for the sake of our marriage — take real care of yourself till this turn is over — I implore you to do so — and then I will arrange to see you as often as possible. I need not say how delighted I would be to meet you, but I am sure it would not be right, so we must put it off. I am not going to let you harm yourself again, and the Dr[2] said you were not to walk before the attack.

When I left you that day I was wretched for a time then I said to myself "You bl---y old blitherer, you've been lonesome for thirty years and now you're sadder than ever because you've got a god-send of a changeling all to yourself." Then I brightened up again at the thought that I had you, and would soon be with you always. You must do the same. Get your health back and be cheerful then all will go well. Tell me more about the Timmy business.[3] It's a queer story, and interests me.

A thousand kisses sweetheart

Your old Tramp

Thanks for envelopes and pencil.

MS, TCD. *LM*, 160

1 A quotation from old Maurya's speech in *Riders to the Sea*.
2 Arthur P. Barry (1879-1938), gynaecologist of the National Maternity

Hospital, Holles Street, whom Molly had consulted about her menstrual difficulties; see I. 371.

3 Perhaps a reference to Timmy the Smith, a character in *The Well of the Saints*, which received its first production at the Abbey Theatre 4 Feb 1905.

To MOLLY ALLGOOD

Lough Bray
Sunday *night* [14 July 1907]

Dearest Love

I wonder how you have been getting on today? Cheerfully I hope. I suppose I shall hear from you tomorrow morning. Yesterday was the worst day there has been since I came out here, I got wet in the morning and in the afternoon I walked down to our little wood and got wet again on my way back. Today there was fog hanging about in the morning so I went up on the Sally Gap road and wandered about in the clouds, writing down my impressions as I went along. Then I came home and had dinner feeling very lonesome and down. After that I got my bike and went off over the Feather Bed mountain, in thick cold clouds again, to the place where I left you on Thursday. Then I turned to the right into Glen Dhu and up through it and Glen Cullen and back up Glen Cree from the Enniskerry end about 20 miles in all I suppose.

Mrs Dunne came out to speak to me as I was passing her cottage, and showed me a post card she had got this morning from F. J Fay to say that there was some talk of *"the girls"* coming out again for a week so he would not yet decide about coming himself. Are you talking of coming? Have you discovered when the company are to begin work again? Of course you can decide nothing till you see how your health goes.

This evening it was very mild so I have been wandering and sitting about till ten o'clock. There has been a very wonderful white fog working about all through Glen Cree, and up the mountain opposite. It reminded me of old evening long ago in Annamoe when I used to be watching "the light passing the North and the patches of fog."[1] I am so sorry you did not see it. There was a Night-jar also whirring in the heather somewhere near our nook, altogether it has been one of the strange Wicklow evenings that have such an effect upon me. Poor Pet it is sad to think of you shut up in Dublin all this evening, when things are so beautiful out here. I'd like to write intimatey to you tonight, but somehow I am tired and nothing very interesting comes under my pen. Your own little imagination, I expect, can read between my arid lines, and see me in Glen Dhu where we did our first flirtations, and passing the lane in Glen Cree where we sat so happily, and mooning about here in the twilight, with a changeling in my scull.

I hope you'll think over all the beautiful things you've seen out here and in our other walks and make a little faery land in your own scull for you to live your changeling's life in when Mary Street is not tollerable. Read your G. Treasury too and 'Aucasin and Nicolette'.[2] There has been a great deal that was unpleasant, my poor pet, in your little life — you have told me a lot now bit by bit — and I want you to get your little mind free and happy and confident and to forget all about the squabblings and uncomfortable moods that you have seen such a lot of. I think if you had more confidence in me you wouldn't be so *tiff*able. I dont mean to say that you haven't confidence, but you haven't got used to trusting me practically in little things. I am glad to think that for the last week we hadn't a single uncomfortable word. That shows that all we want is to be together out and out and then we'll get on "*magnifiquement*"

If you are still *quite* well when you get this trot off and have a look at the pictures in the National Gallery. Another time when you've nothing to do go to the Museum and look through the Case of Evolution, and see if you can make it out by yourself.[3] If you [are] ill keep very quiet but if you are well there is always plenty to do without moping too much. Remember all the years I've mooned about Galleries and Museums by myself picking up my knowledge.

Monday morning | (I give up dates here)

Dearest

I went down to Mrs Dunne's this morning at eleven and a minute after I got in the place was besieged with soldiers getting bread and minerals. In a little while I saw the post boy passing and '*chased*' out after him. He had my rod and three letters from you, my good little angel. Then I sat down under the tree and read your letters. When I came to F.J.F's offer I read 'pooed at' instead of 'jumped at' and I gave you a pat of approbation on the back!! Then when I got further on I found I had made a big mistake. Of [course] I'll be delighted to have you out here again if you come, but I'd rather you got the money from me than from him. Still I dont mind him much poor man. Remember if you are quite normal this time — which we must devoutly hope for — your day will be Saturday so dont make any definite plans till you see how things go. *You must not dream of hurrying up here* before you are quite well. Remember to find out when the company is to meet. I meant to go home on Saturday I am so dull here but if you are coming again of course I will stay on. I find it very hard to pass the long days here by myself, but now I'll be able to fish again. I got a cheque for my Shanachie article[4] this morning for £3. 10. 0 so that will keep me going for a while. I think I'll give Mrs McG. 18s/0d a week that is not too much as I eat a lot. Now I must post this

> Your old H. tramp.

Take care not to go too far in the Park[5] where the roughs hang about.

P.S. I had heard rumours of the Horniman Payne scheme.[6]

MSS, (Sunday night) AS; (Monday morning) TCD, *LM*, 161, 163

1 Cf. *The Playboy of the Western World*, Act I: (Christy to Pegeen Mike) ' . . . and there I'd be as happy as the sunshine of St. Martin's Day, watching the light passing the north or the patches of fog' (*Plays*, Book II, 83).

2 *The Golden Treasury of English Lyrics*, ed. F. T. Palgrave (1861; rev. edn., 1896), and *Aucassin and Nicolete*; JMS mentions Andrew Lang's 1887 translation of the latter, a thirteenth-century legend of Provence, approvingly in his review of A. H. Leahy's *Heroic Romances of Ireland*, vol. I, *Manchester Guardian*, 28 Dec 1905 (*Prose*, 371).

3 In his autobiography (TCD) JMS describes the shock of first reading Darwin; Edward Stephens recalls a discussion with him in November 1902 concerning the case in the National Museum which held 'the skeleton of a man's hand, a monkey's paw, and a bat's wing' (*Prose*, 11 n.).

4 Presumably the first of the series, 'In West Kerry', *The Shanachie*, Summer 1907.

5 Probably Phoenix Park in Dublin, north of the Liffey and easily accessible from Mary Street, where Molly lived with her mother and brothers and sisters.

6 After resigning from the Abbey Theatre, Ben Iden Payne became manager of Miss Horniman's Manchester Playgoers' Club, which advertised its first productions for September 1907.

To MOLLY ALLGOOD

> Lough Bray
> *Monday night* [15 July 1907]

Dearest Love

A very sleepy old tramp is writing to you tonight. I may be going to Annamoe tomorrow[1] and if so I will not get your letter till I come back late at night. I will post this — if I go — in Roundwood or somewhere on the way and then I suppose you'll get it some time tomorrow night.

After dinner today I went down and fished again, and this time I caught *two* little wretches like the last, but I threw them both back alive. I began lower down than we stopped last day, and went on down. I got a lot of rises — some of them good ones — but it was [a] queer heavy day with low water and the fish were only jumping at the fly, not taking it. Still I enjoyed myself and lay about in the sun and thought about you. I never felt such heat when I got home my shirt — with respects to you — was as wet as if you'd dipped in a bucket. On my way home I met the game keeper and he asked if I had an order so I showed him the card. When I got back here I heard F.J.F. had called so I went down again to Mrs Dunne's after tea, and found him there. Then we walked back over the mountain — I went on till I could see the Hell Fire Club,[2] and then I came home. — I had my bicycle with me. I feel better today in my health than I have felt since I was in Kerry last summer. The warm weather is doing me good I think. I hope you are getting on well dearest pet. Good night

Your old Tramp

MS, TCD. *LM*, 163

1 Mrs Synge (see below, p. 162) was spending the summer as usual at Tom-riland House near Annamoe, Co. Wicklow; she wrote in her diary on ? 16 July 1907, 'Johnnie came we sat out in the field and strolled about. He seems better. Had dinner and tea here outside, left about 5.30. Eddie [her grandson, E. M. Stephens] rode part of the way with him.' (TCD)
2 A ruined stone building on the summit of Mt. Pelier, about four miles from Rathfarnham, which was the site of an eighteenth-century club.

To MOLLY ALLGOOD

Lough Bray
Wednesday July 17th [1907]

My dearest Love

I got a long letter from you last night when I came home from an expedition to Annamoe and now at 12 o'clock I have got your little note without a date saying that you want to come up 'to-morrow' that is today and asking me to write to say if I will meet you. You know that there is only one post in here in the morning and one out at 3.15 so that you *cannot possibly* get my answer till *tonight at 8 o'clock!* Putting Urgent on your envelope will not make the Post Office change their arrangements.

Now as to your proposal, my poor little love, I see you are longing to be in the country, but I need not say that YOU MOST CER-TAINLY MUST *NOT* ATTEMPT TO COME. It would be sheer insanity. You are certain to be unwell between this and Saturday and if you took this long walk immediately before it you might lay yourself up for life. You have escaped once, and now you want to break the doctors orders and risk your carreer in the theatre and the happiness of our married life! For a few days pleasure!! What am I say to you. I am terribly uneasy that you may start today without waiting for this and so injure yourself forever. Oh it is cruel of you to make me so unspeakably anxious. I'll have to go off now and sit on the mountain-road half the day to look out for you as the place is full of soldiers and queer tramps that have come about the camp. However your letter seems to imply that you will wait to hear from me. God grant that you will. I half thought of going to Enniskerry[1] when I got your letter and now I wish I had. Great Christ I am so uneasy. You seem to think you are safe because you have escaped once, but for all you know the matter may now be wrong again and a long walk at the wrong time might ruin your health forever.

I am very unwell today with asthma I was awake all night with it. If it continues I shall have to go home. If I get well again and if you get over your period all right you will be able to come up for some days at least. Do try and remember that you are a woman and not a baby. I dont know what to think when you write, as you have done again and again, and ask me to answer at once when it is perfectly obvious that it is not possible to get a letter sent in time. It makes me sad.

Dont think I am angry my dearest love and dont be angry with me. I bicycled up to Annamoe yesterday to see my mother and came back the road across Sugar Loaf where we walked so often last summer and winter. It made me thrill and tremble with tenderness for my little god-send to be on those roads again that I walked so often with you last winter. I was wondering if we shall ever be able to walk so freely again. We certainly never shall unless you are careful. What in the world did you think would become of you if you came up now and got bad suddenly as you did the last time. That long jolty drive back would be the worst thing in the world and what a time you would have if you were laid up in bed in Mrs Dunne's with no one to look after you. I was going to write you a very long and very tender letter today all about my thoughts of you last night but now I am too upset. I may go to Kingstown tomorrow and if so I *may* wire to you to meet me in Dublin. I will if I can

Your old Tramp

Later

My own God-send

I'm afeard you'll maybe think I'm after writing a bit harshly in my other letter so just fancy you feel my arms round you making it all right again with a kiss in your little eye and a kiss in your little ear and forty kisses for each little heathen lip of yours. When I think what a joy it would be to me to have you here again, looking

out for me, and making coffee for me, I get a pain with yearning
for you, but this week, at least, it cannot be.

Do take good care of yourself if you get safely through this
time it'll make such a difference. Remember if I wire to you tomorrow it will be in the forenoon so be in readiness, and remember
if you are the least unwell you are *on your oath* not to come. I am
very dull here now, if you were not coming I'd go home on Saturday
I think, but I am not quite decided. Now with a thousands kisses
and blessings my poor little madcap

Your own old
T.

MS, TCD. *LM*, 164

1 The closest post office with telegraph facilities.

To MOLLY ALLGOOD

Lough Bray Cottage
18.7.07

My poor darling

Your two letters came this morning. I am very sorry for my
poor little pet, but I am glad it has come on before you had time to
do anything foolish. I hope by today you are much better. Yesterday was very hot here too. I went over to Kilikee[1] in the afternoon
to meet you — as you asked me — though I hoped you would not
come. On the way I met F.J.F and Henderson and we lay for a
long time in the heather and talked. Then Henderson went back to
Dublin and F.J. came here to Mrs Dunne's for the night. This morning we have been sitting under the tree at Mrs Dunne's door talking
since eleven o'clock. Now he is gone home. It is too hot to go out
into the sun. This is not a very good place for such hot weather as
there is no shade, one seems to get scorched with the continual
hot sun. Tomorrow I am going to slip down to Kingstown if the
weather permits and come back here in the evening, but I will not
go to Dublin. Please when you get this tonight write me a little
line to Glendalough House to say how you are getting on. Do you
think you will come up here Monday? I will send down the jennet[2]
and trap for you if you do and I will stay on for the week of course.
You could go back the following Sunday evening and be in time for
the Theatre on Monday. I think tomorrow (Friday) you ought to
write to Dr. B[arry] and tell him how you have got on, and ask him
if you should see him again. Tell him also that you are thinking of
going to the country again on Monday. You will have to use a little

thought about our arrangements as there is no post here on Sunday, so that anything you write to me on *Saturday* or *Sunday* I do not get here till eleven o'clock on Monday. Write to me on *Friday night* to this place to say if you think you can come. Then I'll tell the jennet man to keep himself open in case you come on Monday − he is often engaged − Then you can come write to me early on Sunday to say what time the trap is to meet you in Rathfarnham. You had better say four o'clock or so, so that there may be time for me to get him off after the post comes on Monday. I believe F.J.F is coming up for Sunday so Monday would be your best day. I wonder if you will be able to see Barry on Saturday or Sunday it would be a relief to our minds I think if you could see him before you come back. Now do you understand what you have to do. Try and dont muddle things by writing contradictory letters as you did yesterday. There are so few posts here − and no telegraph − that if we once get muddled we'll never get clear again.

The purple grapes[3] are ripe here now I got a lot of them last night on our nook road. The nightjar is singing every night also in the heather. I took F.J. to hear it last night, but he was so busy talking about prononciation that he would hardly listen to it.

It is furiously hot today, and I hardly know what to do with myself. Tomorrow I'll be in Kingstown and on Sunday I'll have to entertain Frank and that will pass me on to MONDAY then there'll be a change and a changeling please godnes.

I had a little asthma this morning but nothing to speak of so I hope it wont trouble me much. The bad attack I had was partly my own fault I drank a lot of whiskey that Mrs McGuirk gave me − not a great deal but a rather large dose − and a lot of tea and fresh bread after my long day at Annamoe, about ten o'clock, and that set me off

Now sweetheart be prudent and take good care of yourself for both our sakes and dont forget the line to Kingstown tonight, and the letter to this place tomorrow Have you anything to read? Get Sally to get you Scott's 'Talisman'[4] for /6d.

Your old Tramp.

If you have to see Dr B on *Monday* perhaps you should not come here till *Tuesday*

MS, TCD. *LM*, 166

1 Killakee House, at the base of Mt. Pelier; from this point Molly would have to walk the steep road to the shoulder of the Featherbed, then down the Glencree valley.

2 A small Spanish horse used to pull carts on mountain roads.

3 i.e. the *fraughans*, or small blue berries; see I. 187.

4 *The Talisman* (1825) by Sir Walter Scott, one of JMS's favourite authors.

To MOLLY ALLGOOD

Glendalough House [Glenageary]
Friday [19 July 1907][1]

Dearest Love

I'm glad to hear you are getting on so well. Yes certainly see
Barry if ⟨he encourages you to go to him⟩ possible. You had better
not decide to come up on Monday *till* you hear what day he wants
to see you. If you fixed Monday and then were delayed by him you
would have no way of letting us know. You dont seem to realize
yet that there is *only one (morning) post to Glen Cree*, as you say
in your last that you hope I got your letter in time to keep me from
going to meet you at Kilikee. I did not — could not — get it till the
next day at 11 o'clock. I think I'll have to take your education
seriously in hand, Eh? This is not a scolding mind but I'm very hot
and very hurried and in a very bad humour because I left two photo
films with my nephew,[2] three weeks ago, and asked him to leave
them in some shop to be developed and he has left them lying,
deliberately, for the three weeks under his nose, and never touched
them. One's relations are the divil!

Of course I will send the trap for you, you *mustn't dream of walking so soon* after your attack it would be madness. Sally can drive
up too if she likes, I pay the trap. I got your first letter this morning
as I met the post man with it near Enniskerry, and then I found the
second here. I hope you have written to me today; — to Lough Bray
— of course. By the way I think you should put 'Co Wicklow' besides
Enniskerry on your letters. Your 'Enniskerry' is sometimes so vague
I dont know how they read it! I had a great evening on the Sally
Gap road last night it was as warm as possible and I lay up in the
heather long after it was dark. If this weather goes on we'll have
great evenings next week. I am not looking forward to my ride up
this evening, it is so hot and the road is so heavy. I broke a spoke
in my cycle this morning, coming down the big hill into Enniskerry,
but I was able to ride on to Bray and I have left it there to be re-
paired. The soldiers all went away from Glen Cree this morning
they began marching past my window at five o'clock, and on up
the Sally Gap road. This is a very dull letter but excuse it, dear
heart. I cant do any better for the moment. I quite agree that some
of my Western Articles are dull. It was very hard to write so many,
always on the same subject — the distress in the West. Tell me by
and by which you thought dull as I want opinions of competent
people — or changelings — before I begin knocking them into a
book.[3]

Did I tell you that I have just got £3. 10 from the Shanachie so I can afford your jennet! I hope against hope that Barry will think well of you, I am sorry to write you such poor stuff when you want something nice to cheer you up. Poor little love I hope you'll soon have me to look after you and cheer you up always. Now sweet heart good bye I am looking forward, you can imagine how much, to having you in Glen Cree. I find Kingstown and the heat and the frousy women *intollerable* today, what must it be in Mary St, you poor little pet its no place for changelings, is it?

Your old Tramp

MS, TCD. *LM*, 168

1 This date has been added in Molly's hand.

2 Probably Frank (Francis Edmund) Stephens (1884-1948), elder son of JMS's sister Annie, who lived near by; he was also an amateur photographer.

3 JMS did not live to complete his revisions of the twelve articles on the Congested Districts in the west of Ireland, commissioned and published by the *Manchester Guardian*, 10 June to 26 July 1905, with illustrations by Jack B. Yeats (see I. 114). W. B. Yeats was to withdraw his support of the 1910 *Collected Works* when the articles were reprinted as originally published.

To MOLLY ALLGOOD

Lough Bray
Saturday 20th [July 1907]

Dearest Love

I have just got your note. I was down waiting at Mrs Dunne's for it for half an hour before it came. I am afraid this letter will be dull too, I cant help it, as I had asthma last night and I am dull myself in consequence. I have told Mrs Dunne that you are coming on *Monday or Tuesday* and asked her to tell her brother to keep himself free to go for you on the afternoon of either day. You must write *tomorrow (Sunday)* and say which day it is to be. If there is *any doubt* about Monday you had better fix Tuesday as there is no way of letting us know on Monday if you cannot come, and it would not do to send the little man down for nothing. I am looking forward very much to having you here again but I am too uncomfortable and too hot to write you a nice letter today. Excuse me dear heart, I cant help it. I hope I wont have asthma next week, I feel as if you would charm it away if you were hear. If you see Barry after getting this ask him if you may LEARN the bicycle now. It is a very [different] thing LEARNING from riding when you know how, and all the straining of flopping about might not be good for you. Yes if Barry allows it, you can get Kerrigan[1] to teach you by all means, but I doubt Sally will lend you her new bicycle to learn on. It is very bad for a new bicycle so she will be foolish if she does. There is heavy thunder rolling all round the glen today but no rain, the air is very heavy and has given me a head-ache.

There is my dinner now I cant write any more Remember to write tomorrow *decidedly* about Monday

Thanks for paper

Your lonely old
Tramp

Dont forget to tell me what *hour* the man is to be in Rathfarnham. I dont think F.J.F will come today it is too thundery.

N.B. This is the last letter you will be able to get from me if you come on Monday. So good bye till we meet Dearest Life I'll be looking out for you. I wish it was Monday now. Bring me a box of matches and bring some coffee if you like.

MS, TCD. *LM,* 170

1 J. M. Kerrigan (1885–1965) joined the Abbey Theatre company in 1906, making his first appearance in Yeats's *Deirdre* and rapidly assuming prominence in the young romantic roles; he went to the United States in 1916 where, except for a brief return to the Abbey Theatre in 1920, he continued to act on stage and in films. He appears to have been a fairly close friend of JMS.

To JACK B. YEATS[1]

Lough Bray Cottage | Enniskerry | Co Wicklow
[22 July 1907]

Dear Yeats

I was charmed to get your letter the other day and to hear that your Rhine trip had come off successfully. I had meant to write and ask you but I've been up here for three weeks and it isn't a good place for writing. I was grieved to see so little of you in London but I couldn't stand any more of the theatre worries so I slipped off on the Monday morning.[2]

This is a rather civilised cottage close to Lough Bray with 13 miles of road with only one house seven miles from here on it — before you meet habitations or cultivation of any kind. I came up mainly to pick up my health but I haven't been very successful. The weather was first too cold, and then too ⟨cold⟩ hot — and now after a tearing thunder-storm that hit a building near by twice yesterday afternoon, there has been a fog for the last six hours that you cant see your hand through with thunderstorms playing in the distance at the cardinal points. The rain yesterday was beyond any thing in my experience, in an hour and a half of it three big rivers leapt out of

the hill opposite and tore the road to splinters. The place is quaint
in various ways though too sofisticated to be altogether in my line.
There is a magnificent four year old youngster in the house who
keeps me amused as I hear him under the door. The other night the
whole family chased him for ¾ of an hour to make him take a pill,
and each time just at the critical moment he managed to get under
the table and begin saying his prayers when they were too pious to
disturb him. Glen Cree Reformatory — that you may have heard
of — is a mile off townwards — and I went through it a week or two
ago and saw an admirable cake-walk danced by one of the convicts,
— and a roomful of the youngsters with a hag — a lay hag — over
them knitting stockings for the institutions.[3] ⟨and⟩ When we went
in the young divils — God help them — blushed scarlet at being
caught at such an ungaolbirdlike employment. It is told that one of
them a while ago made himself a nun's outfit — he was a tailor-
apprentise — and escaped in it, and then before he was caught went
round Dublin and collected £40 for foreign missions.

I go back to Kingstown at the end of this week and stay there
for a week. Then if I am well enough I may go to Kerry for a time.
I spent a day with Masefield when I was in London I dare say he
told you. He seems well but it is pitiable to see him in such an
establishment.[4]

I hope I'll see you while you are in Ireland, I suppose you'll make
a stop in Dublin on your way back.

Please remember me kindly to Mrs Yeats

Yours cordially
J. M. Synge

MS, Yeats

1 Jack Butler Yeats (1871–1957), artist brother of W. B. Yeats, lived in
Devon but frequently visited and exhibited in Ireland; see I. 112.

2 Jack Yeats's letter has not survived, but apparently he and his wife were
on their way to Coole, to visit Lady Gregory. JMS had stayed with the Yeatses
in Devon from 30 May 1907 before joining the company in London on 8 June
for the performances; see I. 365–6.

3 St. Kevin's School, a reformatory run by the Oblate Brothers from 1859
to 1935, was originally one of the barracks built along the Military Road from
Rathfarnham to Aughavannagh after the 1798 insurrection. Mrs Dunne's cottage
stood opposite the main gate. Because so many varied trades were taught the
inmates, the reformatory was almost self-supporting. The cake walk developed
from a Negro contest in walking gracefully, carrying a cake.

4 John Masefield (1878–1968), poet and dramatist (see I. 72), whom JMS
first met in January 1903, was also a good friend of Jack Yeats. JMS had visited
Masefield at his home in Greenwich on 8 June 1907 and is apparently referring
here to domestic arrangements (cf. Constance Babington Smith, *John Masefield:
A Life* [1978], 87–9, 92). The sentence is circled and annotated in another
hand (? Jack Yeats's), 'leave out'.

To MOLLY ALLGOOD

Lough Bray
Monday [22 July 1907]

My dearest Love

I got your two letters half an hour ago, and I have ordered the jennet to meet you at Rathfarnham at a *quarter* to *three tomorrow (Tuesday) wet or fine*. So that is settled. It is just as well you are not coming to day as the roads here are very nearly impassible after the floods yesterday. The Reformatory was struck twice by lightning in the afternoon and the foundation of the bridge at Smith's just below Mrs Dunne's was washed away. I am very glad to hear of Barry's verdict. You must tell me all when you come. I feel it hard to have to get through another day without you. F.J.F sends a card with your message, and says that he and Montgomery[1] are coming out on Tuesday *bad cess* to them. He didn't come on Saturday because of the thunder. I have had two more bad nights with asthma, and I feel very depressed today. You'll cheer me up I hope.

I dont know when or where I shall see you tomorrow, I suppose I'll have these two wretched fellows hanging after me all day. I am writing F.J.F a terrible account of the thunder to frighten him if possible. Bring me a little note paper please tomorrow if you can afford it. Goodnight dearest

Tramp

P.S. I dont think you read my letters I'll tell you why tomorrow.

MS, TCD. *LM*, 171

[1] James Montgomery (1870-1943), who became Ireland's first film censor in 1923; a constant theatre-goer, his name is mentioned frequently in Joseph Holloway's diaries (NLI).

To MOLLY ALLGOOD

[Glendalough House, Glenageary]
Tuesday. July 30th. 1907

Dearest

Did I ever write to you with this thing before?[1] I haven't a pen handy so I am using it now though it doesn't not seem to lend itself to this kind of note.

I am going to tde dentist tomorrow at a quarter to three and after that I'm free, are you free too? Or do you rehearse in the afternoon as well as the morning? Would you like to meet me? I dont know where we could meet . . . . . . A card has come from Henderson to say I am wanted at the Abbey tomorrow[2] so I'll probably go in about twelve, and if so we can lunch together and arrange about the afternoon. I dont know yet what time F.R.[3] is going on Thursday, she doesn't know herself. I have written to my ma that I am asking you down for lunches and teas. It is very uncomfortable here for the moment as my mother ⟨forgto½to⟩ forgot to leave any knives and forks etc. so F. and I are hard up.

Yes we had a great time yesterday. It's wonderful how we always amuse ourselves when we are together. IQm better glory be to . . . . . ⟨for⟩ so we'll hope for the best.

This machine wont wrote sentiment so good bye till tomorrow sweetheart.

TTTTTTTTRRRRRAAAAAMMMMMPPPPPP

TS, Texas. *LM*, 171

1 This letter is typed, inexpertly, and corrected in MS. Although he rarely used it for correspondence, JMS wrote most of the drafts of his plays directly on to the Blickensdorfer typewriter he purchased in 1900; see I. 54.

2 Although Henderson's appointment was to have terminated on 31 July 1907, Holloway was surprised to see him at the Abbey on 20 August (NLI).

3 Florence A. Ross (1870–1949; see I. 184), JMS's cousin and close childhood friend; she was one of the few relatives who shared his interest in theatre and the arts (cf. *My Uncle John: Edward Stephens's Life of J. M. Synge*, ed Andrew Carpenter [1974], 193).

To JAMES PATERSON[1]

Glendalough House | Kingstown
August 2nd. 1907

Dear Mr Paterson

I am very sorry I missed seeing you the other day. I was away in the Wicklow mountains and did not get your note till you had probably left again. In any case I was so far away I could hardly have got down. I hope you will carry out your intention of paying us a thorough visit in Ireland before long.

I was delighted to get your earlier letter, some weeks ago, and to hear that you think so well of my book on Aran.[2] It is a great relief to me to find that it is thought well of after all. It was refused by publishers often in London for three or four years so that I had begun to think it was a failure. I hope to do a book on Wicklow — peasant-life, more or less of the same kind, in the next year or two, and perhaps another on the Kerry Islands.[3] I am working at these matters for the moment so I have started no new play. There have been many worries in the Theatre during the year that have wasted a good deal of our time, but I hope things are going to improve again now.

The company is to visit Edinburgh I believe next December — the first or second week — and I will send you all particulars when we know them. I hardly think I shall go with them this time, but it is possible, and I shall be delighted to see you all again if I do.

I am much the better for my time in Wicklow but alas, I'm not rid of my cough yet. I expect to go off away soon either to Kerry or Brittany where I have friends. Please remember [me] to Mrs Paterson and your party, and believe me with many thanks for your kind and encouraging letter

Very Cordially Yours

J. M. Synge

MS copy, TCD

1 James Paterson RSA (1854-1932; see I. 277), whom JMS had met in Edinburgh while on tour with the company in July 1906.

2 *The Aran Islands* had finally been published by Elkin Mathews, London, jointly with Maunsel, Dublin, in April 1907. Paterson's letter of 23 June 1907 spoke glowingly of the book: 'Not for a long time has anything thrilled me so deeply' (TCD).

3 JMS had visited the Blasket Islands off the coast of Kerry for two weeks in August 1905 (see I. 122-6), but during his lifetime published only one article, in *The Shanachie*, no. 5 (Autumn 1907), on his experiences.

To F. R. SIDGWICK[1]

GLENDALOUGH HOUSE | Kingstown | Co Dublin

August 7th [1907]

Dear Mr Sidgewik

Many thanks for your letter of July 30th, which I would have answered sooner only that I have been away in the country —

I have a short play the 'Tinker's Wedding' which has never been produced and I will be very glad to show it to Mr Granville Barker,[2] but I would like to run through the MS. ⟨first⟩ and make a few alterations before I do so.

We have never acted it here as it would have made a greater disturbance, if possible, than the 'Playboy'.

I do not think the 'T.Wedding' is altogether a satisfactory play and as what merits it has lie in a humourous dialogue that would have to be very richly and confidently spoken, I am not sure that it would be a very wise experiment for Mr Barker to produce it, However as I said, I will be very glad to let him see it and then we can see what he thinks. I have promised to let Maunsel publish it in the autumn.

I suppose if I send the MS to the Savoy[3] and mention your name to Mr Barker it will be all right, or shall I send it to you? I would be interested to know what you might think its chances would be with an English company and an English audience.

Thanking you again

Yours very sincerely

J. M. Synge

MS, Texas

1 Frank R. Sidgwick (1879–1939), a partner of the publisher A. H. Bullen from 1901 to 1907 and founder of Sidgwick and Jackson in 1908. In 1904, during the first ten months of the Shakespeare Head Press, Sidgwick recorded the practical problems of setting up a new press in Stratford in a diary (published by Blackwell in 1975), after which time Bullen moved to Stratford and Sidgwick managed the London office.

2 Sidgwick's letter, on A. H. Bullen stationery, states that he had sent a copy of *The Playboy* to his friend Harley Granville-Barker, who 'writes to me to say that he has heard that you have an unacted play, and wants to see it' (TCD). Granville-Barker (1877–1946), dramatist, actor, scholar and director, who with J. E. Vedrenne (see below, p. 107) established the Court Theatre in 1904, had directed the Stage Society production of *Where There is Nothing* (Yeats and Gregory) in June 1904.

3 Granville-Barker and Vedrenne were in the process of moving from the Court to the Savoy Theatre, a venture which lasted for only one season.

To MOLLY ALLGOOD

[Glendalough House, Glenageary]

August 7th 1907

Dearest Love

It seems quite curious to write to you now, it is so long since I have written. It is so showery tonight I dont think I shall go to the Yeats' after all,[1] I dont want to get wet. I went for a ride last night after you had gone, and I felt a little 'down' as I always do after one of our bad days when we do not get on very well. It is lucky we have so few of them, and that they are getting fewer as we go on. Will you meet me tomorrow at Tara St at *twenty minutes* to *four if it is fine*. We can have a turn in the Park and tea together, I think that is as much as you should do. If it is a wet day I will not go up there would be no where to go. If you are at all unwell or for any reason cannot meet me write to say so *before eleven*. I do not think I shall stay on in town for the night show, I cannot "STICK" these plays any more.[2]

I have nearly finished my article now and I will show it to you tomorrow if it is presentable enough.[3] I hope, my old heart, that you are taking good care of yourself I think you ought to go home and go to bed after 'Kathleen'. I wonder will you get this tonight no, I think, it will be tomorrow morning when you wake up out of your dreams.

I am sorry your visits here dont "go" I dont know why it is. I am rather out of spirits today, I dont know why unless it is because I am not to see my little heart's Treasure, that is enough to make me wretched surely.

I want to go through the Tinkers again before I send it to Granville Barker as some cuts have to be made, — I have just been writing to them about it, — and I want also to read it to you, or let you read it to yourself. This is a dull letter, my dear heart, but I am dull today. It is lonely in this house by myself — Next summer please God things will be different.

I went for my usual ride today around through the Scalp and home by the 'Brides Glen' but it came on to rain on my way home so I had to change when I got in. Do you want the little bag for this tour[4] I will send it to you by the tram if you do. I am sorry you will not get this tonight — I suppose you will be looking out for it — I was too tired to write this morning when I had finished my article. God bless you my thousand loves and give you good luck and good health.

Your lonely old Tramp.

MS, TCD. *LM*, 172

1 John Butler Yeats (1839–1922; see I. 150) and his two daughters, Susan Mary (Lily, 1866–1949) and Elizabeth Corbet (Lolly, 1868–1940; see below, p. 147), frequently entertained the Abbey Theatre company at Gurteen Dhas, Dundrum. Lolly later stated that Lily had had a romantic interest in JMS (William M. Murphy, *Prodigal Father* [1978], 238).

2 As usual, the theatre was open for Horse Show week, but performing revivals only, of *Kathleen ni Houlihan* (Yeats), *The Rising of the Moon* (Gregory), *The Hour Glass* (Yeats), *Hyacinth Halvey* (Gregory), and *The Land* (Colum).

3 Probably his article on the Blasket Islands for *The Shanachie*.

4 The company was going on a two-week tour of Waterford, Cork, and Kilkenny, 11–27 August 1907.

To STEPHEN MACKENNA[1]

Glendalough House | Kingstown
August 10th [1907]

Dear MacKenna

    I expect to be in London for one night next week — probably in Montague Hotel — on my way to Brittany where I am to join

Lebeau[2] for a few weeks for my health's sake. Are you still in London, and if so could you and Madame meet me somewhere in town and share my evening meal?[3]

Yours

J. M. Synge

MS, Texas

[1] Stephen MacKenna (1872–1934; see I. 57), journalist, nationalist, translator of Plotinus, and friend of JMS since the winter of 1896–7 in Paris.

[2] Henri Lebeau, French travel writer and university teacher (see below, p. 218), had been urging JMS for some time to join him on a cycling tour of Brittany.

[3] The MacKennas had moved to London in May or June 1907 after MacKenna gave up his position as Paris correspondent for the *New York World*.

To MOLLY ALLGOOD

Glendalough Ho

August 12 [1907]

Dearest

I got your letter this morning. I fervently hope that you are getting on well and not the worse for your knocking about. I hate to think of you knocking about in Kilkenny yesterday[1] with no one to take care of you! Poor pet.

I was very bad all day yesterday, hardly able to open my eyes with a heavy feverish cold, but I am better today I only hope it wont go to my chest and make my cough worse again. I think about you a very great deal, but I am a little afraid to put much of my heart into this letter for fear it might go astray and be lost. I am VERY lonely.

I heard from Lebeau this morning that he has taken a room for us with two beds ⟨for us⟩ for a month. I dont much fancy sharing my room with a man I know, after all, so slightly especially when I am not very well. It is a nuisance. I am too heavy today to write much, let me know every day how you are my poor love

T.

MS, AS. *LM*, 173

[1] Apparently the company stopped in Kilkenny on their way to Waterford, the first place on their tour, perhaps to arrange lodgings for their final performances the following week.

To MOLLY ALLGOOD

[Glendalough House, Glenageary]
August 13th [1907]

Dearest Life

I got your letter — last night, and I was very much distressed to hear of your bad time on Sunday evening. I cannot understand why *you* went with Sally and Fay, when they could have looked for digs JUST AS WELL[1] without you. However it is too far away and I am too wretched myself to scold you. Let me know again as soon as you can how you are. I am of course exceedingly anxious about you.

I have one of my regular influenza-ish turns with my usual cough as bad as ever — at least the same as ever, but not at all so bad as in the winter. It is very disheartening; but nothing new, of late years I seldom get through a summer without a turn like this. Last year I had it in Glasgow and Aberdeen, when we were on tour. It is very lonely and wretched sitting here all day by myself, I am not able to go out yet. I wish I could write you a nice letter but I'm too miserable in myself, and too uneasy about you to have any little sentiments left in me. I expect you will find me here when you come back. I wont be able to face that long journey for some time yet. Perhaps I wont go at all — or wont go till after the operation.[2] Then I could pick up for both at the same time.

I often think of your story of the moth, — I delight in all your little ways — there's a sentiment at last by grace of God. Do put down your foot and swear once for all that you will take care of yourself come what may — even though the theatre and the Fays and every thing else — except me — should go to pot. I cant help thinking it is a sort of bravado that makes you do things like going out the other night when there was no need. Are you sure of your Cork digs? Is it Opera House Cork? for letters. This will of course be my last to Waterford.

T.

MS, TCD. *LM*, 174

1 Underlined five times.
2 To remove swollen gland from his neck — an undiagnosed symptom of Hodgkin's disease.

To MOLLY ALLGOOD

[Glendalough House, Glenageary]
August 14th [1907]

Dearest Trea.

I got your letter (Tuesday's) this morning — it was a very charming little one, but I am sorry to hear that things are not going well in Waterford. At least I am sorry and not sorry — *too* much touring in little Irish towns would be a dog's life for you, and it would mean doing our *un*intellectual work, L. Gregory's etc, only.[1] I was out for a short time yesterday but I wasn't much the better for it so I am staying at home today. The days seem quite endless here in this empty house and it is not easy to keep up my spirits. However I really am not at all bad this time — I have had no fever except the first day which is a very good sign — so I hope this little attack wont make any further change in our plans than to throw off my Brittany voyage for a week or so. Curiously the last time I was going to Brittany from Paris — in 1900 — I had influenza too, and I remember lying all day in my little room wondering whether I should go or not. I had a turn like this too one year in Aran and it did not leave any trace behind it.

I am glad to see by your letter that you seem pretty well. Do you think you are none the worse for your experience on Sunday? I always feel a little doubtful whether the letters I send to the Theatre will reach you — I am sending this to the Opera House — so I am afraid to put much *depth* into them. Perhaps if I sent this to Waterford you might [get] it but I'm afraid to risk it. I wonder shall I see you before I go away.

Your T.

I I bought a book when I was out yesterday, Thackery's 'Esmond'[2] which has passed a good deal of my time. I will leave it for you. It is quite readable though very 'flat' in places. You ask if I was ever in Waterford. Dont you remember my voyage there last year with Miss T?[3]

P.S. Give me your address in Cork very *legibly* written. Did you get my letter of yesterday?

MS, TCD. *LM*, 175

---

1 Only one of JMS's plays, *Riders to the Sea*, was being performed by the company on this tour.

2 *Henry Esmond* (1852), the historical novel by William Makepeace Thackeray.

3 Agnes Tobin (1864-1939; see I. 309), American poet and translator, whom JMS had apparently met in London some years previously. He accompanied her to Waterford, home of her ancestors, during her visit to Dublin in September 1906; see I. 205.

To LADY GREGORY

Glendalough House | Kingstown
August 14th [1907]

Dear Lady Gregory

I suppose Fay has told you about the takings etc last week. The expenses — cut down to their lowest — were about £30 and the takings up to and including Sat. Matinée were about the same. I do not know what was taken on the last night. Fay told me of your decision about playing the three nights weekly instead of the Saturday only. I hope it will work well, but I dont feel greatly taken with the scheme.

I have been back for a couple of weeks but I have not been often at the Theatre. Fay gave me to understand that he was to have a free hand more or less with these tours etc. to see what he could do with them.[1] I think it is the best plan.

I was much better after my time in Wicklow and I had arranged to go over to join Lebeau in Brittany this week to complete the cure, but very unfortunately, I developed another feverish cold and cough on Saturday night, so I dont know now whether I shall be able to go at all.

I have had rather bad accounts from Waterford. Part of the cottage was forgotten so the programme had to be rearranged the first night. The audience was thin and jeered at Vaughan in the Wise man,[2] and hissed the Rising of the Moon, and Spreading the News — I suppose on the score of the Playboy.

Vaughan said something to me about signing cheques in Henderson's place and that you had told him you were writing to me about it. I think of course as he is managing everything that he will have to sign as Secretary. But I think, now that the business is not quite so much a matter between personal friends as it used to be, that the Directors i.e. two of the Directors should not in future sign blank cheques. Obviously the rule that the Directors must sign is to ensure that they should control and be responsible for all the money that goes out — and I think the method we fell into with Ryan[3] of signing blank cheques 'en bloc' is not a business like one. If you are of the same opinion it would be well to begin the other method now when we are making a change of hands. I do not mean for a moment that I have any doubts about any one in the place but I think it is not well to be too lax.

Vaughan is very energetic and working very well — perhaps as new broom.

I hear vague rumours from Fay that Miss H. is still writing un-pleasantly[4]

Yours sincerely

J. M. Synge

MS, Berg. *TB*, 233

[1] William G. Fay (1872–1947; see I. 79), founder of the Irish National Dramatic Society, the group of actors which became the nucleus of the Abbey Theatre company, had been reinstated as stage manager after Payne's resignation.

[2] Described by Dudley Digges (see below, p. 204) as 'a tall figure in a long black cloak and a large Fedora hat . . . looking like the embodiment of Irving, Tree and Robertson' (W. G. Fay and Catherine Carswell, *The Fays of the Abbey Theatre* [1935], 68–70, 227–31), Ernest Vaughan had performed with W. G. Fay's Comedy Combination in the early 1890s, but was touring as a professional actor during the early years of the theatre movement. After Payne left, W. G. Fay persuaded the directors to appoint Vaughan as business manager. In 1907 he performed small parts in *Fand* (Blunt) and *The Unicorn from the Stars* (Yeats and Gregory) as well as in Yeats's *The Hour Glass* ('the Wise Man'), and resigned with the Fays in January 1908, again going on tour.

[3] Frederick J. Ryan (1870–1913; see I. 83), who served as secretary of the Irish National Theatre Society, 1903–4.

[4] Miss Horniman had not forgiven the company — or JMS and Lady Gregory — for the theatre's and Yeats's falling under the spell of 'the vampire Kathleen ni Houlihan'; she was also convinced that W. G. Fay was incompetent (see *TB*, 223–4).

To MOLLY ALLGOOD

[Glendalough House, Glenageary]

August 15th 1907

Dearest Love

Your letter came all right this morning. There was a post card in the box so I thought for a minute it wasn't there, and I nearly collapsed. I'm sorry Waterford is failing. Dont mind W.G's talk, it is natural enough for him to try and run up his wife. I agree with him that the additional £1 a week all round makes some of the salaries too high. Mrs Fay wouldn't get two pounds a week in any other show in Europe, neither would O'Rourke.[1] This is between ourselves. I wonder what gave you hysterics. I found a book on nursing the other night in a cupboard so I turned up hysteria at once that I might know! They say the patient must resist the attack *herself* that is the great thing, and she might drink a glass of cold water — be sure it is clean if you try it — when an attack threatens.

I think I am better today but I'm not sure. I'm going out for a while I cant stand another long day in here. I thought yesterday would never end, — sitting in these empty rooms from 9 in the morning till 11 at night. I dont know at all when I shall get away, I have a good deal of loose cough still, and I'm very pulled down. I'd give the world and all to have you here these days, little sweetheart. I always have an ocean of beautiful things to say to you when I'm in bed or sitting alone the evening, but now somehow — I'm in a fuss to go out — they've all dissappeared out of my poor old scull! I have been thinking very often of those late evening we had up on the mountain road in Glen Cree, and feeling to you as I felt to you then in that wonderful solemnity and calmness. Many people, little Heart, have never been as happy we were then, at least with a happiness of such a good quality as ours. I feel that we are a great deal nearer each other now, than we were when the last tour was on, I hope you feel so too, and that you are remembering all your promises.

What a long time it seems since we were in Glen Cree, and what a good time it was. Dear little life write me a long letter the next time.

I hope you are getting proper food and keeping yourself well. Do please. I beleive if I was *put to bed* and kept there when one of these colds is coming on — as it was last Saturday when I went to the Abbey — that I'd never have a cough. Will you do that for me. It is amazing how many of my illnesses the last few years have been made serious by my doing something foolish the first day of them.

We're a pair of old crocks I'm afraid. I dont feel too bad today, and I hope I'll soon be all right write to me nicely Sweetheart. I wrote yesterday to the Opera House. Have you got it?

Your old T.

MS, TCD. *LM*, 176

1 After the *Playboy* riots, the players were given a rise in salary. Mrs W. G. Fay (see p. 143) acted under her maiden name, Brigit O'Dempsey. Joseph A. O'Rourke (1882–1937; see I. 254), a tailor by training, played with the company from 1906 to 1916.

To MOLLY ALLGOOD

[Glendalough House, Glenageary]
August 17th [1907]

D----t L---e

I got your letter this morning, but of course none yesterday which made me a little uneasy. I am a good deal better and out again as usual, but I expect you will find me here when you come back.

Could you come and see me I wonder on Wednesday afternoon. Find out what time you are likely to get back to Dublin and let me know. You dont tell me where to write today or when you are going to Kilkenny so I dont know whether this will find you. I am going to *rush* off with it now to the general Post ofce in Kingstown and then it *may* catch the Cork Mail and reach you tonight.

I have no time for more — if you had given me your Kilkenny address I could have written a better letter but perhaps you are not settled yet, I dare say not. Send me your new address as soon as you can and then I'll write again.

T——

I wonder will you think of leaving your address in the Hotel if you go before this comes![1]

MS (with envelope), TCD. *LM*, 177

1 The accompanying envelope is addressed to 'Miss M Allgood Innisfallen Hotel Cork' and on the back JMS has written, 'If not found please forward to c/o National Theatre Company 'The Theatre' Kilkenny.'

To MOLLY ALLGOOD

[Glendalough House, Glenageary]
August 18 [1907]

D.L

I wrote to you yesterday to Cork but I have not any idea whether you will get it or not. Now you write to say you are extraordinarily anxious to hear from me and I am to write at once and then you give me *NO ADDRESS*.[1] I will send this to the Theatre Kilkenny and perhaps you will get it. I am much better I am glad to say, and I expect to get off in a few days. I had almost decided to go on Thursday morning — so that I might see *you* on Wednesday *evening* before I start — but as you are going back to Cork I may go sooner. It is not clear from your letter whether you are going back or not, but that is what I gather.

I would like to write you a fuller letter, but it is impossible when I do not know where to write. I have written every day except the day I did not hear from you. Excuse this note I have a head ache today, and I am not some how in a humour for writing. Send me your Kilkenny address AT ONCE, also tell me when you leave there on Wednesday and whether you are going to Dublin or to Cork. If you dont make things clear we may miss each other on Wednesday if I am still here.

P.S. Thanks for cuttings I am glad things are doing so well in Cork.

I would write you five pages today if I felt quite sure you would get them but it is intollorable to me to think of my letters knocking about, and perhaps in the end being opened and laughed at in the post office. I am a little hurt that when I am so ill and lonely your last letters are so scrappy and short. Write me a better one please before I go. This illness has taken all the pleasure out of the thought of my trip to France I wish I wasn't going now. Be sure to tell me by return what your movements will be. I asked you long ago if you are any thing the worse for Waterford and you have not answered! This is a scolding sort of letter, dont mind it Je t'aime beaucoup! et Je n'aime que toi!

[Unsigned]

MS, TCD. *LM*, 178

1 Underlined five times.

To MOLLY ALLGOOD

[Glendalough House, Glenageary]
August 18/07

Dearest

I wrote a grumpy letter to you this morning as I was a little 'put-out' by the uncertainty you left me in, as to your movements and addresses. Forgive it.

I have had another long lonely day – how different from this day a fortnight or three weeks ago – the day we left Glen Cree – but I took two walks, one of them through the rocky furzy place where we sat one evening when you were down here, so I have got along. I am much better again and my temperature is lower than it has been for a long time a good sign – a proof almost I think that there isn't much the matter. I met Dr Gogarty the other day and he says I ought to get the glands out as soon as ever I can and that I will be all right then.[1] So there is a good hope that I may shake off the delicate condition I have got into the last couple of years. You know I haven't been always like this. One thing is certain I'm not going to kill myself anymore for the Theatre, I get no thanks for it, on any side, and I do no good – at least as things are going now. If the company becomes a success after all as a touring company, and you have to spend half your time fagging round England and Ireland, I fear we will be separated a great deal. It will be worst for me, I think, as you have the variety of moving about and the excitement of playing, but I find being left behind here again and again a very trying and disheartening experience. However there is no use crying over what cant be helped at present.

I find it very desolate by myself here now without, my little changeling, I'm *unused* to being lonesome[2] and I'm not happy for an hour when you're off walking the world. I have just lit the lamp, as old Mary[3] has gone to bed, and I am writing in the silent house. How happy we'd be if you were here with me, little Sweetheart, I never thought that I would come to take anyone into my life so utterly as I have taken you, and how many chances, if they were chances, there have been in it all. It is a great thing that we had those quiet evenings and days in Glen Cree, they will be with us all the winter, the little stream, and the crying birds and the wonderful stillnesses in the evenings. I think sooner or later we'll come to spend a great deal of our time in the country. I wish you'd become a writer, and then we could both have our career living on a hill-top by ourselves. As long as your career is on the stage, of course, we will be tied to towns. I dare say this is all blather that I'm talking, but one's mind likes to look forward into a beautiful and intimate future. I sometimes wonder what your 'ambition' is like or if you have any. Is it chiefly a desire to get applause and get talked about, or is it a real love for acting good plays, and a real desire and determination to do it well. You have real talent I think and real talent of any kind is a very priceless thing so I would be sorry to see you give up the stage unless you could use your talent in some other way. — Suppose you and I write a play together!! Wouldn't that be great! You could supply the actual stage experience and I'll supply the fundamental ideas. Then you can write all the men's parts — I know you like men — and I'll write all the females. We'll do a play at once about life in Switzers — with an act II laid in Miss Fluke's —[4] Then we hire the Abbey and stage it ourselves and make our fortunes and live happily ever after. Now I'm going to bed as that's settled.

Monday morning

No letter from you this morning. I dont know what to do. I have just read yesterday's letter again, but you do not say whether you are all going back to Cork — only that the manager has *proposed* it. It is really *exasperating* not to know as I have to make my plans today. I suppose I had better fix on Thursday for my journey[5] as I could not bare to go away on Wednesday morning without seeing you if you are coming to Dublin that day. You will get this I suppose on Tuesday sometime. If you have time to write on that day, tell me if you can come down here on Wednesday and *what time*. If you get it too late to write on Tuesday *wire* to me on Wednesday morning. Of course if you are too tired after your journey up from Kilkenny to come out here, I could go up for an hour or two in the afternoon if it is fine. I am still coughing a good deal but it is not a bad cough

I am sending this to 'the Theatre' Kelkenny I have no idea whether it will reach find you. I cannot write to you again till I hear where you will be on Wednesday. If I hear you are coming home I will write to Mary Street.

Tramp

MS, TCD. *LM*, 179

1 Oliver St. John Gogarty (1878-1957), unkindly caricatured as Buck Mulligan in Joyce's *Ulysses* and famous for his escapades as well as for his poetry, was later a prominent surgeon and with Yeats a Senator of the Irish Free State. He contributed three plays to the Abbey Theatre: *Blight* (1917), *A Serious Thing* and *The Enchanted Trousers* (1919), all pseudonymously. According to Ulick O'Connor (*Oliver St. John Gogarty* [1964], 132), Gogarty diagnosed JMS's illness as Hodgkin's disease because the glands in his neck were located posteriorally; but O'Connor does not state the occasion.

2 An echo of Nora Burke's speech in *The Shadow of the Glen*: 'and then I got happy again — if it's ever happy we are, stranger — for I got used to being lonesome' (*Plays*, Book I, 39).

3 Mrs Synge's housekeeper, Mrs Mary Tyndal, who had known JMS since his infancy.

4 Switzers was a large department store in Grafton Street, perhaps the shop in which Molly worked for a short time before joining the Abbey full time. A Mrs Flude of the Cottage, Kilbride Road, Bray, is listed in the Dublin Post Office Directory; see I. 302.

5 Evidently JMS wrote this decision to his mother, still in Wicklow, for she entered in her diary for 20 Aug 1907, 'I heard Johnnie is going to Brittany on Thursday' (TCD).

To MOLLY ALLGOOD

[Glendalough House, Glenageary]
Monday Night | 19/VIII/07

Dearest

The post has just come and made my heart jump with delight — for an instant — till I found he had brought a circular for my mother only and nothing from you. Are you getting tired of writing to me? I dont want to be a bother to you, but if we are to keep up during this long separation without drifting, or at least seeming to drift a little apart — as you said we did the last tour — we must get into the way of writing *intimately* and fully. I cannot help feeling a little 'lonesome' tonight — I had a few lines only from you yesterday and nothing today though I have watched for every post. These days have been among the most dismal I have ever spent. It has been too showery to go far, as I am afraid to get wet, so I have been wandering in and out all day, and then wandering about this empty house. I am too restless to read, and too heavy to write so the time hangs terribly.

I am going into town tomorrow to see Roberts about my 'agreements' — which I have never signed — and perhaps old Yeats.[1] I wrote to Lady G. the other day about various matters, and got an answer from *Yeats* — and I fancied rather a stiff one.[2] There is no word of R.G's engagement I wonder if his mother is against it.[3] I wonder what you are doing, and if you are very good? When I think I wont even get answer to this for nearly a week — if you go back to Cork — I get a queer qualm of uneasiness, and lonesomeness. It is a mercy you aren't going to America this autumn[4] — you couldn't go away from me just now I think, we are too united, and still not united enough. There is no good in writing more I may hear tomorrow that you are to be home on Wednesday and that I shall see you I hope to Heaven that I shall. Tonight I hate the thought of going away at all. Are you remembering your promises?

Tuesday morning

Dearest Life

Your letters — two of them came today. I dont know whether to send this to Kilkenny or Cork I suppose Cork is the safest, — you do not tell what hour you leave tomorrow or where I am to write. By the way it would save a great deal of worry if you would put at the bottom of every letter when you are on tour — "Write next
(the address)
to — —— ", or "Write here till (Thursday night)" etc. It is always done when people are moving about. — Of course you would have to calculate roughly how long it would take to get answers. If you get this early on Wednesday and write in time for the night mail, I may get it — I ought to get it — before I start on Thursday morning. Please write me a good letter I'll write to you tomorrow to give you my French address. I dont feel well, I wish now I wasn't going away at all, but I suppose it is best to go. I had a friendly letter from Lady G. this morning, and she tells me of her son's engagement. They are to be married in the autumn and spend the winter in Paris, — at least that is what it looks like though one is never sure of her letters.

By the way I got a *great* qualm of uneasiness when you said casually you are going to leave Sally and 'dig' with someone else. PLEASE[5] dont, Dear Heart, it is better for you to be together, I think, and I will be very anxious and worried if you leave her. What do you know of the other people you suggest? I dont want *my* WIFE to be mixing with Music Hall artists. Now wont you be good? I wish you would tell me more that you are doing, you always promise to and then the moment you get on the road you keep me absolutely ignornant as to what you are doing, who you are going about with, and how you are passing your time, this isn't a scold, my poor little heart, I'm far too lonesome to scold, but I wish you'd write more fully, writing fully of external things leads on naturally into intimate things

Old Mrs Tyndall only spend 8/6 on my food last week, and when she was giving me the change she said she could easily keep two people for the same price. I have four fresh eggs — we have found fresh ones — every day, and two big chops, and cabbage, and marmalade and everything I want. I wonder if we ought to have her. She's a great old gossip and I think she'd think it wasn't proper to attend on an actress, but she manages very well and she "mighty knacky".

Oh God this cough is a fearful worry I am not getting on very well I am afraid, at least there is no change from day to day.

I feel very depressed and wretched, and lonesome. Be a good changeling and write to me nicely my dear old Heart

Your T.

I am uneasy now till I hear where you are staying you ought certainly to be with Sally, I think. Tell me what you decide and please be very good my O. h's L.

MS, TCD. *LM*, 181

1 George Roberts (1873–1953; see I. 80), director, with J. M. Hone and Stephen Gwynn, of the Dublin firm Maunsel & Co. which published *The Playboy* and *The Aran Islands* earlier this year and would publish *The Tinker's Wedding* in December 1907. The studio of John Butler Yeats at 7 Stephens Green North was a frequent dropping-in place for JMS and others.

2 Yeats's letter of 15 Aug 1907 responding to JMS's letter to Lady Gregory of the 14th presented arguments for altering the production schedule and giving Willie Fay a free hand. 'The Theatre is now a desperate enterprise and we must take desperate measures' (*TB*, 235–6).

3 In her letter to JMS of 19 Aug 1907 (TCD) Lady Gregory reported the engagement of her only son, William Robert Gregory (see below, p. 148), to his fellow artist Lily Margaret Graham-Parry (1884–1979), 'a pretty and charming Welsh girl'; the marriage took place on 26 Sept 1907.

4 There had been some talk of the company making an American tour under the management of Charles Frohman (see I. 299), but this came to nothing.

5 Underlined four times.

To MOLLY ALLGOOD
>[Glendalough House, Glenageary] Kingstown
>August 21 (evening) [1907]

Dearest.

I got your note this morning. You dont say how your eye is. I am anxious about, so dont forget to let me know. I was in town yesterday and I coughed so much and felt so ill that I almost decided to give up my French trip altogether — for the present at least — Today I am better, I think, but I find it very hard to decide, I wish you were here to advise me. I am not going in any case till Friday, so I'll have a day longer to think matters over. You see Lebeau and I are to sleep in a Breton village[1] and have our meals at the house of some friends of his who have very kindly invited me. At present however I feel too unwell for that sort of thing so I hardly see the good of spending £10 on a trip that I am not likely to enjoy and that is more likely to do me hard than good. I have more cough now than I had when I went to Jack Yeats, and I was miserable there too ill to enjoy myself in the least.[2] Lebeau wants to take me about touring on our bicycles and I am not well enough for that either, and if I do it I may regularly knock up again. What is more if I go now it will put off the operation till very late, and then the weather will be getting wintry and it will be harder to pick up. On the other hand I am sorry to dissappoint Lebeau.

Well, I think the *case* for *staying at home*, now that I state it at length, is overwhelming. I think Lebeau will have to do without me. What do you think? There is not much use asking you as I shall have to decide before I get an answer to this. If I stay at home I will see you on Monday, then if possible I'll go away for *a week* to somewhere near in Wicklow or to Lucan.[3] Then the first week in September I'll have the operation, and go away about the middle of the month for a couple of weeks to pick up — and *then* if I am all right!!!!!!!!!!!!

I might go to Paris and see Lebeau if he is there at the end of September that would be more possible. However I'll take another night to think things over, perhaps tomorrow morning I'll feel keen to go.

I have been to Bray by train for a walk this afternoon, and I am not very bad still I get turns of coughing and wheezing that are most distressing.

This is a dull letter all about my poor ailments, I was awake last night for a long time and I was 'briming-over' then with things to say to you. Well you'll have them some other time. I am glad 'Riders' is going well; after *Longford* Yeats said it was quite useless for the

provincial tours.[4] I saw a book copy of 'Deirdre' at Roberts' yesterday at 3ˢ/6ᵈ. There is an extraordinary note at the end giving a page
of the play that he had cut out, and then found that it was necessary
after all. He makes himself ridiculous sometimes.[5] Roberts says
about 600 'Aran Islands' have gone, that is very good I think. God
bless you my little life

Your T.

MS, TCD. *LM*, 183

[1] Paimpol, on the Golfe de St.-Malo, north-west of St.-Brieuc.
[2] May–June 1907; see I. 365–6.
[3] An attractive village on the Liffey about nine miles from Dublin, well-
known in the eighteenth century as a spa.
[4] *Riders to the Sea* was one of the plays performed at the Temperance Hall,
Longford, on 12 and 13 July 1906, when Yeats was accompanying the players.
See *TB*, 132–4.
[5] The theatre edition of Yeats's *Deirdre*, with the offending note on p. 48,
was published in August 1907 by Bullen in London and Maunsel in Dublin;
in November 1908 Yeats published a four-page leaflet with further alterations.

To LADY GREGORY

Glendalough House [Glenageary]
August 21st [1907]

Dear Lady Gregory

I enclose the cheques signed. I do not quite understand what
the £250 is, I thought it was £150 that we had from Miss Horniman.[1]

I was to have started for Brittany tomorrow morning, but I do
not feel well and I think I will give up the trip after all, and have
the operation on my neck performed as soon as possible – in a
week or ten days. I do not think I will get better till that is over,
and then I could go away with a lighter heart.

I am astonished at Payne's repertoire.[2] I fear we must be very
ignorant about the classics of the Anglican Drama!

Please give your son my felicitations on his engagement, I wish
him all good luck.

The news from Cork is most encouraging,[3] now if we could capture Belfast we might still do well in Ireland.

Yours sincerely
J. M. Synge

MS, Berg. *TB*, 238

[1] The 'rather . . . stiff' letter from Yeats at Coole had spoken of £150 from
Miss Horniman for the Irish tour, but she had sent £250 in July (*TB*, 235–7).

2 In her letter of 19 Aug 1907 (TCD) Lady Gregory had enclosed a news-paper advertisement for the Playgoers' Theatre company (Miss Horniman's new Manchester venture), whose repertoire was to include *David Ballard* by Charles McEvoy, *Widowers' Houses* by Bernard Shaw, *The Fantasticks* by George Fleming, *Clothes and the Woman* by George Paston, and *The Great Silence* by Basil Hood.

3 Lady Gregory had reported a gate of £26 in Cork.

To MOLLY ALLGOOD

[Glendalough House, Glenageary]
Thursday 22nd. VIII/07

Dearest

I got your wire this morning and your note. I wrote you a lon[g] intimate letter on Tuesday *to Cork* (Opera House) and posted it early so that you should have found it when you arrived on Wednes-day. I also wrote to you yesterday to same address I hope they haven't gone astray. I dont feel very certain about sending letters to these country theatres.

I am glad to hear that your eye has recovered. You dont tell me what you have done about your lodgings. Are you with Sally, or who are you with? You might have told me that I think, perhaps you forgot. I have given up the French trip finally. I am not well enough to go. I met a youth this morning who has just been in Aran. He says the people are deeply offended by my story about the tea being kept hot for three hours![1]

There is no use writing now till I hear if you are getting my letters I am looking forward to seeing you on Monday. I am very down and very lonely.

Your T.

MS, TCD. *LM*, 184

1 Cf. *The Aran Islands*, Part I: 'When the wind is from the north the old woman manages my meals with fair regularity, but on the other days she often makes my tea at three o'clock instead of six. If I refuse it she puts it down to simmer for three hours in the turf, and then brings it in at six o'clock full of anxiety to know if it is warm enough.' (*Prose*, 67)

To MOLLY ALLGOOD

[Glendalough House, Glenageary]
Friday 23rd VIII/07

Dearest Pet

I got your letters one last night one this morning. Last night's did me a world of good I was getting very depressed stuck here with nothing to do after I had finally given up my trip. It is good to write me a warmhearted letter now and then.

This will be my last letter to you on this tour — you will leave I suppose early on Sunday. Write to me on Saturday and then send a line when you arrive on Sunday to say what time you will come and see me on Monday. Old Mary T. has just put her head in to the door and told me I look 'lovely' 'splendid' again now. — I suppose writing to you does me good! I sent the Tinkers to Barker yesterday[1] and I am working now on the MS. as Roberts wants to print it soon. I am longing to see you again I have had an utterly miserable fortnight since you went away.

I have made no plans about next week. I ought to go somewhere I suppose to pick up a bit before they operate on me, but I dont know where to go. I am going to have tea with my niece Ada Synge[2] this afternoon to meet some old man relation of hers who wants to make my acquaintance. I am getting better I think but I am up and down. I was wise probably not to go to France now. Till Monday — I hope.

Your old T.

I may write a line to Mary St to bid you welcome when you arrive.

Your old T.

MS, TCD. *LM*, 185

---

[1] Granville-Barker acknowledged the play on 18 Sept 1907, saying he wished to discuss it with his partner; finally on 2 Dec 1907 he reluctantly decided his company would not be able to 'capture' the 'Irish atmosphere' (both TCD).

[2] Ada Synge (1888–1960), only daughter of JMS's brother Edward.

To MOLLY ALLGOOD

[Glendalough House, Glenageary]
Saturday 24th VIII/07

Dearest

I got your note this morning ⟨and⟩ so I am writing again to Cork as you tell me — I wonder am I to write to Miss O'Neill or to you? — though I haven't much to say exsept that I'm longing to see you. You had better come by the quarter to two I think on Monday, you will want a good rest after your long journey, and I am busy ⟨for the moment⟩ in the morning getting the 'Tinker's Wedding' ready for the press.

I am much better again and I have been out today for a turn on my bicycle. That is a good sign. I had tea with my niece yesterday my brother has a fine big house, and a nice drawing room. Ada was out on the Fleet in the afternoon so she left a note asking me to wait a few minutes till she came back with her friends.[1] So I had plenty of time to poke about their room and look at their curiosities. They have photos of every member of the family on both sides young and old except *me*. It is funy how I am a sort of 'outsider' with them all.

Be very good on your journey and have a good sleep and dont miss your train on Monday. I would die of dispair if you did.

Your old T.

MS, Texas. *LM*, 186

1 JMS's brother Edward Synge (see below, p. 225), a land agent, lived in Bayswater Terrace, Sandycove, Kingstown. The Atlantic Fleet, a section of the the British Navy comprising four battleships and two cruisers, called at several Irish ports during the summer of 1907, and on 22 August anchored off Kings-town in order to coincide with the Kingstown Township Regatta. Sightseers were allowed on board the vessels and the sailors took part in swimming and sailing competitions.

To MOLLY ALLGOOD

[Glendalough House, Glenageary]
August 28th/07

Dearest Child

What about tomorrow? The charwoman is not coming till Friday so I would like you to come here for tea if you can afford it. Will you come down by the quarter to two? If you'd rather come out on Friday we could go to Bray that day or we could do both. Please write tomorrow morning (Thursday) and post it before *eleven* to say what you'd like.

I had a cycle ride today but it was very dusty and unpleasant. I feel very well. I dont know what day I shall go to town, I am waiting till I have finished the Tinkers so that I may take them in to Roberts. I feel twice the man since you came home again, sweetheart, and I grudge every day I dont see you. So I hope you'll come tomorrow.

I have been typing my verses today but I am not working very hard. I got a letter from the Manchester Guardian last night asking me to do them a series of articles on 'Types of Irishmen'![1] If we can bring it off that will be £10 to £20 into my little pocket.

Goodbye Dear Heart
T.

Be sure to write tomorrow morning

MS, TCD. *LM*, 187

¹ C. P. Scott, editor of the *Manchester Guardian* (see below, p. 247), wrote on 26 Aug 1907, suggesting a series of articles 'on various "Types" of Irishmen, which need not be entirely imaginary, but could be reinforced by personal touches and anecdote' (TCD). According to a further letter from Scott on 8 Sept (TCD), JMS replied expressing interest, suggesting Jack Yeats as illustrator, but indicating that because of his health the series could not begin at once.

To MOLLY ALLGOOD

[Glendalough House, Glenageary]
Thursday night [29 August 1907]

Dearest

I found a letter from Miss Tobin, when I got back here this evening, asking me to call on her brother¹ *at once* at the Shelbourne Hotel, so I suppose I must go there tomorrow afternoon. I am sorry that our excursion is off. I shall probably see you at the Theatre *before* one, and if I am not whipped off by Yeats or someone we might dine together — I needn't go to this man till three or four o'clock

Your old T.

MS, TCD. *LM*, 187

¹ Joseph H. Tobin, a San Francisco lawyer.

To MOLLY ALLGOOD

[Glendalough House, Glenageary]
Saturday night [31 August 1907]

Dearest

Dont come till tomorrow afternoon *a quarter to two* please as I feel rather done up and I'm a bit feverish I'd better take things easy tomorrow.

T.

MS, TCD. *LM*, 188

To MOLLY ALLGOOD

[Glendalough House, Glenageary]
September 2nd/07

Dearest Treasurette

You'll want to hear what the doctor said I suppose He thinks pretty well of me — but as I am still a little feverish from Saturday's turn he thinks it better not to have operation till next week. I am to go to him next Monday to make arrangements. Tomorrow I'll take a day at home as I've not given myself much chance of shaking off this last turn.

Then on Wednesday morning I'll go and see Roberts, and look in at the Abbey afterwards about 12 or half past. Of course if you aren't well dont come down I'll have plenty of time to see you towards the end of the week. Write and be careful of your little self.

J. M. Synge (T)

MS, TCD. *LM*, 188

To MOLLY ALLGOOD

[Glendalough House, Glenageary]
Sept. 4th [1907]

Dearest Old Pet

Sally told me today that you weren't well so I hope you are staying safe *in bed* this time and taking care of yourself. There is no need at all for you to go to the Theatre as no show is near. Tell me how you are getting on. You will be well again I suppose by Sunday so that we'll meet again before my turn comes. I was in with Roberts today talking over the proposed American edition of my work.[1] Every-thing looks promising I think. He (Roberts) thinks very well of the Tinkers but its publication may be delayed if the American edition comes off. I hope you aren't very bad this time, let me know as soon as you can how you are, I am anxious to know.

My mother and Miss C.[2] came home all right yesterday and the house is very much upside-down, for the moment, as everything is getting put in order for the winter. My mother enquired very particularly for "Molly". By the way the other night old Mary Tyndall was telling me about some lady in the country and she [said] "She was a nice pretty girl, the best of her family, and indeed the young lady, you had sitting there the other day put me in mind of her. A nice cut of a lady she was."! Now do you feel flattered? You *ought*, because old Mary is might critical. I am sending you one of my American notices[3] to read, did you want more books? Or is there anything else I can do for you? This is a hurried letter so that is why it isn't very intimate. I've heard nothing of Tobin I must write to him I suppose and see if he is still in town. I half meant to go to him today, but then I thought I might as well come home early and save my money. My mother is giving me two pounds towards my house-keeping expenses while she has been away. So I wont come off too badly. Now I'll post this and you ought to get it at six.

Ever your old Tramp

DONT GET UP TOMORROW UNLESS YOU'RE VERY MUCH BETTER, AND IN ANY CASE DONT REHEARSE
Keep the cutting for me.

MS, TCD. *LM*, 188

   1 Suggested by John Quinn; see below, p. 46–7.
   2 Rosie L. Calthrop (b. 1864; see I. 50) frequently spent the summers with Mrs Synge in Wicklow.
   3 By F. J. Gregg; see below, p. 56.

To MOLLY ALLGOOD

[Glendalough House, Glenageary]
Sept. 5th [1907]

Dearest Love

I got your letter this morning I think it was very great shame for you to go to rehearsal yesterday — YOU PROMISED me you'd stay in bed the whole day, however I wont schold you now, as you aren't in good spirits. Let me know how you are getting on — I imagine if you take care now for three or four months you may make yourself all right again, but of course if you WILFULLY[1] break the doctors orders you can expect nothing but a LIFETIME of suffering and ill health. Now it's out — Dont mind me *too* much.

I've nothing very new to tell you I'm just getting along and waiting for my day next week — I dont feel at all uneasy about it, but I wish it was over. I'm sending you some stamps so that you may write to me tonight. You *dont* tell if you would like any books — so I suppose you dont want them — or perhaps you hadn't time to think of asking for them. I was very depressed last night about everything or nothing but I'm cheerful today and so I hope are you. I had a great hunt yesterday for *MS.* of P.B. but I found him at last. If *that* comes off[2] I'll get you a bicycle! Remember it is a profound secret. The Abbey Co will very soon have to make up its mind one way or other as to what they are going to do with me and my work, I'm not going to hang up my carreer on the good pleasure of any of them.

I might see you on Saturday I suppose if you are well enough. What do you think?

I have a number of letters to write this morning so I must stop good bye my own little heart, think about Glen Cree and keep yourself cheerful and take good care of yourself — It's a pity I'm not having my job done this week too so that we would both be laid up, and get it over, at the same time.

I have to write to Quin, and Gregg — the man who wrote the notices in America, — and Lebeau and to the friend of his who invited me to stay over there. All troublesome letters. I hope you pity me. Goodbye again my own treasure

T

MS, TCD. *LM*, 189

1 Underlined three times.
2 See below, p. 49, n. 8.

To JOHN QUINN[1]

Glendalough House | Kingstown | Co Dublin
Sept 5th/07

My dear Quin

I was very glad to get your letter a day or two ago.[2] I have been intending to write to you, for I do not know how long, to thank you for all you kindly did for me in copyrighting 'Well of Saints' and "Shadow of the Glen," and PBoy but I am dilatory about ⟨writing⟩ letters and, to my shame, I let the time slip by. I need not say I am again extremely grateful for your letter, the cuttings, and the advice you give me. I saw Roberts yesterday about Hackett's proposal and I believe he is writting to you on the subject. It seems too soon yet to say anything very definite till we see what Hackell and his firm are ready to offer.[3] If their terms are satisfactory and you think they are in a reasonably good financial position I have no very great objection to working with a small firm. Yeats has published most of his work, on this side, with small firms, and so have I, and there seems to be no reason why I should not do the same ⟨on th⟩ in America. It is most natural after all that work which can never have a really big sale should be handled by firms small enough to be interested financially, in a comparatively small success. The American Macmillan firm opened negociations with me about ⟨a⟩ 18 months ago but they did not come to anything. One member of the firm, I forget his name, who wrote to me seemed anxious to have my stuff but other members, apparently, were against it so everything fell through.[4] Whatever we decide to do I am very strongly disinclined to bind myself in *any way* as to future work. I do not think a publisher has any right to demand any such agreement. Did Roberts tell you that I have another little play "The Tinker's Wedding", (written about the same time as the Shadow of the G.) ready for the press, and in his hands? If the American volume is decided on I think it would be well to include the 'Tinkers' so as to keep all my early work together. It will be a little difficult to calculate royalties. I have retained American rights of Well of Saints and Tinkers (that is in all five acts, three + two) but Roberts has share in Playboy, and Mathews in R to the Sea, and Shadow of Glen (again five acts 3 + 1 + 1) However we can go into that afterwards if it is decided to go on with volume. It would be much simpler to bring out three volumes I. Riders, Shadow and Tinkers, II. Well of Saints. III Playboy, but I do not know how that would work with you in America. Mathew's agreement, (not a very fair one I think,) has only four more years to run from next spring,[5] so his share should not give us much troubl. I entirely agree with you that Mr Yeats would be the best man we could possibly have for the Introduction.[6] He has something so irresistably winning in his personality and way of writting that he would be sure to gain friendship for the plays.

I will write to Mr Gregg as you suggest and thank him for his notices. I was interested also to see the letters you sent me from T. Walsh. He is quite right that early work like 'Riders to the Sea' has a certain quality that more mature work is without. People who prefer the early quality are quite free to do so. When he blames the 'coarseness', however, I dont think he sees that the romantic note and a Rabelasian note are working to a climax through a great part of the play, and that the Rabelasian note, the 'gross' note if you will, *must* have its climax no matter who may be shocked.[7]

As to my manuscript. I work always with a typewriter — typing myself — so I suppose it has no value? I make a rough draft first and then work over it with a pen till it is nearly unreadable ⟨that⟩ then I make a clean draft again, adding whatever seems wanting, and so on. My final drafts — I letter them as I go along — were (G) for the first act, (I) for the second, and (K) for the third![8] I really wrote parts of last act more than eleven times, as I often took out individual scenes and worked at them separately. The MS., as it now stands, is a good deal written over, and some of it is in slips or strips only, cut from the earlier versions, ⟨Of course the great labour was caused by a continual growth in the construction of the play, which forced me to recast continually what I had written.⟩ so I do not know whether it has any interest for the collector.

I have read Shemus MacManus' article it is obviously *preposterous*,[9] Every one knows that since Parnell's death a number of extra-parliamentary movements have grown up in Ireland, — the Gaelic League, largely under Hyde, the agricultural development under Plunket, ⟨and A⟩, the Anglo-Irish literary movement under Yeats, the anti-treating League I think under the priests,[10] but to claim any or all of these for the Sinn Fein, Hungarian policy of "the *boy* Arthur Griffith," is an insult to the intelligence of any ordinary reader with the smallest information about Ireland.[11] God help us indeed if we are to fall into the hands of S. MacManus or any one like him. I am sending you two papers that you may *compare* the accounts they give of a meetin[g] last night. The small type into which the Freeman puts the Sinn Fein incident shows how frightened they are. I would not be surprised if Sinn Fein had a momentary success in *Dublin* — as the so-called Nationalism had in *Paris* at the Dreyfus affaire — but it will never touch the country.[12] I was interested in your idea of a play but it would make this long letter too long if I discussed it now.[13] I have been only middling the last six months or so and I have to go into an hospital and have some swelled glands taken out of my neck in a few days probably next Tuesday. After that they say I will be better. Thanking you again for your kind advice and help I remain

very sincerely yours
J. M. Synge

MS, NYPL

1 John Quinn (1870–1924; see I. 96), the New York lawyer and collector, was a close friend of Lady Gregory and already a benefactor of the dramatic movement when he first visited Ireland and met JMS in 1902. He financed U.S. copyright editions of *In the Shadow of the Glen, The Well of the Saints, The Playboy of the Western World* (Act II only), a service he would later also perform for *Poems and Translations* and *Deirdre of the Sorrows.*

2 Quinn's letter of 23 Aug 1907 (TCD) enclosed copies of Gregg's reviews, two letters from Townsend Walsh, an article in the *North American Review* by Seumas MacManus, all discussed below, as well as a further review of *The Playboy* by William Bullock from the *New York Press*, 21 Aug 1907; he also sent extensive advice about publishing in America, an idea for a play, and general commentary on Ireland and the Irish character.

3 (Edmond) Byrne Hackett (*c.* 1859–1953) had emigrated to the United States in 1899, working first with Doubleday Page & Co.; at this time he was head of the publishing department of Baker & Taylor. In 1909 he became the first director of the Yale University Press, and in 1915 founded the Brick Row Bookshop in New York.

4 See I. 155. The member of the Macmillan firm who wrote to JMS in December 1905 may have been George Platt Brett (1858–1936), who was responsible for the two-volume U.S. edition of Yeats's works, the first volume of which was published in November 1906.

5 JMS's agreement with Elkin Mathews, who first published *Riders to the Sea* and *The Shadow of the Glen* in his Vigo Cabinet Series in 1905, specified a term of seven years and a royalty of 10 per cent. (For the memorandum of

agreement, see *Some Letters and Documents of J. M. Synge* [Montreal, 1959], 7; and see I. 105-7.) His royalty from Bullen (later from Sidgwick & Jackson) for *The Well of the Saints* was 15 per cent. The attitude of his other publisher, Maunsel, towards U.S. publication was perhaps indicated by a letter to JMS from George Roberts of 27 Oct 1906, about the copyrighting of Maunsel's Abbey Theatre series in America (see I. 223): 'If we found it practical for us to secure American copyright', observed Roberts, 'we think you will admit it would be only fair to give us the complete rights for printing and publication in America as well as here, and for a longer period than five years' (TCD).

6 Quinn had advised publication in one volume only, retaining JMS's Preface to *The Playboy* and W. B. Yeats's introduction to *The Well of the Saints* in addition to a general introduction by J. B. Yeats, of whom he wrote: 'He has an extraordinary gift of expression and writes in a very winning way', using almost exactly the same words in a letter to W. B. Yeats (*Prodigal Father*, 324). On 15 Sept 1907, J. B. Yeats wrote to his son, 'I am quite ready to do [the introduction] provided it is done on approval (by which I chiefly mean my own approval)' (J. B. Yeats, *Letters to his Son W. B. Yeats and Others*, ed. Joseph Hone [New York, 1946], 100).

7 Townsend Walsh (d. 1941), biographer of Dion Boucicault, circus aficionado, former dramatic critic for the *New York World*, was at this time business manager for the actor Otis Skinner. In two letters to Quinn about *The Playboy* he spoke (7 Mar 1906) of the 'farce': 'As a picture of Irish life, even among the wild folk of the most primitive places along the western coast, it seems unduly grotesque,' adding a comment which Quinn would himself pick up: 'If Synge had made Christy murder a peeler instead of his father, the Nationalists would have crowned him a genius.' On 13 Mar Walsh wrote again, confirming that he believed *Playboy* inferior to previous work: 'The great charm of his "Riders to the Sea" was its absolute spontaneity and lack of effort. As in Mr Yeats' "Cathleen-ni-Houlihan" the characters spoke simply and with real feeling, and whenever there came a speech full of pregnant imagination it seemed precisely right and apposite.' He singled out two speeches — Michael James's description of the wake and the Widow Quin's dismissal of Pegeen as 'itching and scratching' — as being 'superfluously coarse'. (Both TCD)

8 ˙ Quinn had offered to buy the MS of *The Playboy of the Western World*. Actually, JMS reached draft 'F' for Act I, 'K' for Act II, and 'L' for Act III (*Plays*, Book II, 294).

9 Seumas MacManus (1869-1960; see I. 57), prolific poet, playwright, novelist, and essayist, who would become one of the most vitriolic attackers of *The Playboy* in America in 1911, divided his time between Ireland and the U.S. after his first wife, the poet Ethna Carberry, died in 1902. He was referred to by Lady Gregory and Quinn as 'Shame-us MacManus', primarily because of his support of the Sinn Fein policy of Arthur Griffith (1872-1922; see I. 106). MacManus's article, 'Sinn Fein', in the *North American Review* (vol. 186 [1907], 825-36), extolled the Young Ireland Party, 'under the guidance of a Dublin boy named Arthur Griffith' and including 'probably three-fourths of the national thinkers in Ireland', and implied that the Gaelic League, the 'Buy Irish' movement, and even the anti-treating movement had been initiated by Griffith and the Sinn Fein movement.

10 Douglas Hyde (1860-1949; see I. 55), scholar, poet, translator, had founded the Gaelic League, whose aims, under his presidency, were cultural rather than political: to revive Irish as the national language and to create a modern Irish literature. Sir Horace Curzon Plunkett (1854-1932), pioneer of agricultural

co-operation, first president of the Irish Agricultural Organisation Society (1894) and vice-president of the Department of Agriculture and Technical Instruction for Ireland 1899–1907, was the author of *Ireland in the New Century* (1904) and other books and essays dedicated to the slogan, 'Better farming, better business, better living'. The League against treating in the public-house exacted a pledge from each member neither to accept nor to pay for treats.

11 In 1904 Griffith published in the *United Irishman* a series of articles, *The Resurrection of Hungary, a Parallel for Ireland*, in which he advocated the abandonment of parliamentary action and passive resistance to English rule in Ireland. Following the example of the Hungarians under Déak after 1848, the Irish Members of Parliament were to form a national assembly in Dublin which would set up tribunals to supersede the courts. Griffith named his policy Sinn Fein ('We Ourselves').

12 Under the heading 'Dublin Corporation. Monthly Meeting. Sinn Fein and the Mansion House', the *Irish Times*, 3 Sept 1907, reported in detail the Lord Mayor's refutation of charges concerning rental — and reasons for not renting — a room to committees 'condemning himself and his own house'. On 5 Sept 1907 the *Freeman's Journal*, under the heading 'Scene Outside the Mansion House', briefly reported the story in small type. The case of Captain Alfred Dreyfus, unjustly convicted of treason in 1894, excited intellectuals in France for more than a decade until, in 1906, he was exonerated.

13 'Take some word like Sinn Fein,' Quinn had written, 'and trace a hero like "Shame-us" MacManus or Griffith who thinks he is a nation builder and who surrounds himself by some women and a lot of young asses who look upon him as a statesman and a nation builder . . . . and laugh at them. Show their mixture of cunning, bragging and hypocrisy . . . . . two of the great weaknesses of Irish character — their tendency to brag, their lack of that fine sense of honor in dealing with other people in intellectual matters, and their subservience to priests.' (TCD)

To MOLLY ALLGOOD

[Glendalough House, Glenageary]
Sept. 6th. 07

Dearest Treasure

I got your letter this morning and I am glad to hear that you are getting on so well. Take care now you dont make yourself bad again. I will go up tomorrow by the train that gets to Tara Street at *five minutes past two* so meet me there then, and we can go to the Park or somewhere. If there is anything to stop me I'll wire to you at Mary Street before one. My little old cousin[1] — who first took me abroad is to be in Kingstown tonight and it is just possible that she may annex me tomorrow, but that is not probable. I've got a very sore eye again, but it is the lid and not like yours. I hope it will get better soon.

I have been out riding with Miss C[althrop] the last two days, round the lane between the Chimney and the Scalp yesterday and round through the Scalp today. My mother told her all about you so we have been talking about you, and she wants to meet you. How would you like that? I might take her to the Abbey next week, if there is time before the operation. You wont get this in time to answer about tomorrow, so if you are not a[t] Tara St I'll take it for granted that you aren't coming. Dont come if you do not feel well, and do not come, of course, if it is wet. I must post this now so that you'll get it in the morning. I was doing other things this morning sorting my papers so I did not write.

For ever and ever
Your old T.

P.S. Your letter has just come. Yes the letter was from Tobin, he says he was at the Abbey one night and was delighted with the show.

Do not on any account, please, have anything to do with Mrs Vaughan[2] I blushed red all over at the very thought of it. It could be of no use to you and would finally ruin your health. Who is paying Mrs Vaughan? Is Sally? Or Who? Isn't it splendid that you have got over this turn so well? Now when I'm spliced up too we'll be grand. I am going off to see my old cousin now I dont know when I saw her last. By the way Tobin went off to Killarney the day I called on him and when he came back old Yeats told him I was in *Wales*! So he did not try and see me. Old Yeats must be doting.

Now till tomorrow, sweetheart isn't it an age since we met.

T.

MS, TCD. *LM*, 191

1 The pianist Mary Synge (b. 1840; see I. 26), a cousin of JMS's father, lived in London; she had been responsible for his going to study music in Germany, where he stayed with the von Eicken sisters (see I. 8 ff.).

2 Perhaps the wife of Ernest Vaughan; according to Holloway (NLI) she accompanied the players on tour in November 1907, playing the small part of the old mother in *The Country Dressmaker* (see below, p. 63) when Sara Allgood's illness in Glasgow required a shifting around of cast. I have been unable to find any further reference to her or her activities.

To MOLLY ALLGOOD

[Glendalough House, Glenageary]
Sept. 9th/07

Sweetheart

I'm sending you Macbeth, Hans Anderson, and the little book of old Welsh stories[1] — written 900 years ago — that you once asked me for. I hope you'll read them and like them, though they'll need a little bit of an effort from your lazy madcap head to lift out of

Mary Street into that wonderful and beautiful old world. Hans A.
I know you'll like. I coughed a great deal this morning, so I'm not
going to the doctor till tomorrow. I have been doing a good deal
all last week so one day of rest will be good for me. Let me know
how you are and if you are well of your cold.

I am sending these early so I haven't much to say.

Please take great care of the Mabinogion, — as you did of Aucassin and Nicolète.

I'll write to you again when I've seen the doctor tomorrow

Your old T.

MS, TCD. *LM*, 192

---

¹ Hans Christian Andersen's fairy tales, first translated into English in 1846,
were frequently reprinted in various editions; *The Mabinogion*, a collection of
eleven Welsh tales from the 'Red Book of Hergest', was translated by Lady
Charlotte Guest, 1838–49.

To MOLLY ALLGOOD

[Glendalough House, Glenageary]
Tuesday Sept 10 '07

Dearest

I am surprised at not hearing from you today I hope that you
got the books all right and that you are all right yourself.

I have to put off my affair another day — worse luck — as I
have a threatening of a little cold today — the merest threatening
only — so there is no use fixing for the job as it could not be done
unless I am quite well, and it would be a great bother to fix the day
and hour and then have to put it off. I hope to go without fail
tomorrow. This cold was brought on by a bungle the servants made
about not airing my night garments. My eyelids are sore again today.
How are yours? I am eaten up with impatience now to get this
business over, these days of waiting are intollerable

I cant write

Your old T—

MS, Texas. *LM*, 192

To MOLLY ALLGOOD

[Glendalough House, Glenageary]
Tuesday evening | 10th. IX.07

Dearest Life

I have just got your letter I am *furious* with *myself* for having
frightened you by my silly talk. I do not think there is practically

any danger in this operation — I would put it stronger only that I dont want to boast — so cheer up and keep a good heart. I heard today that the surgeon is away and wont be back till Thursday so there is another delay. I must see you again of course. Will you meet me tomorrow *(Wednesday)* at Tara Street at *20 minutes* to *three.* If you cannot, *write before eleven* if I cannot — if I am stopped or not well I will wire to Mary Street. Of course I wont go if it is wet.

Now my poor sweetheart be happy we ought to be very thankful that it is possible to get rid of this beastly ailment that is upsetting me so much. How are you. I dont mind O'Rourke's teaching you to cycle, but I confess I get a qualm when I think of you going for walks with a taylor! *Take* care he doesn't see this! Till tomorrow your old

                                      T.

MS, TCD. *LM* 193

To MOLLY ALLGOOD

                               Westland Row Dn
                     [11 September 1907] 4.04 P.M.
Miss M. Allgood 37 Mary Street Dublin   Missed you Tara please write

                                    Synge

Telegram, Texas. *LM*, 193

To MOLLY ALLGOOD

                   Glendalough House [Glenageary]
                                  Sept.11th 07
Dearest Love

Your letter did not come till *six o'clock it is stamped 1.P.M.* You must have posted it *late* for the eleven ⟨for the⟩ post. I went off to town and stood about Tara Street for half an hour or more I felt very uneasy about you and I got a great headache from anxiet[y] I thought you must have been run over or something. I hope I may not be the worse.

If I am all right tomorrow as I hope — I shall be at Westland Row, at 25 minutes to three if you are able to get there to meet me. If there was any doubt about your letter being in time you should have inquired at the Gen. Post Office, and wired instead. I feel shaken all over by the anxiety I have been in, I dont know what would become of me if any thing *did* happen to you, I'd never survive I think. I must post this now I suppose you will have got my wire. You deserve a good scolding for dragging me off to town by your carelessness I suppose to stand about in the damp when it is so important for me to keep in good health however I'm so over-joyed to hear that you are all right I haven't the heart to say any-thing to you.

Dont ride *too* far at first.

Your old T.

I wont wait tomorrow so be in time if you come to W. Row.

MS, Texas. *LM*, 194

To MOLLY ALLGOOD

[Glendalough House, Glenageary]
September [12th][1] 07

Dearest Treasure

I saw the doctor and surgeon all right and the operation is fixed for 12 o'clock on Saturday so I am go to in tomorrow evening. I got a qualm when I left you today and sat down in the doctors waiting room, but as soon as I saw him and started off for the surgeon's I felt as gay as if I was going to order a pair of boots. When I had seen Ball I went off to the hospital and engaged a room.[2] Then I got some tea in O'Brien's and went off and saw old Yeats[3] and came home by the quarter to six. Tomorrow I shall have to stay quiet so I fear I will not be able to meet you — I cannot ask you here as people are coming[4] — perhaps it is just as well for us not to be together we would feel queer and uneasy all the time and then when I see you getting uncomfortable I begin to get 'qualmy' myself. Ball says the glands will come out 'beautifully' and that I will be much the better for it, so cheer up now and dont *dream* of being *uneasy*. You can enquire for me about 2.30 on Saturday the address is "Elpas" 19 Lower Mount St.

You must write me a very nice cheerful letter when you get this. I hope I didn't depress you about the bicycle I hardly know what to advise. It seems *foolish* not to take a little time and make sure you are getting the best value for your money when your comfort and safety for the next five years or so depend on your choice. Besides you will want clothes and you have very little money to spare with your debt in the theatre and your "trousseau"! coming on. However I dont want to be a spoil sport, but I would be very anxious about you if you went riding much now without me to

look after you, and I am afraid you might over-do it if you hadn't
me to warn you.

You'll get this, my own heart's treasure, tomorrow morning,
so write to me if you can in time for the evening *6 o'clock* post
here. When I'm in Mount St. I'll write to you to the *Abbey* when
I'm able to write of course I wont be able for *some time*. (Do please
take care of yourself I feel anxious about leaving you so long)

It is *just possible* I may wire to you tomorrow to come down by
the *quarter to three*, if it is very fine and I feel very well. You will
find the wire at Mary St about one if I wire. I would meet you at
Glenageary and have a little walk   dont be disappointed if I dont
wire as it is quite uncertain.

Post Script. Now I've had supper. I think I have told you everything.
Be cheerful and well when I come out again — you weren't looking
at all well today — and then we'll have great times. Of course I'll
write to you again tomorrow if I dont wire you to come down here.
Read your books and learn your parts and be happy my sweet pet,
I feel worse about you moping and making yourself miserable than I
do about my own affair.

Remember it is very doubtful about tomorrow so dont count
on seeing me. I must be careful now. A thousand blessings your
old Tramp. If you come down we'll have tea out so dont worry
about your 'get up'.

MS, TCD. *LM*, 194

1 Misdated 11 Sept.

2 Sir Charles Bent Ball (1851–1916), Regius Professor of Surgery, Dublin
University, had an office at 24 Merrion Square North. The Elpis Nursing Home,
19 and 20 Lower Mount Street, had been established by JMS's brother-in-law
Harry Stephens (see I. 106) and Miss Margaret Huxley, relative of Thomas
Huxley, the biologist, and matron of Sir Patrick Dun's Hospital in Dublin.

3 There was a branch of Johnston, Mooney & O'Brien Ltd. at 38 Stephens
Green North, near J. B. Yeats's studio. The elder Yeats wrote to W. B. Yeats
on 15 Sept 1907, 'I saw him [JMS] the day before the hospital business and he
was in good spirits, wanting to see Jack about a book on Irish types he is medi-
tating' (*Letters to his Son*, 100).

4 Mrs Synge's diary for 13 Sept 1907 reads, 'Hall door varnished and had to
be open all day, made it very cold. Johnnie fearful of getting cold . . . . Mamie
and Kathleen [Robert Synge's wife and daughter] came to tea rather late and
then Robert came in.' (TCD)

To FREDERICK J. GREGG[1]

Glendalough House | Kingstown | Dublin
Sept. 12th/07

To Fredrick J. Gregg Esq

Dear Sir

My friend Mr John Quinn sent me several very kindly notices of my plays and "Aran" book — a week or so ago — which he told me were written by you.[2] Ever since I read them I have been intending to write to you, but I have let the time slip by, and now I can write a hurried line only as I am just packing my bag to go into an hospital where I am to have an operation on my neck tomorrow morning.

I am particularly grateful for any outlying friendship that the "Playboy" has been able to gain for himself, as although our actual 'row' in the Abbey was ⟨distinctly⟩ invigourating, the peculiarly ignorant malignity of some the articles and letters that followed it — in the Irish Press — gave one a sort of disgust for the whole business. I hope to be at work again in a few weeks, but I do not quite know what my next ⟨work⟩ play will be like. The "Playboy" affair brought so much unpopularity ⟨to⟩ on my friends Lady Gregory, Mr Yeats and the individual players of our company that I am placed in rather a delicate position. I am half inclined to try a play on 'Deirdre' — it would be amusing to compare it with Yeats' and Russells'[3] — but I am a little afraid that the "Saga" people might loosen my grip on reality. — Let the circumstances be my excuse for this 'scattered' note, which is written only to give myself the pleasure of thanking you sincerely for the sympathy you have shown my work.

Very faithfully yours
J. M. Synge

MS, Lilly

1 Frederick James Gregg (1864–1927), an old school friend of W. B. Yeats and George Russell (AE), now a journalist in New York.

2 Two unsigned notices of JMS's work appeared in the New York *Evening Sun*, the first, on *The Aran Islands* (6 July 1907), observing that 'Mr Synge's work has an originality, a strangeness, which places it quite apart from that of any of his contemporaries', and the second on *The Playboy of the Western World* (10 Aug 1907).

3 The close involvement of George William Russell ('AE', 1867–1939; see I. 95), poet, mystic, and economist, with the theatre movement ended about 1905. AE's *Deirdre* was first produced by W. G. Fay's Irish National Dramatic Company 2 Apr 1902; Yeats's *Deirdre* was first produced by the company at the Abbey Theatre 24 Nov 1906.

To LADY GREGORY

Glendalough House | Kingstown
Sept. 12th 07

Dear Lady Gregory

I was glad to get your letter and card some time ago, but I am sorry to say I missed Yeats, as I was not quite well and the day was so bad I could not go to town. I have been hanging on ever since waiting for the operation, but at last it is fixed for tomorrow, so I hope my troubles will soon be over.

I have not been to the Theatre for some time but things are going smoothly there I believe.

I hope your play has got on well and will be 'in' for this season.[1] I have not made any attempts at a play since, I have been so bothered with my health, and I have had so much other work to do — Kerry and Wicklow articles chiefly that I am going over.

I suppose you and Yeats will be here some time in the autumn. After all the storms in the Abbey the present lull makes me almost feel that it is dead or dying. I wonder how things will turn out. I do not think Fay will be able to do much, that is worth doing, unless we keep with him, and over him.

This line is just to let you know why I am so little to the fore!

Yours sincerely
J. M. Synge

MS, Berg. *TB*, 238

1 Probably *Dervorgilla*, first produced at the Abbey on 31 Oct 1907.

To MOLLY ALLGOOD

Glendalough House [Glenageary]
Sept. 13th. [1907]

My own dearest Love

I couldn't get you out to me today, I was inclined to sneeze and the weather was threatening so it would have been madness to run the risk of givin myself cold. I am very sorry not to have seen you, yet in some ways it was better not not, ⟨see you,⟩ I feel perfectly hard, and fearless and difiant now, but if I saw your little sweet face looking mournfully at me I'd get sentimental and qualmish at once. I'm really not at all uneasy the doctors and nurses and all of them take it so utterly as a matter of course, they reassure one. You mustn't think of being uneasy either. I'm going in there to be cured I hope, and it isn't at all as if I was going to the wars. How would you like it if I was a ⟨guady⟩ "gaudy officer"[1] getting poted at by the Boers or some one? Did I give you the address? It is "Elpas" 19 Lower Mount Street. If you like to come down there at about 3 o'clock tomorrow and inquire for me you can, but perhaps the telephone is the simplest way. Perhaps they will call be 'singe' you'll have to spell it S.Y.n.g.e as Fay does in his article.[2] The little skit, by the way, isn't at all bad. It's six o'clock now and I'm looking out for a letter from you. I hope one will come. Dont for get you've promised *not to ride in traffic*!

I feel wonderfully gay! I'm going in by the quarter past eight this evening so I haven't much longer to wait. The worst time will be tomorrow morning waitin about without any breakfast till 12 o'clok! at the hospital. I dont believe you'd like me a bit if I was a kind of cast-iron man who didn't know what it was to be ill? If I was like that I wouldn't be able to sympathise with you, when you aren't well. ——

Your letter has come do try and be happy. If you know how I am counting the hours till I can get you for my very own! Meanwhile try and keep philosophical and cheerful — a certain amount of wretchedness is good for people when they're young — I wouldn't be half as nice as I am if I handn't been through fire and water!!!

My spirits are going up, and up, and up, they always do when I get into a good tight corner. The only weight on me now is the thought that you are unhappy. Of course I'll have qualms tomorrow but after all it's an interesting experience to break the monotony of ⟨course⟩ one's daily. I believe if I was a woman I'd have a big family just for fun! I wish you could see me grinning over this letter and you'd get as cheerful too, by this time tomorrow of course I'll be pretty flat. Now Good bye for a few days my own pet, treasure, life, love, light and all thats good

Your T.

MS, Texas. *LM*, 196

1 A phrase from *The Playboy*.
2 The article is unknown; perhaps an unsigned 'paragraph' for one of the company's tours.

To MOLLY ALLGOOD

[Elpis Nursing Home, Dublin]
[18 September 1907]

Dearest
Going on splendidly   Write to me as often as you like. It is a

good plan for you to come with F.J.F, I'll tell you when   Of course I'm rather weak still

I mustn't write more, I think of you a lot

T.

MS, TCD. *LM*, 197

To MOLLY ALLGOOD

[Elpis Nursing Home, Dublin]
Sept 20th '07

Dearest L

I got your note yesterday and I hope will get one tomorrow. How are you, my little pet, I'm getting on very well, but it's terribly slow. I'm afraid of having people in to see me JUST YET as I'm a bit too weak still, and I dont want to give myself a longer time than necessary. Sir C. Ball is going to take off the dressings tomorrow and then if all is well perhaps he'll let me up. Write me a good letter now. I got the one you gave W G. [Fay] all right. Dont cycle *too* far. A thousand blessings

T.

MS, TCD. *LM*, 197

To LADY GREGORY

[Elpis Nursing Home] 19 Lower Mount Street | Dublin
Sept. 20th [1907]

Dear Lady Gregory

The operation — a rather severe one as it turned out — went off all right last Saturday, and I'm getting on very well. They talk of letting me up tomorrow. I'm able to see people now if W B. Y should be in town again.[1]

Yours sincerely
J. M. Synge

MS, Berg. *TB*, 239

---

[1] Evidently Yeats, who was as usual spending the summer at Coole, did not come up to Dublin again until the theatre opened for the season on 3 Oct 1907; he wrote to Quinn on 4 Oct, 'I am to see him to-day for the first time. When he woke out of the ether sleep his first words, to the great delight of the doctor, who knows his plays, were: "May God damn the English, they can't even swear without vulgarity". This tale delights the Company, who shudder at the bad language they have to speak in his plays. I don't think he has done much this summer owing to bad health but he will probably set to work now.' (*The Letters of W. B. Yeats*, ed. Allan Wade [1954], 497)

To MOLLY ALLGOOD
                    [Elpis Nursing Home] 19 Lower Mount St | Dublin
                                             21 Sept 1907[1]

Dearest
    I'm in a great hurry, writing this. I'm up today and better but
I'm ANXIOUS[2] about you   You oughtened to be unwell *now*. It's
not the time. I hope you haven't done too much cycling   For my
sake don't go tomorrow. *I'm very distressed*
                                             Your old T
I hope to see you about Tuesday. Blessings on you. I heard today
the[y] were all right not tubercular in any way I am overjoyed.[3]

MS, TCD. *LM*, 197

    1 The address and date are written in another hand, possibly by Rosie
Calthrop who visited JMS at Elpis on that date.
    2 Underlined four times.
    3 'Some months before his death Mr. Synge got the idea that it was con-
sumption he had and he would not see Molly. This was, of course, the greatest
pain to her, but he was at last convinced by the doctors that there was no
danger to her.' (Lily Yeats to John Quinn, 31 May 1909, NYPL)

To MOLLY ALLGOOD
                              [Elpis Nursing Home, Dublin]
                                        Monday | Sept 23rd/07
Dearest
    I got your two little notes all right I am relieved to hear that you
aren't unwell.
    I was out in the garden yesterday for half an hour, and today
they have taken the stitches out of neck, so I shall soon be all right
now I hope. I am very shaky of course still.
    Will you come and see me tomorrow with F.J.F, about 4 would
be a good time.
    Dont be disappointed if I seem queer and flat, in this sort of a
business one feels worse the first days one is trying to get about
again, than any other time. Please bring me an ounce of Three
Castles[1] and some papers, — I dont know whether there is anything
in the Theatre Library that I haven't read, and that is readable, ask
F.J.
                                             Your old T.
MS, TCD. *LM*, 198

    1 'During rehearsals of his play, he would sit quietly in the background,

endlessly rolling cigarettes. This was a typical gesture, born more of habit than of any desire for tobacco — he gave away more cigarettes than he smoked . . . . He used to sit timidly in the wings during plays, rolling cigarettes and handing them to the players as they made their exits.' (Maire nic Shiubhlaigh, *The Splendid Years* [Dublin, 1955], 41) In his reminiscences of JMS, James Starkey ('Seamus O'Sullivan') also recalled 'the unmistakeable perfume of the caporal tobacco which he smoked continuously in cigarettes which he rolled in the French fashion' (TS with MS additions, TCD).

To MOLLY ALLGOOD

[Elpis Nursing Home, Dublin]
Sept. 25th/07

Dearest

Sir C.B. has just been in and says, I am '*well*' and may go home as soon as I like. I think I'll go tomorrow morning so you can write to me here if you write *tonight* or to *Kingstown* otherwise. Remember the time has come now for *you* to be careful of yourself. I feel in great trim today and ready for any thing. Your grapes were *magnificent* I was enraged when I opened them that I had not done so when you were here so that you might have had some too. I was so full the pleasure of seeing you I could think of nothing else. Isn't it *great* that all this wretched business is over!

T.—

The only thing this pencil can do is *underline* so I do *it OFTEN!*

MS, TCD. *LM*, 198

To MOLLY ALLGOOD

Glendalough Ho. [Glenageary]
Sept [27th]¹ 07 | *Friday*

Dearest

I got your nice little note all right yesterday morning.

I came back here before dinner, and, of course, felt very tired all the evening so that I couldn't write to you. Can you come and see me tomorrow (Saturday) afternoon? If you can, and *if you are all right*, — come down by the quarter to three and come to the House. Write <u>BEFORE</u>² eleven tomorrow to say if you can come If anything happens here to make it impossible for me to have you I will wire to Mary Street in the morning.

I feel a good deal better now, but I am rather shaky still. That is to be expected. I dont know at all yet when I shall get away for my change. I am sorry to have to leave you again, but of course it is quite necessary now that I should have a good change before the winter. Goodbye old pet

T.

MS, TCD. *LM*, 199

    1 JMS has written '25th' with a question mark.
    2 Underlined five times.

To MOLLY ALLGOOD

[Glendalough House, Glenageary]
Sept 30th 07

Dearest Love

I got your letter this morning and I was delighted to hear that you are getting on so well, remember to go on taking care of yourself. I am doing very well indeed, I wear a collar now when I go out, and I was able to take quite a good walk this morning, round through the furzy place where we sat one evening near Kileney Hill, and I am going out again now.[1] I am beginning to think that I will only go to Kerry for my change after all, I dont feel very much inclined for Brittany while my neck is at all sore. However we'll see. Yes I hope we'll soon be 'fixed' as you call it. I dont know what to advise about the table linen. If you get it you'll have to pay for it and I dont think you've any money. Anyway dont get much, as we may have to go into lodgings, after all, and then we'd have no need for it at once.

By the way I want *you* to get a *Note Book* and write down everything you read, who it is by, when he lived, and any particulars that you think you would like to remember. I have a wheelbarrowful of such notebooks (every one who reads seriously keeps them), and you will find it no trouble, and the greatest use. Do try, — to please me, because you know I'm ill still! Wont you? You are reading a lot of books that very few ordinary people read and it is a pity for you to let everything go in at one eye and out at the other. In a few years you'll be the best educated actress *in Europe*, and I want you to take a pride and pleasure in your progress. 'Nish,[2] dont you feel that I'm nearly well again, as I'm setting off to lecture you? Be good, write soon, take care of yourself, and we'll have great times presently.

T.

MS, TCD. *LM*, 199

    1 Mrs Synge's diary (TCD) records Molly's visits and JMS's progress: 'Johnnie

took a walk nearly an hour, seems stronger' (27 Sept 1907); 'Johnnie passed on Albert Road . . . M. Allgood here' (28 Sept); 'Johnnie improving, walked 1½ hours' (30 Sept); 'Johnnie out from 2 till past 8' (6 Oct).

2 Apparently one of Molly's favourite expressions; it probably comes from the Irish admonitory 'now!' (*anois*).

To MOLLY ALLGOOD

[Glendalough House, Glenageary]
Oct 2nd. 07

Dearest

I am most distressed at not hearin from you this morning. Are you ill or what ⟨is⟩ has happened? Please write by return. The last line I got was written on Sunday and this is Wednesday. You never left me so long without news of you before, and as I'm not very strong yet, I have worked myself up in to a fuss.

I am getting on all right but I am very much bothered by this numbed finger they have given me. It annoys me more than the glands ever did all the time I had them. I am going to Sir C. Ball today if it is fine. I dont know I shall go away at all after all. My mother is making me pay for my time in Elpis so I dont know if I can afford a trip. If you dont write today I'll go in and see you to find out what is the matter.

Your old T.

MS, Texas. *LM*, 200

To MOLLY ALLGOOD

[Glendalough House, Glenageary]
Saturday night | Oct 5 [1907]

Dearest Love

I'm very fond of you tonight. I've managed to have tomorrow clear — thanks be to God — so come down by the quarter to two dont miss it. I'll meet you at the train if I can and take you on to Bray but if I'm not there come down to the house. I wish it was tomorrow.

I'll tell you then all about the play as I understand it and criticise the acting.[1]

Your T——

MS, TCD. *LM*, 201

1 *The Country Dressmaker*, by a new playwright, George Fitzmaurice (1877–1963), received its first production on 3 Oct 1907; Molly played two small parts, Min Dillane and Maryanne Clohesy.

To MOLLY ALLGOOD

[Glendalough House, Glenageary]
Monday Night | Oct 7th 07

Dearest Life

How are you tonight? I wonder what you've been at all day, I've been very busy and I'm very tired now. First I typed my new Kerry Article[1] from 9.30 till 11, then I cycled till 1, then I had dinner and a smoke and cycled again till 4, then I typed till 5.30 and went up to my sister's to bid my cousin[2] goodbye, till 7. Then supper and now its 8, and I'm writing to you. Have you done as much as that? I'm beginning to wish you weren't so lazy. You'll have to stir up one of these days and give up snoosing till one o'clock, *soon*, I hope. Nish! are you wounded in your tenderest feelings? This is a silly letter, but I'm too tired to write; that is why. Do you know what I've been thinking you ought to write some Irish Theatrical Articles for the Evening Telegraph and make enough to get a bicycle. I'm sure you could write as well as Henderson — you've no idea how easy it is till you try and how soon your ideas begin to stream out of your mind — and of course I'd help you to put them in trim. I wish you'd try; you'd find it much more amusing than 'Nap'.[3] And you'd get money instead of spending it.

Hadn't we a great time yesterday? I wasn't at all tired or the worse, I hope you weren't either. I was thinking last night it's rather remarkable how well we seem to know now, how we're getting on at a distance. I felt 'as sure as sure' on Saturday night that you and Daussy were talking or something,[4] and there you were, playing him off for Lady G's benefit. That feeling for people at a distance is quite a well-known fact between people who are in close sympathy. It's called 'telepathy', as I dare say you know. I think we'll be married by Xmas, as we're long enough like this. I wonder if I should go out in the cold to post this or if I should leave it till tomorrow. I think I'll go so that you'll have it when you wake. Blessings Dear One

Your T

N.B. This is a long letter because I've written very small.

MS, TCD. *LM*, 201

---

1 'In West Kerry. To Puck Fair', published in *The Shanachie*, no. 6 (Winter 1907), 233–43 (*Prose*, 277–9).

2 Mary Synge.

3 A card game the players frequently played in the green room.

4 Udolphus ('Dossie') Wright (1887–1952; see I. 95), electrician and actor of small parts, was the only member of the company JMS seems to have been jealous of. See I. 176–80.

To LADY GREGORY

Glendalough House | Kingstown
Oct 9th [1907]

Dear Lady Gregory

I have heard nothing more of special Matinée, so I suppose it is going to take place.[1] I am settling to go South on Saturday morning, so if we are to have a directors meeting it would be best to fix on some time tomorrow if that is convenient to you and Yeats.

I see no advertisement of tomorrow's show in I. Times and there was no paragraph about it in stage column on Saturday.

In haste

Yours
J. M. Synge

MS, Berg. *TB*, 240

[1] On 11 Oct 1907 the Abbey players presented *Riders to the Sea*, *Kathleen ni Houlihan*, and *The Rising of the Moon* for the companies of Herbert Beerbohm Tree and Johnston Forbes-Robertson, who were performing in Dublin.

To MOLLY ALLGOOD

[Glendalough House, Glenageary]
Oct. 9th. 1907

Dearest Love

Jack Yeats didn't come yesterday after all, so I had a very long day here by myself. Didn't I tell you it was going to rain 'cats and dogs', I hope you realised what a damn fine prophet I am! I got your little note yesterday morning all right. Yes Sunday is a delightful memory, may we have *many many many* more like it. I'm going in to see Parsons[1] today and I'm going to Ventry on Saturday, tomorrow there will be a Director's meeting I think, and on Friday the matinee so I dont quite know when and how we're to meet. It's a great nuisance, and I suppose after the matinée on Friday they'll have all sorts of business to do and people to see. It's high time to put an end to these snatched interviews. Write at once and tell me what *times* you are free on Thursday we might meet for a lunch or tea before the meeting if it can be managed. I'll wire to you tomorrow if I can when I hear from you and Lady G. So tell me what hours you'll be at home and what at the Abbey. Good bye my own love, I've written five (5) letters this morning, business ones.

Your T.

MS, TCD. *LM*, 202

1 Dr Alfred R. Parsons (1864–1952; see I. 236) of 27 Lower Fitzwilliam Street, JMS's general physician.

To EDWARD GARNETT[1]

Glendalough House | Kingstown | Co Dublin
Oct 10th/07

Edward Garnett Esq
Dear Sir

I received your play this morning just as I am setting off for the country where I will have great pleasure in reading it carefully

Meanwhile let me thank you for your goodness in sending me a copy. I do not see how the English Drama is to develop if the censorship remains as it is.[2]

In haste

very truly yours
J. M. Synge

MS, Texas

1 Edward Garnett (1868–1937), well-known publishers' reader who encouraged, among others, Joseph Conrad, John Galsworthy, Edward Thomas, D. H. Lawrence, and Dorothy Richardson; the model for Bosinney in *The Forsyte Saga*, he published two novels, a collection of prose poems, and three other plays besides *The Breaking Point* (1907).

2 The play was probably Garnett's *The Breaking Point*, recently refused a licence by the Lord Chamberlain's office; it was performed privately at the Haymarket Theatre, London, in April 1908. A licence to perform had also been refused to Granville-Barker's *Waste*, and among JMS's papers are two telegrams from Granville-Barker urging him to sign a memorial disapproving of censorship 'as unconstitutional' (26 Oct 1907, TCD). JMS was one of 71 dramatists signing a formal letter of protest against the office of censor, as 'autocratic in procedure, opposed to the spirit of the Constitution, contrary to common justice and to common sense' (*The Times*, 29 Oct 1907, 15).

To JOSEPH HONE[1]

Glendalough [House, Glenageary][2]
Oct 11 [1907]

Thanks for yours. I think I can have article[3] easily by Nov. 1st. I have done most of it already.

J.M.S

MS postcard (photo), Blackwell

1 Joseph Maunsel Hone (1882–1959; see I. 229), one of the founders of Maunsel & Co. and editor of *The Shanachie*.

2 The postcard is postmarked Killarney, 12 Oct 1907.
3 Probably 'In West Kerry. To Puck Fair' for *The Shanachie*.

To MOLLY ALLGOOD

> c/o Mrs Kevane | Sea View
> Ventry | Dingle | Co Kerry
> Oct 13 (?) 07 | Sunday | night | !

Dearest Love

At last I have got to work at a letter. I sent you a card yesterday with my address which I hope you got — I gave it to clergyman to post in Kilarney as I could not get at a post-office myself   Today there was no post from here so this will go tomorrow and you'll get it on Tuesday. I hope you wont be very dissappointed tomorrow when the post man goes by.

I did not get here till ten o'clock last night, the trains were so late. Then at Dingle I found they had only sent a little flat cart with a jennet for me and my luggage and bike so I had to ride four miles in the dark on very wet muddy roads. However I got here in great spirits and I wasn't anything the worse. Today I've been walking nearly six hours on the mountains in heavy showers of rain — like the ones we had at Glen Cree — and I feel very well except that I am a little inclined to have asthma, but I hope it may keep off. I enjoyed my day's walking here very much, but I had qualms of loneliness every now and then. Still it wasn't like the old loneliness — the loneliness before I knew you — as in a way now you seem to be with me even when you're miles away.

I wonder how you got on at Darley's[1] today, tell me all about it. — I ate too much duck for my dinner today and I've got a pain — so I can't be emotional! I had a very amusing journey from Tralee on to Dingle with a quantity of country people. The carriages are like tram-carriages, and there was such a crowd — mostly of women and girls — that I and an old man had to sit on a flour sack, at the end. We had a great talk and every one in the carriage stopped and leaned out to listen. They couldn't make out who or what I was — here everyone is known by sight — sitting up on my sack with my typewriter on my knees. The old man said I was a Kerryman, that I was dressed like a Kerryman, and talked like a Kerryman and therefore I must be a Kerryman. Then he asked what was my calling — I put him off, and talked vaguely about my travels. Then an idea struck him, "Maybe you're a rich man" he said. I smiled as much to say I was, "And you're about 35?" he said. I said I was. "And not married?" I said no. "Well" he said, "you're a damn lucky man travelling the world with no one to impede you." Afterwards he got out and I fell into the hands of another old man who had got in. We talked about the fishing season, and the Aran fishing etc. Then he turned a knowing eye on me. "Begob" he said, "I see you're a fish-dealer!"

Now I've given you a guinea's worth of "article"[2] so never say I'm not generous!

The sea is right under my window with a beautiful moon shining on it. — How I wish you were here. I am delighted to have seen this place in winter — it is winter here — as I will be able to strengthen my Kerry book very much. My poor little pet try and be happy. If you nothing to do all day you ought to go to the National Gallery or the Museum, it would be a variety you will make at home. Now I've to write up my book diary so goodbye dear love. The lodgings are comfortable   1000 blessings

Your old [T.] Fishmonger

MS, TCD. *LM*, 203

[1] Arthur Darley (1873–1929) occasionally performed traditional Irish music on his violin at the Abbey Theatre and had accompanied the players on their lengthy tour in 1906; see I. 170.

[2] JMS later used this material for his third article on West Kerry, in the Winter 1907 *Shanachie*.

To MOLLY ALLGOOD

c/o Mrs Kevane [Ventry, Co. Kerry]
Tuesday [15 October 1907]

Dearest

I have just got your note. I could not help the delay in writting. I was dead tired on Friday night and had all my packing and settling to do. I started before eight on Saturday. I have been very bad indeed with asthma so I am leaving here again at once. It is too bad. I hoped so much from this trip. I may be a couple of days at Killarney or somewhere on my way home so you cannot write till you hear from me again. I shall be home by Saturday I expect at the latest.

Certainly I am an afflicted poor devil. I am all right now however fortunately it only takes me at night.

Goodbye dear Heart

Your T.

MS, TCD. *LM*, 205

To MOLLY ALLGOOD

Ventry
15 October 1907 | 2.50 P.M.
Miss M. Allgood 37 Mary St. Dublin.   Leaving   Dont write here again

Synge.

Telegram, TCD. *LM*, 205

To MOLLY ALLGOOD

Glendalough House [Glenageary]
Oct 17th/07

Dearest Pet

I got home last night after all. The asthma has rather renewed my cough — for the time being — so I thought it wisest to come home and get myself better as fast as I can. I wrote to you on Tuesday to say that I was leaving Ventry and I gave the letter — with one to my mother — to the people in the Hotel in Tralee to post but they must have forgotten them or something as my mother's letter did not come till this morning! When did you get yours? The letter you wrote me on Saturday only reached me *this morning* — my mother sent it on late so that it did not get to Ventry till after I had started. It made me feel very penitent — my poor love — for not writing to you on Friday, but I couldn't have written anything worth while. Are you glad to hear that I'm home to you again? I'm glad to think I'll soon see you again, but of course I dont like being driven home by asthma. I've a nasty cough still, but I'm not at all ill, and I hope it wont last. My sweetheart I'm looking forward so much to seeing you. Write me *by return* when you are free to-morrow *if you can*. I might wire to you to meet me tomorrow afternoon, if it is fine and I am well enough. Do not count on it however, I will go to the Saturday matinée to see the new Shadow of the Glen, so I'll see you then in any case,[1] and then SUNDAY!

My trip cost me about £3.10.0 but I'll get it all or most of it back by articles I hope, now my dear treasure goodbye till very soon I hope you're very good, and thinking of me and that you forgive my not writing on Friday.

Your old T.

MS, TCD. *LM*, 206

[1] Molly was again playing Nora Burke in a revival of *The Shadow of the Glen* whose new cast included Arthur Sinclair as Dan Burke, F. J. Fay as Michael Dara, with W. G. Fay in his former part as the Tramp.

To LADY GREGORY

Glendalough House | Kingstown
Friday [18 October 1907]

Dear Lady Gregory

I got a violent attack of asthma at Ventry so I had to pack up and come home again on Wednesday. I am still coughing very much from the effects of it, but I hope to get to the matinée tomorrow to see the new cast of "Shadow of Glen"

I shall be here now indefinitely

Yours sincerely
J. M. Synge

MS, Berg. *TB*, 240

To MOLLY ALLGOOD

Glendalough House [Glenageary]
22.X.07

Dearest Heart

I didn't write to you yesterday as I was waiting to hear from Lady G. but no letter has come. I dont know how we're to have our 'rehearsal' unless we have it in the Abbey.[1] I suppose I'll hear from her Ladyship tonight

I got a 'Deirdre' fit yesterday and I wrote *10* pages of it in great spirits and joy, but alas I know that that is only the go off. There'll be great anguish still before I get her done if I ever do. Write to me. How are you. I'm afraid to propose to meet you anywhere for fear you may be unwell. I had a little bicycle ride yesterday afternoon, and enjoyed it, but I croaked a good deal in the night. By the way I saw houses advertised in yesterday's Irish Times for 6/0, 8/6, 9/0, 10/0 a week. I wonder where they are. The address was Tully, House Agent, Parliament St. would you like to send a line to enquire. They'd stick on the price or something if I enquired from this address. However I'm sure they're hovels.

I have worlds of work to get through now. I was so tired last night I kept falling asleep in my chair — a rare thing for me. Write dearest.

Your old Tramp

MS, TCD. *LM*, 206

---

1 *The Shadow of the Glen* was to be given a professional matinée on 25 Oct 1907 in honour of the English actress Mrs Patrick Campbell (1865–1940; see I. 75) and her company, who were performing at the Gaiety Theatre, Dublin, in the week of 21 Oct. During the early days of their courtship, JMS had coached

Molly in the part of Nora Burke — hence his signature, 'Your old Tramp', referring to the Tramp who lures Nora into the countryside with his sweet-singing speeches of nature.

To MOLLY ALLGOOD

                 Glendalough House [Glenageary]
                              Oct 23rd/07

Dearest Child

I was delighted to get your note last night. I didn't fix on a re-hearsal for a number of reasons, the first that it is *probably* better for you to stay quiet today as you will have to work in the evening. Further it would have cost 0/6 for a wire 1/0 for my train and 2/0 for teas, that is 3/6 in all and we wouldn't have had much to show for it, so I am staying at home. You know I'm to be married soon! I am not at all sure that you are not better without a rehearsal with me — *one* so soon before the show would be more likely I think to embarrass you than anything else. I would rather you went through the part yourself (I mean rehearse yourself) using your own intellect and taste and let us see what you can do with. All you have to do is to be *simple and natural* as you used to be.

I dont think I'll go to Hedda Gabler tomorrow I dont like being out in the late train till this cough is better. I'll go to her Matinée on Saturday and see Magda, that will do me very well, I'm sure I wont like her at all — from what I have heard and seen of her.[1] By the way if you are unwell tomorrow night I HOPE YOU WONT GO.[1] It would be very very bad for you rushing down to the Gaiety. PLEASE dont, REMEMBER what you've been THROUGH[3] and dont have it, or worse over again.

I expect to have MacKenna out here to see me tomorrow after-noon and then he'll be at the show I hope on Friday I'll introduce you to him afterwards so wash off your make up well and dont powder yourself before you come down!! And also have on your best face and get into some part of the Green Room where your left profile will very telling. Nish! It's too bad to go through all this week without seeing you, but what's to be done I cant take you out to walk, and I must have fresh air myself. By the way if you'd really like me to hear Nora before the show we could run through it at the Abbey perhaps at 1.30 on Friday or earlier if there is no rehearsal. What do you think of that? This is an extra long letter as I'm not seeing you today. I was very lonesome after you went away on Sunday. Yesterday I went to Killiney in the train and walked up to the church where we once quarelled I enjoyed part of it and part of it I was lonesome. Today I'm going on my bicycle. I'm printing the films[4] today. They aren't much good. I must have left them too long. This isn't very intimate I'm afraid, Dear Heart, but I've just eaten a big dinner and that's against sentiment. Be good and be happy and for *Heavens sake take care of* yourself.

Later

Post Man

Just heard from Mackenna to say he's coming tomorrow, so we wont meet till Friday hard luck! Of course I'd have you out walking with me only that this is not a time for you to walk. With Mountains of love

Your old T.

MS, TCD. *LM,* 207

1 Mrs Campbell had invited the company to her performance of Ibsen's *Hedda Gabler* at the Gaiety Theatre on Thursday evening, 24 Oct 1907; during the week she also performed in Sudermann's *Magda*, and *The Notorious Mrs Ebbsmith* and *The Second Mrs Tanqueray*, both by Pinero.

2 Underlined five times.

3 'Please', 'Remember' and 'through' are underlined six times.

4 Probably the films JMS took while in Kerry; see Lilo M. Stephens, *My Wallet of Photographs* (Dublin, 1971) and I. 48.

To LADY GREGORY

Glendalough Ho [Glenageary]
Monday [?28 October 1907]

Dear Lady Gregory

I have read the Unicorn[1] with great interest — I am sure it will make a stir.

All the same I think we were probably right in putting it [off] as we did for Manchester, — a play like it, that is so off usual lines, has so many possibilities of unexpected failure or success. I suppose F. J. Fay is to play Martin? A great deal will depend on how far he can make himself '*felt*'[2]

I am leaving this at Nassau[3] and Act III back to Abbey.

Yours
J. M. Synge

MS, Berg. *TB,* 241

1 *The Unicorn from the Stars* by Yeats and Lady Gregory, a rewriting, chiefly by Lady Gregory, of *Where There is Nothing* (1901), which had been written in haste by Yeats, Lady Gregory and Douglas Hyde; see I. 89.

2 Evidently the directors had contemplated a first production of *The Unicorn from the Stars* during the company tour to Manchester later in 1907. When the play was first performed at the Abbey, on 21 Nov 1907, Frank Fay, rumour has it, fell asleep out of sheer boredom (James Flannery, *W. B. Yeats and the Idea of a Theatre* [1976], 229).

3 A temperance hotel in Nassau Street where Lady Gregory usually stayed when in Dublin; see I. 174.

To KAREL MUŠEK[1]

Glendalough House | Kingstown | Co Dublin
Oct 28/07

Dear Mr Musek

It is a long time since I have written to you — you must excuse me however as I have been very unwell this summer though I am now in good health again. Everything is going well at the Abbey Theatre. We gave a special matinée to Mrs Pat. Campbell, the well-known actress last week, and she was so much interested, she has promised to play for us in the Abbey, next year in one of Mr Yeats' verse plays.[2]

I am working on a new play, and I am publishing a little comedy 'The Tinkers Wedding', next month that I wrote some years ago. Have you translated any of the 'Playboy' yet? I have had some very good reviews of it — of the book — from America recently; and we hope to play it in Edinburgh in December.

Has the Shadow of Glen been done yet at your 'national theatre? I got your post card from England in the summer,[3] and was glad to get it. I hope you had a pleasant holiday there. May we hope to see you in Ireland again some day?

Please make my compliments to Madame Musek, and believe me

very sincerely yours
J. M. Synge

MS, Berg

1 Karel Mušek (1867–1924; see I. 109), Czech translator of JMS's work, and actor and régisseur of the Bohemian National Theatre, Prague.

2 'She made a beautiful speech from the stage of the Gaiety promising to return in November next year to play at the Abbey "in Deirdre by my dear friend and your great Poet",' Yeats reported to Florence Farr (Josephine Johnson, *Florence Farr: Bernard Shaw's New Woman* [Gerrards Cross, 1975], 156).

3 Neither Mušek's postcard nor his reply to this letter have survived. *The Shadow of the Glen*, performed at the Inchover Theatre in Prague on 7 Feb 1906, did not receive its promised production at the National Theatre there until 22 Aug 1907, when the translator took the role of the Tramp.

To MOLLY ALLGOOD

Glendalough Ho [Glenageary]
Tuesday Oct 29th [1907]

Dearest Love

I have just got your letter thanks.

Meet me at Tara St tomorrow at *twenty-five* minutes to *three* if it is fine, and bring my cape with you. I'd better not go up I think if it is wet. I coaxed another thread of smoke out of the fire when I got home but that was all. My mother didn't say anymore about you, I didn't expect she would. That will come in good time.[1] Mac-Kenna said more nice things about you and Sally yesterday. I had tea with him and then dinner and then we walked out as far as Booterstown. He is coming to Ireland I think in the spring so we'll have them for neighbours in Rathgar.

I walked round by Loughlinstown to day at a great rate as I am trying to get rid of my stomach!

Yes Sunday was a great day. I hope tomorrow will be fine enough for us. I have been slaving at my Kerry article all day I hate putting the last touches and getting the spelling and punctuation right it bothers me.

Till tomorrow

Your old T.[2]

MS with envelope, TCD. *LM*, 209

1 Mrs Synge entered in her diary for Sunday, 27 Oct 1907: 'Mollie came at 4, staid till 9. We had a talk on China.' (TCD)

2 Molly has written in pencil on the back of the envelope, 'What is the meaning of an otiose epithet'.

To MOLLY ALLGOOD

[Glendalough House, Glenageary]
Nov 1st 07

Dearest Love

This is a hurried *after-dinner* line only, to wish you good day and many of them. I hope I'll hear from you tonight with news of Dervorgilla[1] there was a cold notice in the Irish Times.

I worked hard and I think well at Deirdre this morning if I go on like this I may have it done for this season if I only escape illness. I walked round by Kilmacangue — or *Kilmacanick* as we call it — all round Little Sugar Loaf and back into Bray through Wind Gates yesterday in 2½ hours! When I got out of the train at Glengeary I was so stiff I could hardly walk. I haven't gone so fast for years.

Our black-berry lane — where we fought — was full of blackberries, and all the country was fine. Its a pity you weren't with me.

I'll be in tomorrow I hope. It's just possible that I'll go away with Lady G. and W.B.Y after the show as there may be things to discuss. I'll see you of course on Sunday. How seldom you write to me now! A little while ago you wrote every day

Your old
Tramp

MS (photo), NLI. *LM*, 209

---

1 Molly played the role of Mona, the old servant, in *Dervorgilla* by Lady Gregory, which had opened the previous night at the Abbey.

To MOLLY ALLGOOD

Glendalough Ho [Glenageary]
Saturday night Nov 2 [1907]

My poor little Pet

I have felt very bad ever since I had to run away from you, and saw you ducking in behind the scenery. I couldn't help it my sweet genius — you are a genius after your Mona and that's no lie. Will you forgive me? I heard nice things about that I'll tell you tomorrow.

Come down by the *quarter* to *two* dont miss it, and if its fine we'll go off and have tea in Enniskerry and come home slowly under the stars — in the balmy beautiful night. Wont that be great. If its *wet come here*. I'll be counting the hours till I see you. I'm afraid I'm a great fool to be so upset by missing my little talk with you and dissappointing you. Never mind my treasure soon we'll be together for ever with the help of God   Dont be late dear Heart tomorrow

Your old T——

MS, TCD. *LM*, 210

To MOLLY ALLGOOD

Glendalough House [Glenageary]
Nov. 9th/07

Dearest

I haven't had dinner today yet; but I've been working at Deirdre till my head is going round. I was too taken up with her yesterday to write to you — I got her into such a mess I think I'd have put her into the fire only that I want to write a part for YOU, so you mustn't be jealous of her.

I am very glad you came down on Wednesday and gave me a little glimpse of you, I am *living* on that. I suppose I wont see you now till Sunday. I will not go to Matinée, there is no use.[1]

I am keeping pretty well but I am very tired, worn-out, with anxiety about Deirdre. Since yesterday I have pulled two acts into one, so that — if I can work it, the play will have three acts instead of four, and that has of course given me many problems to think out. As it is I am not sure that the plan I have is a good one. Ideas seem so admirable when they occur to you and then they get so doubtful when you have thought over them for a while.

Write me a full intimate letter, my dear love, I am weary and depressed, and lonesome. I wish we were together.

Florence Ross came yesterday and there is some talk of Ada Synge coming also as one of her brothers is ill. Remember we go out *early* on Sunday if it is fine and get a good long day together. I hope it may hold up but the glass is coming down again. I wonder shall I hear from you today before you get this. I hope you have written me a nice letter it would put heart into me

Your old Tramp

MS, TCD. *LM*, 210

1 On 7-9 Nov 1907, the company was performing *Hyacinth Halvey* (Gregory), *The Hour Glass* (Yeats), and a revised version of *The Land*, returned to the Abbey by Padraic Colum who had withdrawn himself and his plays in January 1906 to help his fellow seceders found the Theatre of Ireland (*TB*, 90-1).

To MOLLY ALLGOOD

Glendalough Ho [Glenageary]
Saturday Nov 9th/07

Dearest Heart

It looks as if it would be fine tomorrow, if it is be sure to come down by the *quarter to eleven* and we'll have a great day with the help of G——. I had a long ride this afternoon — the country was radiantly bright wonderful and I was as happy as seven kings.[1] I had nearly forgotten what it was like to be in good health, and to have hearty spirits. I only wished that you were with me — but though you weren't, you were putting a glow into my heart of hearts all the same, my blessings on you. I finished a second rough draft of the Sons of Usnach[2] today. So I have the whole thing now under my hand to work at next week.

If it is not fine tomorrow come here as usual by the quarter to two.

I hope against hope that it may be fine tomorrow so that we may have a royal radiant day together.

I must post this now. I wrote to another address about lodgings in Terenure today. It does no harm to enquire.

Till tomorrow

Your old T.

MS, TCD. *LM*, 211

1 Perhaps a reference to a drawing and scenario, 'Comedy of Kings', discovered in one of his notebooks (*Plays*, Book I, 230).

2 It was not until four or five months later that JMS finally decided on *Deirdre of the Sorrows* as the title.

To MOLLY ALLGOOD

[Glendalough House, Glenageary]

Monday Evening | Nov 11?/07

Dearest Pet

I am a little dissappointed and uneasy at not hearing from you tonight you promised to let me know how you were after the long walk, I hope I shall hear tomorrow morning. I am going to post this to you tomorrow early so that you may get it in the afternoon to make up a little for the 'Ball' you've given up for me. I was wonderfully happy last night thinking how good you had been to me, my dear heart, I'm afraid I've often written to say you'd put me in the blues — do you remember the horrid incident this time last year before I went away?[1] — but this time you've made me OVERFLOW with delight. I hope I dont seem very unreasonable, I'm sure bye and by you'll be glad that you've chosen a good *style* of life, there is a 'style' in life as there is in acting, or painting or writing — but this is dry stuff I didn't mean to write.

I hope you aren't too tired today, why didn't you send me a line? I never felt better than I did this morning and I had a long satisfactory time at Deirdre. Afterwards I went out on my bicycle but it was very damp or something and I got a headache and didn't enjoy myself much. What a day we had yesterday!!! The people I wrote to about the rooms did not answer me at all, which is queer, so I wont be able to go and look at them tomorrow as I intended. This is a very dull letter I'm afraid and I wanted to write a particularly nice one today when I am so full of love and delight in you my little treasure — I am tired, so shut your eyes and imagine I've got my arm round you and am just resting my poor old head on your little shoulder.

Tuesday

No letter this morning I am dreadfully uneasy about you, if I have made you ill again I will never forgive myself. <u>WRITE BY RETURN</u>[2]

Your old T.

P.S. I'm just off to Rathgar for the lunch with this good man.[3] It is a bother as we might have met today, but I daresay it is better for you to be quiet today as your time of rest is coming near.

I want to show you my Deirdre some day soon perhaps I can on Sunday.

My blessing on you, little Changling, you have made me very happy, you are so good to me now, giving up your ride with O.R,[4] and now your Ball.

T.

MS, TCD. *LM,* 212

    1 See I. 244–5.
    2 Underlined four times.
    3 Probably Edward Adderley Stopford (1843–1919), whom JMS had first met in London with his cousin Edward Synge; see I. 259–60. Stopford had recently moved to Dublin to work with Horace Plunkett in the Irish Agricultural Organisation Society.
    4 Probably J. A. O'Rourke.

To ELKIN MATHEWS[1]

Glendalough House | Kingstown
Nov 12th [1907]

Dear Mr Mathews

I have given Miss Jones permission to act the ⟨little⟩ two plays for a charity at Chesterfield,[2] so I write to tell you as you request.

By the way, I have not received a copy of the second edition,[3] could you kindly send me one whenever convenient.

I hope it is still selling.

Very truly yours
J. M. Synge

MS, TCD

    1 Charles Elkin Mathews (1851–1921; see I. 106), bookseller and publisher, in 1905, of *Riders to the Sea* and *The Shadow of the Glen.*
    2 Gladys Jones, who in a letter to JMS of 8 Nov 1907 (TCD) described herself as a 'professional actress', produced the two one-act plays in aid of the Victoria Home for Nurses, Chesterfield, herself playing Nora Burke and old Maurya.
    3 There were new editions of the two plays in 1907 and 1909.

To MOLLY ALLGOOD

Glendalough Ho [Glenageary]
14/11/07

My dearest Love

I got your two letters on Tuesday and was very much relieved. It is hard not to see you this week, but I could not appoint to meet you today or yesterday as your time was so much taken up and you must be tired out. I shall be at the Matinée[1] but I fear I am nearly sure to be carried off by the directors as I have not seen them for nearly a fortnight.

I cannot live this way any longer — I nearly died of loneliness and misery last night while you ought to be here to comfort me and cheer me up. Do take care of yourself this *time* if you get a pain in your back or anything we will be afraid ever to take a long walk again, and our long walks are such a delight to us. I was very depressed last night, were you? I suppose you were at the Merry Wives,[2] I wonder if you liked it. I am working myself sick with Deirdre or whatever you call it. It is a very anxious job. I dont want to make a failure

On Tuesday I lunched with my friends at Rathgar and then we went to the lecture on Japanese art at the Alexandra College. It was interesting enough but heavily delivered.[3] If you get this in time please write me a line. I think it is a *bad* plan you have started of writing so seldom now. I get sad for the want of a little sympathetic line that wouldn't take you a minute

Your old T.

MS, TCD. *LM*, 213

1 The Abbey company gave a professional matinée on 15 Nov 1907 for the companies of John Martin Harvey (see below, p. 128) and F. R. Benson, both of which were performing in Dublin; JMS attended the matinée with Hugh Lane, to see a programme of *Riders to the Sea*, *Kathleen ni Houlihan*, *The Rising of the Moon*, and *Hyacinth Halvey*. Benson was reported in the *Freeman's Journal* for 16 Nov 1907 as praising the plays as beautiful 'art, and . . . true, and I feel humiliated in listening to them when I think of the ordinary drama of the day'.

2 F. R. Benson's company at the Gaiety Theatre was presenting *The Merry Wives of Windsor*.

3 Alexandra College for women in Dublin advertised in the *Irish Times* the Hermione Lectures for 1907: a series of four lectures on Japanese art by Laurence Binyon (1869–1943), of the Department of Prints and Drawings, British Museum, from 11 to 14 Nov at 4 p.m. The lecture on 12 Nov was entitled 'The Chinese Renaissance of the 15th Century'.

To MOLLY ALLGOOD
Glendalough House [Glenageary]
Nov 15/07

Dearest Love

How are you today? I was tired after all the compliments, but I am as usual now. About tomorrow; if it is *wet* come by the quarter to two or the quarter to three, as you find it most convenient, and if it *fine* come by the quarter to *three*, so that I'll have time for a little walk, That will leave us three hours together. No great thing but I suppose we must be satisfied.[1] Of course I DEPEND on you not to come out at all if you are not well *enough*.

I was too busy with Deirdre to write to you this morning so — as you can see — this is an after-dinner note. I wonder which of my letters it is that you like so much. You mustn't mind my letters being a little dry these times, because I am pouring out my heart to you in Deirdre the whole day long. I am pleased with it now, but that doesn't mean much as I go back and forward in my feelings to my work every second day — at least when they are in this stage. I am half inclined to write to Old Yeats and ask him straight out to sell me your picture.[2] Would that be a good plan? If it goes to the Abbey we'll see no more of it.

Now do take every possible care of yourself my own treasure of the world.

Your old Tramp

P.S. Your notes have just come. My poor Changling to worry your little self about nothing! Dont you trust me?

I am very sorry to see by the first that you speak of being very ill. Perhaps we should not walk tomorrow if you aren't feeling well dont bother about it! *I hope you'll feel well!*

MSS, (letter) (photo) NLI; (PS) TCD. *LM,* 214

1 An echo of old Maurya's famous speech at the end of *Riders to the Sea.*
2 The portrait of Molly by J. B. Yeats now hanging in the Abbey Theatre is dated 1913; this earlier picture — or sketch, as it is later described — has not been traced.

To JAMES PATERSON
Glendalough House | Kingstown | Co Dublin
Nov 15th [1907]

Dear Mr Paterson

Our little company is going to pay you another visit so I send you three or four circulars and perhaps you would kindly give them to any of your friends who [are] interested in our work.[1]

I shall not be over with the Company this time but we are still looking forward to seeing you some day in Dublin.

I hope Mrs Paterson and your party are well. I had an operation done on my neck a couple of months ago and some swelled glands taken away. Since then I am glad to say I have been in good health again, and I am hard at work on a new play and a book on the wild coasts of Kerry and their people

Very Cordially
J. M. Synge

MS copy, TCD

---

[1] The company was to visit Edinburgh and Glasgow as well as Manchester on its tour, 24 Nov to 15 Dec 1907.

To MOLLY ALLGOOD

Glendalough House [Glenageary]
Tuesday night | Nov. 19th [1907]

My dear Hearts Love

I went to the Abbey today to meet Poel[1] and was sorry to hear that you are unwell. I am in a fever of anxiety to know how you are I nearly telegraphed to you but then I thought you would write. Write at once for Heaven's sake. I am eaten up with uneasiness. I never know how much you are the very breath and soul of my life till something goes wrong. Are you worse than usual? Or are you only being wise and taking care of yourself?

I was greatly pleased with Poel who is most enthusiastic about my work[2] We dined together Poel and the three Directors — every now and then Poel launched out into praise of my work, and it was amusing to see Lady G dashing in at once with praise of Yeats' work. They have put off the "Well of the Saints" till *Lent* I feel angry about it, and sick of the whole business I wish you were here, I feel lonely tonight. I am going off to Kingstown with this in the hope that it may reach you tonight — it is five o'clock now. Goodbye, Dearest Love. If no letter comes from you this evening I will be WRETCHED INDEED.[3]

Your old T.

P.S. Is there any possibility of getting the sketch, please let me know; also send me news how you have been this turn it is not fair or right to keep me in distress and anxiety.

MS, TCD. *LM*, 215

1 William Poel (1852–1934), actor and producer famous for his emphasis on verse-speaking and reinterpretation of Shakespeare in terms of Elizabethan techniques. On this visit to the Abbey he was sufficiently impressed by Sara Allgood to ask her to play Isabella in his production of *Measure for Measure* for Miss Horniman's company in Manchester in April 1908, and during the summer of 1908, he was asked by the Abbey Directors to instruct the players in verse-speaking; see below, p. 150.

2 The indefatigable Frank Fay had sent Poel copies of *The Well of the Saints* and *The Playboy of the Western World* some time in the spring of 1907, and received several lengthy letters in reply, praising JMS's plays in general, as having 'given me more pleasure than any others of this age' (5 July 1907, TCD), and *The Playboy* in particular as 'one of the best that has been written in modern times . . . . Every line of his dialogue is vital and stirs equally the emotions and the intellect . . . . Mr Synge's play will have to be reckoned with by all future historians of the Stage and the further time moves forward the more will the work stand out as unique of its kind and it will hold its own beside all writers of genius.' (26 June 1907, TCD).

3 Underlined three times.

To MOLLY ALLGOOD

Glendalough House [Glenageary]
Nov 20th/07

Dearest

I have got your two letters — the one this morning seemed a most bitter and cruel one, and upset so that I could hardly do my work. I got home yesterday at a quarter-to-five (with a headache and coughing worse than I have done for months) — and as soon as I got a cup of tea I wrote to you and rushed off with it the Post Office at *Kingstown Station* where I found after I had posted it that I was three minutes late. I could do no more.

Your second letter does not tell me how you have been ⟨[*illegible*]⟩ so I am uneasy and miserable still. I am afraid I am not so well as I have, or else it is the worry — on top of my fatigue with Deirdre — that is knocking me up.

I believe that I am to go to tea with Poel after the lecture to-morrow,[1] so perhaps I can see you on Friday afternoon I heard them saying that you are not going till Monday after all. So we may have Sunday

I am BITTERLY DISSAPPOINTED that we have lost the sketch of you, why did you stop me writing to him — you promised to write. L.G[regory] I should think has paid for it.

Excuse this letter I will be a long time before I quite get over the blow you gave me this morning. I am glad you are better. *Be cheerful* and take care of yourself

Your old T.

MS, TCD. *LM*, 216

1 William Poel gave an illustrated lecture on the Elizabethan playhouse at the Abbey Theatre on 21 Nov 1907 at 2.30 P.M.

To JAMES PATERSON

Glendalough House | Kingstown | Co Dublin
Nov 22/07

Dear Mr Paterson

We are greatly obliged for your kind help in 'spreading' our circulars,[1] help now is peculiarly valuable to us as the *financial* future of our movement — this of course between ourselves — is giving us a good deal of anxiety and it is important for us to be able to make a little money in towns like Edinburgh where our work gets the sort of audiences that it needs.[2]

I am very grateful indeed for your kind promise to give me my picture.[3] I shall be delighted to have it — as I need hardly say. I often remember the two pleasant mornings I spent in your studio

Cordially yours
J. M. Synge

MS copy, TCD

1 Paterson had replied on 16 Nov 1907 (TCD) requesting twenty more prospectuses of the tour.

2 Miss Horniman's disenchantment with the company was now so great that she had made it clear no further subsidy would be forthcoming after 1910; meanwhile, her interest was centring more and more on her Manchester venture (*TB*, 234 ff).

3 On 16 Nov 1907 Paterson reported to JMS that his 1906 crayon drawing of him (see I. 277) reproduced as frontispiece to Edward Stephens's *My Uncle John* and still in the possession of the family) 'still makes the round of the Galleries, and will be at the Fine Art Society Exhibition with others in February. When its wanderings are over I am going to ask you to hang it up in some corner as a small return for much pleasure given.' (TCD) In 1908 Paterson took two studio photographs of JMS, and based on these earlier works painted a posthumous portrait reproduced in Maurice Bourgeois, *John Millington Synge and the Irish Theatre* (Dublin, 1913).

To JOHN G. WILSON[1]

Glendalough House | Kingstown | Dublin
Nov 22/07

Dear Mr Wilson

I am sending you a few circulars of our next visit to Glasgow — you will excuse me, I hope for troubling you again!

[I] am not going round with the company this tour as I have too much literary work on my hands, but you will I hope see Mr W. G. Fay whom I think you have met.

Remember if you, or any of your friends, come to Dublin that we will always be delighted to see you at the Abbey Theatre.

With best wishes

Yours sincerely

J. M. Synge

MS, AS

1 John Gideon Wilson (1876–1963), whom JMS first met when he was a bookseller with John Smith & Sons, Glasgow, moved to London in 1908; after working with Constable, then taking over James & Evans, he joined the firm of John and Edward Bumpus Ltd., eventually becoming chairman and managing director (1941–59).

To MOLLY ALLGOOD

Glendalough House [Glenageary]

Nov 2$\frac{2}{3}$/07
?

My dearest Heart,

I have a queer lonesome qualm in me today all the time I am working — I dont how we would get on if you went to America! How are you my dear child? I am watching all the points of the compass to see if you'll have a fine day tomorrow, I hope the gods I mean the saints will be kind to you.

I am not going to John Bull[1] or the Abbey today, I haven't been quite so well this week so I'm going to be very careful now for a day or two till I recover the lost ground. I do not feel the slightest inclination to go and see Shaw — I'd rather keep my money for Esposito's concert tomorrow and hear something that is really stirring and fine and beautiful[2] — though I dont suppose I shall go there either, — that would quiet my poor lonesome gizzard. It is queer how *hollow* I feel today, my poor changeling, but still I have been working well and hard and I am not unduly depressed. I know you wouldn't like me to be *too* cheerful.

Write me full satisfying letters every day please that will keep me well. I am kicking myself today because I forgot to make you *swear* yesterday that you'd write your promised article on this tour I mean while you are on tour. F Ross has got her article on Skerries quite clear and good now after three corrections. Why wont you do the same?[3] There is dinner Goodbye dear love.

J. M. Tramp.

I shall write to [you] as M. O'Neill on Tour. I hope you wont forget to send me the Manchester address in a legible form.

P.S. I've opened your letter again to remind you to put on your warm under garments for the journey. It makes the greatest difference travelling I know by experience. Its very cold out here today and I expect you'll have it very sharp tomorrow   Remember all your swears   Goodbye again old Heart

MS, TCD. *LM*, 217

1 William Poel's company was performing *John Bull's Other Island*, the play Bernard Shaw had originally written for the Abbey Theatre in 1904 but which was rejected by the directors as unsuitable for their company to act; JMS had thought it would 'hold a Dublin audience, and at times move them if even tolerably played', but objected to the Grasshopper scene and 'the Handy Andy-like scene about carrying the goose' (M. J. Sidnell, 'Hic and Ille: Shaw and Yeats', *Theatre and Nationalism in Twentieth Century Ireland*, ed. R. O'Driscoll, [Toronto, 1971], 173–4). Apparently, in an effort to assist the Fays after their resignation, Yeats wrote to Shaw asking him about the possibility of work for them in London, in particular in a revival of *John Bull's Other Island*; Shaw's reply to Yeats of 16 Jan 1908 is in NLI.

2 The *Irish Times* for 23 Nov 1907 announced that 'the next Sunday orchestral concert will take place tomorrow at the Antient Concert Rooms at 4 o'clock. The band, under the conductorship of Signor Esposito, will open the concert with Herold's Overture to "Zampa".' The programme was also to include 'practically the whole of' Mendelssohn's incidental music to *A Midsummer Night's Dream*, the prelude to the third act and the shepherd's air from Wagner's *Tristan und Isolde*, and Rossini's overture to *Semiramide*. Michele Esposito (1855–1929; see I. 135), Italian pianist, composer, and professor of pianoforte at the Royal Irish Academy of Music, was conductor of the Dublin Orchestral Society from 1899.

3 Florence Ross's article has not yet been discovered; nor did Molly, apparently, write an article on the tour (cf. I. 348).

To MOLLY ALLGOOD

> Glendalough House [Glenageary]
> Sunday 24th Nov. 07

Dearest Love

Your little scrawl, your *charming* little scrawl I should say, has just come and cheered me up very much though I dont like the thought of going off for a cold lonely walk today in our old haunts. I wont go till after dinner. Yesterday afternoon I walked out through Loughlinstown — I [wonder] if you've remembered to remember where Loughlinstown is? and on to Killiney and back by train from there, in time for a bout at Deirdre.

I heard the boat blowing its horn this morning at a quarter past eight and I got hollow again at the sound of it. However I'm not really unhappy this time because I trust you very fully ⟨to be good⟩, and three weeks wont be long going over as we're both so busy.

I have been building castles in the air this morning to no end — a sign I suppose that I am really in good spirits. I saw the Abbey coming to grief — I sometimes think it is doomed in its present shape — then I saw Martin Harvey[1] or someone taking up my work and money beginning to come in by the wheelbarrow full! Then in about ten years I saw *us* starting a little Dublin company of our own with you as as leading lady of course and first stage manager! Then by that time Dublin will be better educated and I saw big houses coming in, and a real Irish Drama getting on its legs at last thanks to the enthusiasm of the extraordinarily gifted and subtle actress *Mrs* J. M. Tramp! That is what we must live for, and to do that you must keep off the English Stage which would destroy your peculiar and subtle talent which I am getting to understand better than you do.

I think if the Abbey breaks up soon we might go to Paris for a while, and then you could be my literary secretary and at the same time study the French stage and the French art of speaking. — of course your French blood[2] predestines you to be the bringer in of the essence of the French tradition for the Dublin stage! Nish!!!!!!!!! !!!!!!!!!! I hope you will not keep up your feud with F.J.F. first because he is a man — with all his drawbacks — that deserves sympathy and friendship rather than anything else; and also because you *can* learn, and *ought* to learn, a great deal from him — taking of course nothing he tells you for granted, and testing everything by your own intuition.

I wonder will you think this a dull letter. I suppose you are nearly half way across the Channel by this time, I hope you are not sick. Be sure to write every day and to write fully telling me how you are and everything else.

I suppose you will get this tomorrow (Monday) morning, and probably the next of my letters will reach you on Wednesday. Now I must write to Lebeau.[3] Many blessings on you, my dear treasure,

Your old Tramp.

MS, AS. *LM*, 218

1 Martin Harvey, who had earlier expressed a wish to produce *The Playboy*, had written to JMS on 17 Nov 1907, praising both *Riders to the Sea*, 'your singularly impressive play . . . . Mr Stephen Phillips has been haunted with it ever since Friday, and last night the old woman paid him a visit in his room!', and *The Playboy*: 'I wish it had been my good fortune to have had the opportunity of interpreting that delicious creation.' (TCD)

2 Little is known of Molly's family background; see *LM*, xviii–xix, and below, p. 116.

3 On 24 Feb 1908 Lebeau replied from Vendôme to 'your long and so interesting and cordial letter dated Nov. 24 . . . in which you speak of your wedding and many other things' (TCD); JMS's letters to him have not yet been traced.

To MOLLY ALLGOOD

Glendalough Ho [Glenageary]
Nov 26th 07

Dearest Life

Your letter came this morning a very good one too, I'm afraid I haven't much to tell you today. I went up on Sunday to Kilmaca-nogue and up our little lane round little Sugar Loaf and on to Bray. There was snow on the back Hills and a gray whitish cloud stretching round the horizon, with the Sugar Loafs black against it, that made me very mournful. Before I got to Bray it got quite dark and rained a cold drizzling rain, and I felt as lonesome as the Almighty God — out in the night by myself and you far away talking and laughing with the the company.[1] Yesterday (Monday) I went into town and spent a while in the National Gallery and then paid for my fishing-rod at last! In the evening I was very depressed it seemed as if I was put down at the bottom of a black well for three weeks of solitude.

This morning I got your letter which did me good, also a card from MacKenna to say that he is over again and wants to see me tomorrow.[2] That will make a little break.

It is very wet today, *pouring*, but I have written 7 pages of Deirdre this morning and I am very cheerful but very tired. My mothers friend came last night[3]   It is a nuisance trying to keep up small talk at meals. I am to go to the Dentist on Thursday and I'll enquire about you. I got a rather favourable answer to an enquiry about a digs at 39 Rathgar Rd. I may go and look at it on Thursday. It is furnished so I am not sure that it will do. — Excuse these scraps of paper it is all I have in my *reach*

By the way I looked into 'Riders to the Sea' the other day and I saw a stage direction (*in a whisper*) before your speech Is it (B) it is? No wonder I am not pleased when you wail it out. —[4]

Do you remember your first show of Nora at the Midland? And how you sent me a message that you wanted to see me after it, and beamed with delight when I praised you for it? It is unfortunate that our life separates us so much — "I am not used to being lone-some,"[5] now, and I feel it very much more than I did.

Dont let this letter depress you, I am right and working hard, so the time will slip away. Be very good my dear Heart, and write very often and very fully.

Your old lonesome
Tramp

P.S. I wouldn't think badly of Poel — it is age and nerves most likely that makes his eyes 'shifty', with highly strung people, passing expressions are often misleading. There is a great storm rising it is well you aren't on the sea today. I dreamt last night I was introducing you to my nephews.[6]

MS, TCD. *LM*, 219

1 Probably a reference to Christy Mahon's speech in *The Playboy* when in Act Two he describes to Pegeen his lonesome journey through Mayo (*Plays*, Book II, 109).

2 This card from MacKenna, who was living in London, has not survived.

3 Miss Barry, a lady missionary who dedicated herself to converting Roman Catholics to Protestantism, was visiting Mrs Synge from 25 Nov to 17 Dec 1907.

4 Cathleen whispers this line to the keening women who accompany Bartley's body on stage (*Plays*, Book I, 23).

5 A variation on Nora Burke's speech after the death of Patch Darcy in *The Shadow of the Glen*.

6 JMS's sister Annie's sons: the older, Francis (Frank) Stephens, was an apprentice in Harry Stephens's law office, Fred Sutton & Co.; Edward M. Stephens (1888–1955), at this time a student at Trinity College, later a solicitor, was to become his uncle's beneficiary and biographer.

To KAREL MUŠEK

Glendalough House | Kingstown | Co. Dublin
Nov. 26th/07

My dear Mr. Musek,

Many thanks for your kind note and news.[1] This is a line merely to tell you that the money you kindly sent me has not reached me. I have waited all the week in the hopes that it would come but it has not. Could you send me the date when you sent it that I may make enquiries. I suppose you have the receipt? By the way if there are more fees I hope you will keep your share as translator, I am always glad to get even small sums as I am not a millionaire! Our company is playing in Manchester this week, Glasgow next week, then Edinburgh. We open in the Abbey Theatre again on Dec. 26th.

Yours sincerely,
J. M. Synge

MS copy (Mušek), TCD

1 Mušek's letter, presumably informing JMS of royalties paid for the produc-

tion of *The Shadow of the Glen* in August 1907 at the National Theatre in Prague, has not survived.

To MOLLY ALLGOOD

Glendalough House [Glenageary]
Nov 28th 07

Dearest Life

What a chapter of accidents. I am *proud* of you, for coming out so brilliantly and saving the reputation of the company forever.[1] Let me know as soon as ever you can how everything is going, and how you are yourself. Dont knock up. I am all right. Yesterday I spent the afternoon with MacKenna first at Bewley's and then at the Arts Club.[2] I made a lot of enquiries from him about the way one gets married, but he did not know things very definitely as he was married in England. He thinks you must register yourself *three* weeks before hand with the registrar of your district and fix the day. I can do nothing till I find a digs, but I am going off to Rathgar tomorrow to look round. By the way if things go the same as last time you will be unwell the week between Edinburgh and Christmas. What are we to do? I am going out of this as soon as ever I can, and then we'll have to do our best. If the worst comes to the worst, we can get married on a Saturday to Monday while our shows are going on.

We had a long talk with Count Marciekivez at the Art Club, yesterday. There seems to be some scheme in the air — *this* is absolutely private not A WORD of it to SALLY OR[3] the COMPANY — of buying up the old Queens [Theatre] and starting a sort of municipal Theatre to play all the *good* plays of the day on a wide basis, not mainly Irish ones, but including Irish ones. If that comes off there will be a hope for *us* after the Abbey is buried. I am going to frequent the Art Club and see what is going on[4]   It may be all talk.

I am writing this in a hurry as I am going to the Dentist[5] at 2 o'-clock   I corrected the final first proofs of the Tinker's Wedding, yesterday and this morning I have finished (?) the Preface to it. The play is good I think, but it looks mighty shocking in print.

Tell Sally I hope she is better, and to take care of herself for her sake and ours

With many blessings
Your old Tramp

Send me your Glasgow address again.

MS, AS. *LM*, 221

¹ In Manchester Sara Allgood fell ill with tonsilitis, and the company doubled on parts, Molly taking the roles of Maurya in *Riders to the Sea* and Mrs Delane in *Hyacinth Halvey*. Willie Fay further blotted his copy book with the directors by sending his wife Brigit O'Dempsey on in place of Sara in *Kathleen ni Houlihan* and *Dervorgilla*, without announcing the change of cast to the audience. (See *TB*, 242–6.)

² Bewley's was a coffee house in Grafton Street. The newly established United Arts Club was soon to become a centre for artists, writers, and musicians.

³ Underlined three times.

⁴ Count Casimir Dunin-Markiewicz (1874–1932), husband of Constance Gore-Booth, founded the Independent Dramatic Company later that year; but most of the plays produced were by himself, and the company's early productions were presented at the Abbey rather than at the Queen's Theatre. JMS did not join the Arts Club until late February 1908, though he frequented it in 1907.

⁵ G. Wyclif Yeates, 25 Lower Baggot Street; see I. 98.

To LADY GREGORY

Glendalough House [Glenageary]
Nov 28th [1907]

Dear Lady Gregory

I am sorry to hear that you are not well. I will finish the play tonight and send it to you with my opinion —¹

I suppose you have heard of the catastrophe at Manchester — that Miss Sarah Allgood has tonsilitis and cannot leave the house, so that Miss O'Neill is playing all her parts! They seem to have got through wonderfully well. Fay went off as usual without giving them his address so they could not get hold of him to let him know what had happened till Tuesday! That, of course, between ourselves.

The address of the French man I thought your son might like to know is

Monsieur Lebeau
80 rue Claude Bernard, Paris.

I like him greatly. I hope I shall see you before you leave Dublin. I am still hard at work on Deirdre

Yours sincerely
J. M. Synge

MS, Gregory. *TB*, 242

¹ *When the Dawn is Come* by Thomas MacDonagh; see below, p. 91.

To LADY GREGORY

Glendalough House [Glenageary]
Nov. 29th 07

Dear Lady Gregory

I return the 'Fragment'. It is hard to know what to do with it. It has real dramatic gifts of characterisation and arrangement, and general power of building up something that can stand by itself, but the treatment of the hero at the end is so sentimental and foolish I hardly see how we can stage it. It would [be] well perhaps to write to the author telling him how much we are interested in his work — and saying that we have no plan for his play at present but that we might do it towards the end of the season. Meanwhile we would suggest that he should carefully revise the part of his principal character who would be likely in his present form to appear ridiculous on the stage —[1] Then if he revises — I think it is a case where Fay's judgement would be useful, and we might be guided almost by reasons of utility. It is good *promising* enough to play if it would be useful to us, and crude enough to refuse, if it would be likely to do us harm. — That is my *very hasty* view of the matter

I hope you are better

Yours sincerely
J. M. Synge

I am sending the MS to you, as you may want to look at it again. ⟨Send me your address I am not sure⟩[2]

MS, Berg. *TB*, 243

[1] 'A Fragment' was the first tentative title for *When the Dawn Is Come*, by Thomas MacDonagh (see below, p. 146). In a letter of 3 Dec 1907 returning the MS to MacDonagh, Yeats quoted Synge's comments as from an unnamed reader to whom the play was submitted 'for final judgment' (Edd Winfield Parks and Aileen Wells Parks, *Thomas MacDonagh* [Athens, Ga., 1967], 101).

[2] For this cancelled message see below, p. 92.

To MOLLY ALLGOOD

Glendalough House [Glenageary]
Nov [29th][1]/07

My own dearest Life

I am writing you an extra line today as I could not write to you anywhere tomorrow. I will write on *Sunday* to Glasgow — I suppose you will get it there sometime during the day, dont be dissapointed if it does not reach you in the morning.

My dear child I'm at my wits end to know what to do — I am

squirming and thrilling and quivering with the excitement of writing Deirdre and I *daren't* break the thread of composition by going out to look for digs and moving into them at this moment. Meanwhile my mother's visitor drives me nearly to distraction though I only see her at meals. One thing is absoluty certain as soon as ever we find a digs now we must be married *even* if you *have no holidays*. Let me get Deirdre out of danger — she may be safe in a week — then Marriage in God's Name. Would you mind a *registry office* if that saves time? I dont know whether it does or not, but we might be married *here* in a registry office perhaps when you come back if I have not got 'digs'. Write very often I am so eager to hear every day. I went to the dentist yesterday, but there was nothing serious to be done. He gave me the name of a young but reliable and cheap dentist where you can go and use his (my man's) name so that you will be sure to be well treated.

Your old Tramp.

I have got your picture (photo) framed and put it up in my little study. It looks very nice, *of course*.

Send Glasgow address I am not sure where I have put yours. I have a letter to Lady G. on my table and I have just written this last message on her letter by mistake!!!

MS, AS. *LM*, 220

---

1 Misdated 27 Nov.

To MOLLY ALLGOOD

Glendalough House [Glenageary]
December 1st 1907

Dearest Love

Your little note came this morning, you dont say if Sally will be able to play in Glasgow, is she better?

This is a grey cool Sunday morning, I wish we were going off for a day in the mountains I am tired and I haven't the heart to go by myself.

Yesterday I went out on my bicycle and when I got as far as Carrickmines just as I was mounting, after a hill, the wheel bent into the brake and jammed, so I had to take off the brake and wheel the thing home. There was a spoke broken apparently that I had not noticed, if the wheel had gone when I was spinning down a hill I'd have got a fine come down! I am beginning to feel the strain of this hard work very much, I wish you were here to take my thoughts off it, and cheer me up for a while. I didn't go to sleep till two last night my poor nerves were so excited — indeed I'm sleeping badly nearly every night. I finished the (G) i e the 7th revision or re-writing of the III Act yesterday. It 'goes' now all through — the III Act I mean — but it wants a good deal of strengthening, of *'making personal'* still before it will satisfy me. I wish you'd read a lot of the best things — G Treasury, Shakspere and so on — I'll have to rely a good deal on your criticism and if you dont read what is good you wont know what is good — you wont know really and surely, no one can — and what I'll do then? Anyone with a quick taste and intelligence — and you have them ten times over — who reads and knows the masterpieces of literature can very soon tell whether some new work is rubbish or a masterpiece too. Nish. That's your Sunday lecture!

I hope you're very good my own dear dear life, not rolling your dear little eyes, or playing cards and remembering your swears! By the way do you know you've spent £25 since this time last year on *Nothing*? You gave your Mother £25 we'll say — you didn't really give so much — I bought you two dresses and paid for all your outings. Dossy paid for your amusements on tour and going to theatre, F.J.F. paid for one of your weeks in Glen Cree and I paid for the jennet. What's become of the other £25. For that you should have got two beautiful dresses £10 and a bike £5, and £10 pocket money, but I dont know where it's all gone. I'm afraid you're not old enough to be trusted with money! This is not a scold my poor sweet treasure, but a little gentle kind of a warning. That is harmless isn't it.

I'm going to Parsons tomorrow to show him my neck, its swelling a little again, but nothing much.

My cough is keeping nearly all right which is a good sign. I hear Lady Gregory has had influenza so I'm afraid to go in there for fear of catching it.

We'll easily get 'digs' of some kind when we want them temporary furnished ones if necessary till we can settle into our permanent ones. Did I tell you I have got Jack Yeats sketch of the stoker framed and the glass put into the etching?[1] I am quite proud of them, I have them in my little study and they look very nice. That is my first step towards furnishing! Nish! *I'm* as unpractical an ass as you are — that's the worst of it — fancy marrying and setting up with no furniture but three pictures and a suggawn chair[2] and a fiddle! Yet that's what I'm at now. This is a long rambling letter with not much in it I'm afraid. Is it too long?

I am not seeing anyone and I have nothing interesting to write about. I got the last 'page' proofs of the 'Tinkers' last night it will be out in a few days now. That will be my *third* book published this year.

Your old Tramp.

Write at once

By the way you've worked out a *most elegant* 'hand' for the outside of my envelopes at least, is it a fine pen or what?

MS, TCD. *LM*, 222

1 The sketch by Jack Yeats is unidentified. The etching was *A Courtyard, Venice*, by JMS's cousin Edward Millington Synge (see below, p. 116).

2 *Sugan* or *suggan* is the Irish term for a hard twisted rope made of straw or heather; JMS bought his *suggan* chair during his trip to Kerry in October 1907.

To MOLLY ALLGOOD

[Glendalough House, Glenageary]
December 3rd/ 07

My dearest Life

I am looking out for a letter from you — it is a quarter past one and the post passes at half past. If none comes I — I — I — I'm writing this beforehand that I may have something to send you in any case. How are you all? I was in, with Lady G. and Yeats yesterday and they told me that Sally had been left behind in Manchester — poor wretch — it is too bad.

Lady Gregory went out to call on Mrs Russell[1] in the afternoon and Yeats set to to find out my stars. He says there is a very big event coming off in my life in the next month — a good one on the whole though with unusual circumstances and some breaking of ties. Isn't it curious? He evidently had no idea what it was — and I pretended not [to] know either — he thought it had something to do with the theatre or going to America. At the end he said "If you were a different sort of man, I'd say it was a wild imprudent love-affair." Nish!

No post yet I'm very anxious — it is the hour now I must watch out — Here he is, a letter!

I am so very sorry to hear of rows, do try and keep cool and quiet it is not worth while to make yourself ill or uneasy for anything our friends may say. There is nothing like keeping a check on one's self then no one can gain a point anywhere. I am very uneasy about you, my poor dear Life, away there with no one to advise or help you. Try and be happy and quiet and do your work and let the rest slide. You'll be coming home to me in 10 days now, and then we'll be together all ways my dear love.

I told Yeats the story of my Deirdre last night. He was very much pleased with it I think. *He asked* me to get the hour of your birth and date, I think he believes in you a great deal — we all do — I could say more that would please you perhaps but I had better not. I wonder when you will get this I shall be *very anxious* for further news.

Does the rug keep you comfortable? I am so glad you have it this cold weather, it is very cold here. I must go to the post now. Good bye my hundred treasures remember you are my little wife and keep as quiet as I did when I had words with our friend.[2]

Your old Tramp.

P.S. Curiously I dreamed on Saturday night that Fay was in some way skoffing Sally's illness. You see I keep an eye on you!

I have got the £3 from Prague, all right at last.

MS, TCD. *LM*, 224

---

1 Mrs G. W. Russell, née Violet North (*c.* 1868–1932), who married AE in 1898 when they were both members of the Dublin Theosophical Lodge.

2 During this tour the antipathy between W. G. Fay and the company was becoming more and more obvious; he tried to persuade Sally to perform before she had recovered, and severely chastised Molly for arriving late to rehearsal (see *TB*, 245–8). For JMS's 'words with' Frank Fay, see I. 341–2.

To MOLLY ALLGOOD

Glendalough House [Glenageary]
Dec. 4th/07

My dearest Love

How are things going? I hoped there would be a letter today to reassure me — yesterday's was so stormy but none has come. I do not wonder; you must find it hard to get time to do anything.

Dear Love do write me a nice letter, I am uneasy about you somehow. I am *glad* Dossy is there to look after you. Nish! Never say I am jealous again.

Little Heart you dont know how much feeling I have for you. You are like my child, and my little wife, and my good angel, and my greatest friend, all in one! I dont believe there has been a woman in Ireland loved the way I love you for a thousand years. When that is so, what do the Fays matter? Be punctual and polite, and do not lose your temper, then nothing they say can have any power over you.

Now I am going to town.

Write a lot to

Your old lonely Tramp.

MS, TCD. *LM* 225

To MOLLY ALLGOOD

Glendalough House [Glenageary]
Dec 6th/07

My dearest Treasure

I got your letters and the cuttings yesterday but I did not manage to write to you as I had written the day before and I was very busy. I have several rather important things to tell you. I have had long talks with the Directors and we have come to some important decisions which you will hear of in good time. Meanwhile you are to stop Kerrigan leaving the company — if he is taking his notice seriously[1] — just tell [him] to stay on till he has seen the Directors this PRIVATELY from me. If he is not really meaning to leave dont say anything about it. You know, I suppose, that we are to have Miss H. subsidy for *three full years* more — if nothing unforeseen happens — that is great news for 'US-TWO' — as by three years I ought to have a much better position than I have now and I think we'll come through all right — so that it is really worth while to fight the battle on and we the Directors are going to do it at all risks. We have just got a really excellent play from a new young man[2] — in many ways really clever and good so that we wont run short of work this season. I was at the New Arts Club *debate*[3] with Yeats the other night and I was delighted to find him the favourite and star of the evening with a crowd of young men hanging on his words — new clever young men who have nothing to do with all the worn out cliques   Trinity College also is becoming vehemently interested in Irish things so that if we can only get *good plays* we may strike a new audience any day. Remember the Abbey is so small and our expenses are so small that quite a few people out of the crowds who go to Martin Harvey, say, would put us on our feet. So keep your spirits up and Sally's up, for my own have come up greatly. MacKenna is coming over very soon[4] and he will be of the greatest use to us I think on the Irish Press. I remember I spoke gloomily about the Abbey a few days ago, but somehow the new play and the new sympathetic people at the Arts Club have given me new hope. Long may it last.

Yeats got a wire on Wednesday night to say Sally was taking Devorgilla   Did she get there in time.[5] I think the directors must know that we are getting married, they probably have no idea that it is so close. We talk about you and the communications I have with you, quite frankly of course. Now be discreet and dont let Kerrigan or anyone leave. THIS IS VERY PRIVATE it is likely that on any further tours one of the Directors will go also — so perhaps you and I will be on the road again together before too long. Nish!

I wonder shall I hear from you today. I have written you two extra letters and you haven't written one *extra letter* to me. You little *B. Rose!*[6] I was touched and obliged and grateful for your list of the Chaucer. I think the 8/0 or rather 6/0 one is the one I want. If it is complete and fairly good print that is the one. If not probably the one in three vols 3/0 net would do, but the 6/0 one I imagine is many times the better.[7]

I went to Parsons the other day he thinks I am *"grand"*, my neck and chest are very satisfactory. I had not been quite well this week with queer pains in a portion of my inside, but he couldn't find anything the matter so I hope it is nothing.[8] I am very anxious now of course as the time — our time is coming on — I am better today. Remember not to over do yourself *next week*.

I hope you understand Dear Heart that when I write about money-matters, it is for *our sakes* not for my sake.

I am going in to see Roberts today to try and arrange a copy-right reading of the Tinkers, we may publish it next Tuesday if all goes well.[9] I have written a preface I wish I had you here to advise me about it. Good bye my one treasure

Your old Tramp

Send me your *Edinburgh address* again please, I'll write there next on Sunday.

P.S. Your letter has just come I am sending on cutting to Lady Gregory. It was a *very great shame* to do *what they did*. I mean Vaughan and Fay.

MS, TCD. *LM*, 226

1 Molly had apparently written that J. M. Kerrigan, after a quarrel with W. G. Fay, had given notice.

2 'Norreys Connell', pen name of Conal Holmes O'Connell O'Riordan (1874–1948), actor and author of many plays and novels, who briefly succeeded JMS as a director of the theatre in 1909. His one-act play *The Piper, an Unended Argument* was produced on 13 Feb 1908 to a puzzled, sometimes angry audience; two other plays, *Time* and *An Imaginary Conversation*, were produced in 1909. He became president of the Irish Literary Society in 1937.

3 The organized programme of the United Arts Club frequently included a debate on Wednesday evenings.

4 MacKenna finally moved from London to Dublin in early April 1908, his wife following in July.

5 While Sara Allgood was ill, *Dervorgilla* was replaced after the first night by *The Rising of the Moon*. Brigit O'Dempsey took Sally's roles of Mary Cahel in *The Gaol Gate* and Bridget Gillane in *Kathleen ni Houlihan*, while Molly played Kathleen, and Mrs Delane in *Hyacinth Halvey*. Sally returned for *The Hour Glass* on Tuesday, 3 Dec.

6 The 'pretty operetta' *Briar Rose, or the Sleeping Beauty* was performed in the parochial hall of Christ Church, Kingstown, several times during this season, in aid of the local missionary fund.

7 A letter of 7 Dec 1907 (TCD) from W. S. Sime, Bookseller, 120 Sauchie-hall Street, Glasgow, reports the forwarding of the Chaucer, 'as ordered this day', at a price reduced from 6/6 to 5/–.

8 These pains eventually led to the operation the following year, at which an inoperable growth was found. After JMS's death the family blamed Dr Parsons for not taking the symptoms more seriously at the outset.

9 *The Tinker's Wedding* was copyrighted on 21 Dec and finally published on 27 or 28 Dec 1907.

To LADY GREGORY

Glendalough House [Glenageary]
Dec 6th/07

Dear Lady Gregory

I send you the papers in case you have not seen them. Fay did not slip programmes or announce in any way that Miss Sarah Allgood was not playing, so the papers have let his wife off easily. Miss S. Allgood is not unnaturally very much annoyed at having Mrs Fay masquerading in her name. Otherwise I have heard of no fresh troubles.

I met Lane in town yesterday and he tells me they have arranged to go on with the gallery and open in January[1]

Yours sincerely
J. M. Synge

I read Casey's play last night. I was *enthusiastic* after the first act, but I didn't think the others so good. I wont call him a genius yet, till I see his next play.[2]

P.S. I have just got news again from Glasgow and a Herald cutting which I send.

I hear a lady reporter got hold of Sally Allgood *after* Devorgilla in the stalls and asked her if she was Miss Sarah Allgood and if so who were the ladies they had been seeing, and Miss Sarah told her that she had just come, and appeared for the first time that week. The press, they say, is very angry.

Will you please send on my news to Yeats if you are writing.

MS, Berg. *TB*, 244

1 Lady Gregory's nephew, the art collector and critic Hugh Percy Lane (1875–1915), knighted in 1909 (see I. 262), was primarily responsible for the new Municipal Gallery of Modern Art at 17 Harcourt Street, to which he loaned some of his paintings and of which he was honorary director. The gallery was officially opened on 20 Jan 1908 with an exhibition reviewed by JMS in the *Manchester Guardian* on 24 Jan 1908.

2 William Francis Casey (1884–1957) contributed two plays to the Abbey:

The Man Who Missed the Tide, first performed 13 Feb 1908, and *The Suburban Groove*, 1 Oct 1908; in 1913 he left Dublin for London to join *The Times*, of which he served as editor 1948-52.

To MOLLY ALLGOOD

[Glendalough House, Glenageary]
Dec 8th [1907]

Dearest LOVE

This is the second day without a letter and I need not say that I am ⟨greatly⟩ disappointed and ⟨most anxious and upset⟩. (I'm *not now* as I understand Dear Heart.) I have not got your Edinburgh address — you gave it to me but I am afraid I have lost it — so I will not be able to send you this till I hear from you. ⟨I wish you would [write] me the merest line —— two words rather than leave me without news. I make myself ill with uneasiness.⟩ (*Amn't I a born ass*?) I dare say you were very busy your last day in Glasgow and perhaps missed the post — and that has spoiled my day. (I will be cheerful in spite of it, but I got an AWFUL *qualm* when the post passed!) It seems *years* since you went away, I feel like a blind man or a deaf man, or something queer and horrible ever since I cant *live* now without you. Thank Heaven in a week now the tour will be over.

I am getting better I think, but I'm not altogether flourishing yet. Nothing much is the matter but I've queer pains in my inside. They are going away I think. I got a letter from Brodsky yesterday asking for particulars for an article he is doing on *my work* for Australia.[1]

Your old Tramp

P.S. I realize that I'M a fool, your letters never come till midday from Glasgow so I *could not* hear from you this morning if you posted yesterday as usual. I ought not to send this perhaps but you wont mind my being lonesome.   T.

I've found your address so this goes. Good Luck!

P.S. I wonder how all your affairs are going now. Keep every body quiet till the tour is over, then there will be oportunities of saying anything that has to be said.

I told Lady Gregory about Sally — she *very* STRONGLY disapproves of what was done — I mean about letting Mrs Fay appear in Sally's name.[2] This is *private*, but you can tell Sally if you like that we disapprove of the course that was taken, but there is no use, for the moment, crying over spilt milk — it will not happen again.

I hop with delight when I think how nearly the tour is over. I have never known such a long fortnight.

Your very lonesome old Tramp.

Take care of yourself my own dear Treasure. Be cheerful.

MS, TCD. *LM*, 228

1 The Australian journalist Leon Brodzky (see below, p. 102) wrote to JMS from London on 4 Dec 1907, 'Having finished and sent out to Australia an article giving a general account of the Irish Theatre, I am now engaged on an article devoted to your work exclusively' (TCD).

2 Lady Gregory wrote to JMS on 7 Dec 1907, 'It was disgraceful & I should think actionable putting Mrs. Fay to play under Miss Allgoods name' (*TB*, 245).

To MOLLY ALLGOOD

Glendalough House [Glenageary]
Dec 10th [1907]

Dearest Love

I wired to you this morning to look for the letter I wrote on Sunday to the address you gave me before the tour. You must find it some-how. Try the General Post if it is not at the 'digs' Mrs Strathdee 26 Grindley Street, and if that won't do write to the Dead Letter Office — they will tell you where at the G.P.O Edinburgh. It is intollerable to think of my intimate letter to you being opened and laughed at in the Post Office and then sent back to me here "Tramp", Glendalough House ⟨I feel more humiliated at the thought than words can tell you. I shall be the laughing stock of the servants and the whole family, and all because you didn't think it worth while to send me a post card with your address,⟩ and because I — ⟨poor fool⟩ — thought you would be lonely getting into Edinburgh and finding no letter for you on Monday. I thought you valued my poor letters, such as they are, but now you have left me half a week without your address. You could have written on Sunday I suppose if you had cared to. However this is not to scold you, only I feel sad somehow. Dont, for a moment get it into your head that I am writing crossly my poor little heart. I dont want to make you unhappy for a quarter of a second. You are my whole life remember.
⟨Your address I am sorry I have written at such length.⟩ The Chauser came yesterday it is charming Dear Heart and I'm *very grateful indeed*. I am enquiring about a 'digs' and will have one soon I hope. I am better I think, but I've queer pains still a little. I am off to town now 10 o'clock to arrange about Tinker's Wedding copy-right show which is on tonight I believe.

I needn't say that what you write about the money — the money I lent you — *is nonesense.* All I have is yours now and you know it. Why is it that you get so get so careless about my letters when you have been such a little time away? It makes me a little low Dear Heart though I dont suppose you mean it. I'm afraid you've taken up what I said about the money quite wrong I never wanted you to send me any, *I never give it a thought.*

The Chaucer was only 5/0 post free so they sent me 1/6 back I've bought another book with it   you are a good little changling after all. I was in Lane's new gallery today. They have my portrait by old Yeats *not* a good one.[1]

Be sure to read this cheerfully it isn't a schold.

Take care of *yourself this week*

P.S. Deirdre is getting on I think, but slowly now. I over-worked myself for a while and I'm taking it a little easier now. In any case at this stage one cannot go fast. I am so glad to think the tour will be over now in four days it has seemed interminable — months since you went away.

Please write by return to say if you have got my letter. Dont let this letter upset you in any way I am writting in a very great hurry Dearest Treasurette.

> Your old Tramp with many blessings.

MSS, (page 1: 'Dearest Love . . . life remember.') AS; (remainder: ⟨Your address . . . blessings.') TCD. *LM*, 229

---

[1] This portrait was commissioned by Hugh Lane and presented to the Municipal Gallery. Begun in 1905, J. B. Yeats worked at it, between making pencil sketches of his subject, for at least two years.

To LEON BRODZKY[1]

Glendalough House | Kings town | Co Dublin
Dec 10th/07

My dear Brodzky

I have not had time till today to answer your letter, please excuse the delay. I dont quite know how much you want in the way of autobiographical particulars, I'll be very brief and if you want more you can send me queries.

I was born 1871 near Dublin   I entered Trinity College in 88 — and took my degree B.A. there in /92/   Meanwhile I gave most of my time to music, and was took Scholarship ⟨of⟩ in Harmony and Counterpoint at Royal, Irish Accademy of Music in 92.   In 1893 I went to Germany to study the language and music, and in 94 — I

gave [up] music and took to literature definitely. Jan 1st/95 I went
to Paris and spent six or seven winters there the summers in Ireland
with one visit to Italy to learn the language. In 1898 I went to the
Aran Islands — I had known the Co Wicklow peasantry — we always
spent long summers there — intimately for years — ⟨but⟩ and found
the subjects of most of my plays there. Since 1903 I have lived in
or near Dublin and worked in connection with the Irish National
Theatre ⟨Compan⟩ Society, and the Abbey Theatre since it was
opened. So much for my auto.

I am bringing out another play next week 'The Tinker's Wedding'
and if you can hold over your article I will send you a copy. I am
publishing it only; it is *too* dangerous to play. I dont know whether
you know my book "The Aran Islands" — it throws a good deal of
light I think on my plays.

At present I am writing a 'Saga' play on the story of Deirdre, but
it is an experiment chiefly to change my hand, and there is no use
speaking of it ⟨yet⟩, I think, in your article. I am also doing a book
on Kerry to follow up the Aran Islands and describe my times with
the Kerry peasants.

I hope your play[2] will be very successful, as you say, it must be
hard to work at it and journalism. There is no work I that require
such slow care as writing a play.

Sincerely yours
J. M. Synge

MS, TCD

1 Leon Herbert Spencer Brodzky (1883–1973, see I, 173), who changed his
name to Spencer Brodney on being appointed editor of the London *Weekly
Despatch* in 1914, eventually became editor of the *New York Times* monthly,
Current History, later founding his own journal, *Events*. Early in 1906 he left
Australia for London, to work as a journalist. Two articles, 'The Lesson of
the Irish Theatre', *The British-Australasian*, 9 Aug 1906, and 'Towards an
Australian Drama', *The Lone Hand*, 1 June 1908, apply his general obser-
vations of the Abbey Theatre company from performances he saw in Hull in
July 1906. The article projected here, completed in 1908, was rejected for
publication, and 'sent to an Irish friend in Australia' in 1915. An unpublished
article written in 1925 recalls his 1906 impressions of JMS, 'with that simple
charm and utter lack of any sense of self-importance . . . that simplicity and
sincerity' (TCD). Apart from three letters from JMS, all Brodzky's notes and
other correspondence with and concerning him have disappeared.

2 Brodzky apparently wrote and produced two plays, the (unidentified)
one mentioned here and *Rebel Smith* (New York, 1925).

To MOLLY ALLGOOD

[Glendalough House, Glenageary]
Dec 11th/07

Dearest Little Heart

Your letter has come   I am so glad you got the other I felt upset about it yesterday. I wrote part of my letter yesterday to you twice over I was so afraid of saying something that might upset you I hope it was all right.

I am counting the hours till we meet. This is a most lovely day and I am just off on my bicycle for a ride to the Skalp or some-where. By the way when do you get home and what day do you leave your present address. There should not have been 'card' in the wire. I put "Letter sent etc" Write to me every day now I cant hold out any longer. In a hurry your old

Tramp

Yes I *often* dream of you.

MS, TCD. *LM*, 230

To LEON BRODZKY

Glendalough House | Kings town
Dec 12th [1907]

Dear Brodzky

I am writing to my publishers to ask them to send you a copy of the Aran Islands. The Tinkers Wedding will not be out till next week.

I wrote one play — which I have never published — in Paris, dealing with Ireland of course, but not a peasant play,[1] before I wrote "Riders to the Sea". By the way 'Riders' was written *before* the Shadow of the Glen, though Shadow of the G. was the first played.

I look on the "Aran Islands" as my first serious piece of work — it was written before any of the plays. In writing out the talks of the people and their stories in this book — and in a certain number of articles on Wicklow Peasantry which I have not yet collected — I learned to write the peasant *dialect* and *dialogue* which I use in my plays.

Though I wrote 'Riders' and 'The Shadow' for Fay's company, I had been out of Ireland so much that I had never ⟨seen⟩ met any of the company or seen them act, at that time[2]

This is a disconnected sort of letter but perhaps these stray points will interest you. Let me hear if you want any more information, and also please let me know if they send you the A. Islands all right.

Yours sincerely
J. M. Synge

MS, TCD

1 *When the Moon Has Set*, finally published in 1968 (*Plays*, Book I, 153–77).

2 Although he did not see Fay's company perform until December 1902, JMS had been impressed by the performance of Douglas Hyde's *Casadh an tSugain*, produced by the Irish Literary Theatre with Yeats and Moore's *Diarmuid and Grania* on 21 Oct 1901, and directed by Fay; see his article for *l'Européen*, 'Le Mouvement Intellectuel Irlandais', 31 May 1902 (*Prose*, 378–82). *Riders to the Sea* and *The Shadow of the Glen* were both written during the summer of 1902.

To MOLLY ALLGOOD

Glendalough House [Glenageary]
Dec 13th/07

Dearest Love

Your letter came last night at six o'clock and gave me a pleasant surprise, they dont generally come at that hour.

I laughed at your cranky morning scrawl. You little B. rose you ought to have more sense! I am overjoyed to think that I shall see you so soon again. If you are very tired after your journey on Monday and *unwell* perhaps you ought not to come down on Monday. It might be too much for you. I could meet you in town perhaps. Of course we must meet as soon as ever we can, but you must not start off by making yourself ill. My inside is making me uneasy — I was rather worse after my bicycle ride the other day. I hope it is only fancy, but I think I'll have to go to Parsons again. Yes I see they are doing A.E.'s Deirdre at the Abbey tonight. Madame M. is Lavarcham I think. There was an absurd "puff" about the play in the I. Times today written evidently by one of themselves.[1] They should have more sense. I can hardly believe that this is the last letter to you on tour I cant write now you are coming so soon take care of yourself on the journey and be *very good*.

Your old Tramp

Let me know of course if there is any change in your time for arriving   J.M.S.

MS, TCD. *LM*, 231

1 The Theatre of Ireland, formed in June 1906 by the nationalist seceders from the National Theatre Society Limited (see *TB*, 82–3, 96–119), occasionally

hired the Abbey Theatre for its productions; a revival of AE's *Deirdre*, on their agenda since the beginning, was finally produced on 13 and 14 Dec 1907 with Countess Markiewicz playing the role of the old Nurse/Druidess, Lavarcham. A full column in the *Irish Times*, 13 Dec 1907, improbably under the 'Books of the Week' section (AE's *Deirdre* was not then published in book form) and signed by an unidentified 'A.H.T.', recollected in loving detail the play's first production in 1902, by W. G. Fay's company. The notice quotes lengthy passages from the play, making brief reference only to 'the eve of the production of "Deirdre" by the players of Ireland at the Abbey Theatre'. Constance Markiewicz, née Gore-Booth (1868–1927), Irish revolutionary and the only woman among the leaders of the 1916 Easter Rising, in the opinion of many squandered not only her beauty but her artistic talents in her nationalist fervour. In addition to being an acting member of the Theatre of Ireland, she became leading actress in her husband's Independent Theatre Company the following year.

To MOLLY ALLGOOD

Glendalough House | Kingstown
Dec 14 [1907]

Dearest Heart

I got your letter (Friday's) last night, I am glad you had one pleasant day at least during your tour.

Isn't grand that you're coming back at last — I am counting the minutes till tomorrow — This tour has been intollerable and interminable, I seem to have been sitting here making myself old with looking on the days and they passing me by for the last ten years.[1]

I wonder how you are. It is likely to be foggy tonight so you may be late getting in tomorrow morning. I think Tuesday would be a better day for you to come out here. My mother's friend goes away on Tuesday morning early, so she'll be fussing about all day on Monday. Will you meet me in town tomorrow Monday afternoon and have tea somewhere, I couldn't let a day pass without seeing you. If you are tired and not up for much I could meet you at *twenty* to *four* at Tara St. and just go as far as the D.B.C.[2] Or if you are pretty fit I could meet you at *twenty to three*. Of course if you are *feeling done up you* had better stay quiet, and wait till Tuesday. I wont go up unless I get a letter *posted before eleven*, or *a wire* to say the hour and place. A wire would be the safer perhaps as the post is getting clogged with Xmas letters. If you do not meet me will you please write as soon as you can to say how you are. Also please tell me if Kerrigan still means to leave, and if so give me his address and tell him I would like to see him before he does anything definite. You need not, of course, say anything of this to the Fays.

I wish to -

- -
- - - - - - - - - - - - - it was tomorrow.

I'm better I think, I haven't got digs yet I'll tell you why to-morrow, a thousand blessings

Your old T.

MS, TCD. *LM*, 232

   1 JMS is parodying Nora Burke's speech in *The Shadow of the Glen*: 'Isn't it a long while I am sitting here in the winter, and the summer, and the fine spring, with the young growing behind me and the old passing . . . ' (*Plays*, Book I, 49)
   2 A Dublin Bread Company tea room in Sackville Street (now O'Connell Street), fairly near Molly's home at 37 Mary Street.

To LADY GREGORY

Glendalough House | Kingstown
16/12/07

Dear Lady Gregory

I have not been able to see Kerrigan yet, I hope to do so in a day or two as soon as I can get in communication with him. It seems he wrote a letter to the Directors giving his reasons for resigning, and gave it to Fay to forward to them. Fay it seems has suppressed it, unless you or Yeats have got it. If Fay has done so it will give us a possible means of getting the resignation ⟨revised⟩ re-tracted. Fay appears to have used violently bad language to Kerrigan and he bases his resignation on that. I have heard Fay on one occasion using impossible and unmentionable language to the scene-shifters to perhaps Kerrigan may have some reason for what he has done. Fay has called the company for a rehearsal tomorrow (Tuesday) morning as usual and said nothing to them about holidays. If as I understand you are in favour of holidays will you please write to Fay at once and tell him to let them off for a few days. I think it would do good to let them have a few days rest — to quiet down. I do not see any need to have the meeting at once — now that they are safe back they are not very likely to do anything rash for a ⟨day⟩ week or two. It will be much more possible to come to some understanding when their excitement and irritation has cooled down a little.[1]

I hear Mac has been offered a 'shop' but as he has come home it does not look as if he was going to accept it.[2] Miss Sarah Allgood is looking out too I am told. This sounds very bad but I do not think it will come to anything Mac has been going away for the last year or more and nothing ever comes of it

I am writting to Miss Sarah Allgood to tell her that there is going to be a meeting in January, and to ask her not to do anything in a hurry I was not at all surprised to hear that she had written in to Payne. I told you I think that she applied to Vedrenne when we were in London.[3] I do not blame her. They are in want of money and people tell her she could get wonderful salaries on the English stage, and Fay and Vaughan tell her that we are no use, and cannot last.

Vaughan, by the way, has been impresing on the company that they are scandalously under paid! and making himself popular. I will give you any more news that I get.

Yours sincerely
J. M. Synge

By the way Sarah Allgood has been advised to have her tonsils taken out I believe. I hope she will not go to a quack and have her voice ruined. She is very much afraid of spending money. I am advising her to be careful and not in a hurry.

MS, Berg. *TB*, 249

1 Evidently conflict between W. G. Fay and the members of the company outside of his immediate family had become so serious that the entire company was threatening to disband; Lady Gregory and Yeats hoped for an open meeting, at which 'they will decide to go on or drop off, & we shall have more hearty work' (see *TB*, 247–9).

2 Francis Quinton ('Mac') McDonnell (1883–1951; see I. 141), stage name 'Arthur Sinclair', was one of the leading actors with the company 1904–15; he became Molly Allgood's second husband. A 'shop' is a limited engagement.

3 Miss Horniman wrote to Yeats that Sara Allgood had applied to Payne as manager of her Manchester company, but that she 'did not wish to take anyone' from the National Theatre Society as long as it holds together' (*TB*, 247). John E. Vedrenne (1867–1930), lessee and joint manager with Granville-Barker of the Court Theatre, London, and later of the Savoy, in 1907 became lessee and manager of the New Queen's Theatre, London.

To LADY GREGORY

Glendalough House [Glenageary]
Wednesday 18 Dec /07

Dear Lady Gregory

I met Kerrigan to today and had a long talk. He is *ready*, — *eager*, — to come back to us. He speaks of Fay quite simply and without temper. On the day in question he was in time for his cue — he only comes on in the 2nd Act — but Fay swore and cursed at him and spoke badly to him personally — as he puts it — but there was nothing out of the way. Kerrigan, however lost his head and temper and gave notice. He says Fay is unfortunate in his manner with them; at one time too confidential, and then the next lowering himself by undignified personal abuse so that none of them can feel any respect for him. The letter I spoke of was a line or two only. Mac, Kerrigan says, is very much against Fay.

On the whole Kerrigan seemed quite satisfactory, and in sympathy with our ideas. He is ready to stay with us, and fight our battle as long as we will have him.

Then I went on and found Fay. He seemed depressed and nervous, and, I think, quite decided to go if he does not get what he wnats. He put his case very quietly and well, and he has a good deal to say for himself. He has written to you I understand, so I need not go into all he said.[1] He is very bitter against Miss O'Neill. She is, I dare say, hard to manage, all artists with highly excitable tempers are, but I know a whole series of little things by which Fay has broken down his authority with her. One of the things he is most deeply 'hurt' about is the fact that Miss Sara Allgood when questioned was *shabby* enough to admit that she was herself.[2] Fay, it seems, thought there would be a penalty if he changed the cast and he was trying to trick the Management. As no penalty was claimed he was evidently wrong!

⟨I think⟩ If we gave Fay the power he wants we would lose the two Miss Allgoods, Mac, and, of course, Kerrigan. Otherwise we shall I fear lose the "Fay family" as Kerrigan calls them. (I think we shall have to lose the Fays.) He, Fay, as it is, flatly refuses to have Kerrigan back, he is putting Vaughan into the Yankee part! in the Dress-maker[3] that is why he cannot give holidays. He is in favour of closing for a fortnight after the Stephen's night show and getting a rest, and then putting things on whatever new basis we decide on afterwards. I do not know if that will seem best to you and Yeats. I think the matter is so very important, that we *three* MUST MEET and talk it over with Fay, and then with the company.[4] I am sincerely sorry for Fay; he has put himself in an impossible position by a generally unwise behaviour that he is largely unconscious of. Please send this to Yeats. I am writing him a line merely to say I have seen Fay.

Yours sincerely
J. M. Synge

What shall I say to Kerrigan? I told him I would try and smooth matters down so that he might come back, but it does not look hopeful unless Fay goes.

MS, Berg. *TB*, 251

1 On 1 Dec 1907 W. G. Fay had sent the directors a set of proposals including the termination of all contracts, the actors to be re-engaged by him personally for the season only, the power to dismiss them resting with him, and no appeal to any authority other than his. Complaining of the lack of discipline within the company, he mentioned in particular Molly's unpunctuality, that she was 'exceedingly difficult to manage on the summer tour and uses her intimacy with Mr. Synge to do as she likes'; 'the trouble started', he said, 'with Paynes coming'. (*TB*, 245)

2 i.e., not Brigit O'Dempsey; see p. 98.

3 *The Country Dressmaker* (Fitzmaurice).

4 Although the directors met on 4 Dec and rejected Fay's proposals, Yeats and Lady Gregory were attempting to avoid direct confrontation — and Fay's resignation — until the company could meet and elect members to 'consult with the Stage Manager and Directors as to rules of discipline' (*TB*, 246). JMS remained the only intermediary until 11 Jan 1908, when the directors' reply was submitted to Fay after the company returned from Galway.

To W. B. YEATS[1]

Glendalough House | Kingstown
18/12/07

Dear Yeats

I have seen Kerrigan and Fay, and I am writing full particulars to Lady Gregory and asking her to send on letter.

Kerrigan is very anxious to come back, he is very keenly interested in our work and wishes to stay with us to the bitter end. Fay refuses flatly to have him back.

Fay seems very sad and very depressed and I think very decided to have his way or leave us If we gave him his way, we would lose the two Miss Allgoods and, I think, Mac, and Kerrigan who is already gone. Fay suggests that we close the theatre for a fortnight after the Stephen's Night show — it has to be painted I believe — and meet during that time to arrange matters, if they can be arranged. What do you think. It is essential in such a matter that the three directors should be together.[2] What shall I say to Kerrigan? I told him I would try and arrange matters so as to get him back.

Yours
J. M. Synge

MS, Berg. *TB*, 251

1 William Butler Yeats (1865–1939), poet, dramatist, and co-founder of the Abbey Theatre, JMS's fellow director; see I. 125.

2 The directors' reply to Fay's proposals included a reiteration of aims: 'That it be explained to the Company that this Theatre must go on as a Theatre for intellectual drama, whatever unpopularity that may involve. That no compromise can be accepted upon this subject, but that if any member find himself

unable to go on with us under the circumstances, we will not look upon it as unfriendly on his part if he go elsewhere, on the contrary we will help all we can.' (*TB*, 246).

To MOLLY ALLGOOD

Glendalough House [Glenageary]
Dec 18th/07

Dearest Heart

What about tomorrow? Where shall we meet? Can we meet? I wonder if you are rehearsing in the evening? You had better write to me before eleven and be sure to post in time to say if you will come out or if I should meet you in town. If I am to meet you I might not catch the quarter past two train if the post is late   Then I could go by the next   write anyhow. If there is any put off I'll wire.

I saw Kerrigan and Fay today

I must run with this to the post

Your Old Tramp

MS, TCD. *LM*, 233

To W. B. YEATS

Glendalough House | Kingstown
Dec 19th/07

Dear Yeats

I have received cheque-book etc, and your letter.[1] I will see to the deposit business the first day I am in town — tomorrow or next day. I understood the money for salaries was in a separate account now, that could be drawn on by Vaughan and Fay, however I will find out if they need money. Vaughan I suppose is our Secretary now so that it is his signature that will be needed for the deposit money. Do you know if there is any minute recording his appointment?

As to the other troubles, I wrote hurried notes to you and Lady Gregory last night, and I have thought over matters a good deal since. Yesterday in his depressed mood Fay — I think — really meant to leave if he does not get autocratic power. One does not know what he may think in a fortnight. Further in going over our talk again ⟨in my mind⟩ I can see a carefully hidden, but bitter animosity against the Allgoods — both of them. It is the same feeling that he had against the Walkers and Roberts two years ago,[2] and that he has had since against Miss Horniman, and the Directors in varying degrees. I do not see any hope of *peace* while he is at the head of the company. I like him in many ways, in spite of all draw-backs, but I do not think he is now suitable for his position, especially as his wife is using his irratabil[it]y for her own ends. His perfectly definite refusal to remain stage-manager if Kerrigan is brought back, is a plain issue on which to work, but it seems not a sufficiently broad one. The difficulty of our position is that Fay's claims are logical and reasonable if he was the right man for the position, but are impossible when we take into consideration all the details of his personality which we have learnt by long co-operation with him.

If it was possible for Lady Gregory to come up now — her presence is essential if anything is to be done — I half think it would be better for you to come over and clear things up at once, as it is a matter where we want to work on clear issues, and not on compromises that will only lead to worse confusion. The danger of delay is the danger of compromise, and none of us want an arrangement that will lead to a fresh crisis in two or three months.[3]

I was pleased with Kerrigan yesterday he seemed really intelligent and in sympathy with what we are trying to do. I told him, vaguely, of what we propose to put before the company, and he seemed to think the plan would work. He admits the need of discipline to the fullest.

One other matter. I think Miss M. Allgood's unpunctuality is very serious, but it is not, as Fay thinks, merely agressive insubordination. She is just as unpunctual in everything she does. Further, on this tour when she had her sister seriously ill in rough theatrical lodgings, and was playing and learning new heavy parts, a reasonable stage-manager would have treated her with a little extra consideration, instead of singling her out as Fay has done.[4]

Yours
J. M. Synge

P.S. My Deirdre is impossible without Kerrigan.

I think in future — I suggest at least — that there should be a permanent committee — The Directors — Stage-manager — and two or three of the company elected by themselves, who will keep up a link between us and the rank and file and aid discipline. I am all for more democracy *in details*.

MS, Berg. *TB*, 254

1 Yeats wrote from London on 18 Dec 1907 enclosing a letter from the manager of the National Bank Limited and Yeats's cheque — returned by the bank — for £17.10s: his attempt to reimburse the National Theatre Society for the extra expenses of the production of his revised *Deirdre* on 1 Apr 1907

(TCD), with a supply of signed salary cheques for JMS's counter-signature. Yeats also quoted from a letter he had received from Willie Fay complaining that Molly had been late for six of seven rehearsals on tour and that Sara Allgood had refused to attend the next rehearsal called for (*TB*, 253–4).

2 Mary Walker (Maire nic Shiubhlaigh; d. 1958) and her brother Frank (Prionnsias MacSiubhlaigh) had been members of W. G. Fay's Irish National Dramatic Society until joining the seceders of the Theatre of Ireland early in 1906; see I. 80 and *TB*, 117–18 for theirs and George Roberts's resignations.

3 Yeats replied on 20 Dec 1907, 'It is [im]possible for us to put the company as Fay wishes into the power of one we know to be unjust and untruthful. I too think that compromise is out of the question or drifting on — but I wont act without Lady Gregory as the loss of Fay affects her work chiefly . . . . If he is to stay it should be as a defeated man. I believe him to be unfit to manage the company.' (TCD)

4 Lady Gregory wrote privately to Yeats *c*. 22 Dec 1907, 'We shall have to snub Synge and Molly in the end — her being late in assignations with him is no excuse for her upsetting rehearsals' (Berg), but agreed, reluctantly and finally, that W. G. Fay must go (see *TB*, 254–62).

To MOLLY ALLGOOD

Glendalough [House, Glenageary]
Saturday | 21/12/07

Dearest Life

The doctor says I'm all right so come down tomorrow by the quarter to eleven — dont miss it — if its fine. The doctor made me nervous the last time I was there, thats why I went back today. If its wet tomorrow of course, come by the quarter to two   If I'm not at the eleven train — by any chance — come to the house.

By the way I heard from Quinn today   He is going to take the Playboy MS after all and send me whatever he thinks it is worth! He is also going to guarantee an edition of all my plays in America next spring.[1] Nish! This is all between ourselves of course. So till tomorrow

Your old Tramp

MS, AS. *LM*, 233

1 Quinn's most recent suggestion to George Roberts of Maunsel & Co. was to approach Scribners of New York; nothing came of the plans.

To LEON BRODZKY

Kingstown
23.12.07

Best wishes. Remember that the Kerry 'stuff' that is in the Shanachie is more or less raw-material only. We will send you the Tinkers at once   It was to be out today

Yours
J.M.S.

MS postcard, TCD

To MOLLY ALLGOOD

Glendalough House [Glenageary]
Dec [23]¹/XII/07

Dearest Love

I see that the carols are on tomorrow at Patricks² and I think we'd better go to them. Will you meet me at Tara Street at 20 to three tomorrow (*Tuesday*) afternoon and we'll go. If its wet — very wet — I wont go. My mother says I ought to give you an umbrella for Xmas would you like that?

Hadn't we a great day yesterday   This was a magnificent day here but I'm told it was wretched in town.

I rode round near the Scalp and through Loughin's town and I've done a great day's work also — I *must* work again, but I've got lazy somehow. I'm very well I hope you weren't too tired   If you cant meet me tomorrow send me word. If its wet come out here if you can.

Your old Tramp

Only dont miss me.

MS, TCD. *LM*, 234

  ¹ Misdated 22 Dec.
  ² St. Patrick's Cathedral, Dublin.

To W. B. YEATS

Glendalough House | Kingstown
Dec. 23rd 07

Dear Yeats

In order to draw the mony from the Deposit, the receipt, itself, must be endorsed by two Directors and Secrtary, then the whole can be drawn out, what we want deducted, and the rest put back, on a new Deposit Receipt. According to Vaughan the £17, is to go into the 'running expenses account' in the Munster and Leinster Bank, and not into the ordinary account of the National Bank, where

Miss Horniman's guarantee fund is kept only. I found the receipt all right, but I think, as we have waited so long, it will be easier to settle the matter when you come over. The Deposit receipt is rather a valuable document to set adrift on the Xmas post.

You do not give me any direction as to what I am to say to Kerrigan, and he is anxious to know what we are going to do. If Fay is allowed to keep him out, he will try and get rid of any other members of the company that he does not like, by the same simple means, I am afraid. If Kerrigan will wait, it will, I suppose, be easier to deal with his case when you are over.[1]

On Saturday — ⟨I was at the Abbey copy-righting the Tinkers after the rehearsals⟩ — I found that the Galway contract was fully signed on both sides, it had just come in, but Fay was going to break it on the pretext that the Galway man had delayed some days, a week I think, in sending back his — the Galway man's — half of the contract. I did not think that that was a desirable thing to do, especially as Lady Gregory is a Galway person, so I told them they had better go, and got them to wire a proposed bill to Lady Gregory for her approval.[2] Not having Kerrigan the plays will suffer a good deal. Still it is not possible to force him back for the moment.

I suppose Lady Gregory will go to Galway, the date is the 6th of Janury. Vaughan says we are likely to lose thirty pounds on the trip — That should have been said when the matter was proposed not after the contract has been signed on both sides.

It seems bad management, somewhere, that the theatre should be painted now, when we have important work coming on, and not during the three weeks when the company was away.

Things are now, apparently, as usual.

Are the company to have a holiday, if theatre is being painted and there is nothing special to do?[3]

Yours sincerely
J. M. Synge

TS (MS emendations), Berg. *TB*, 259

[1] Yeats replied on 25 Dec 1907 that for the time being he would prefer Kerrigan to remain out so as not to confuse the issue with Fay (*TB*, 260–1). On 30 Dec he wrote to JMS enclosing a letter to Kerrigan, now missing (*TB*, 267).

[2] The Galway bill proved to be the last straw for Lady Gregory, who accused Fay in a letter of 26 Dec 1907 to Yeats (Berg) of being 'insubordinate' in insisting he had the right to choose plays for Galway, a right she insisted upon for herself (*TB*, 261–2).

[3] This last sentence is added in holograph.

To MOLLY ALLGOOD

Glendalough House [Glenageary]
Dec 28th /07

Dearest Love

I was too busy and too tired out afterwards to write to you yesterday. Are you all right? I think it is too cold and wretched to go out for a long day tomorrow. Come down by the quarter to two — and if it is very fine perhaps I'll meet you at train and take you for a walk or else we can be here. Come here of course if I'm not at the train. Dont bring rug or picture with you in case I meet you.

I have no fresh news since except that I'm hard at work as usual and that I'd pains in my inside last night. I think it's the cold. Keep yourself as warm as you can the wind is very bitter.

We'd a nice little time on Thursday hadn't we? I heard your train passing up after I got home, and I pitied you for having to wait so long. No word from Mrs Cassidy yet.[1] Till tomorrow

Your old
Tramp

MS, TCD. *LM*, 234

[1] Another enquiry about digs.

To LADY GREGORY

[Glendalough House, Glenageary]
[30 December 1907]

[p] 2

The company would have done anything when they came home, but now after the break and Xmas festivities they are probably in a less bitter frame of mind. Their complaints against Fay are quite real, I think, but they are not easy to formulate, as they are based on a general and *growing* dissatisfaction with Fay's bad temper, untruthfulness, and his whole attitude towards them. You write that we 'must give Fay a good pretext for leaving'[1] and Yeats writes 'Fay is looking for an excuse and we must try and keep him from getting one'.

I think we will all agree that Fay will have to go out, and that all we want is to bring things to a climax and to get the business done in such a way as to leave both him and us in as good a position as possible. I am inclined to think his 'proposals' when on tour and our own views as to a more democratic atmosphere in the company — by means of comittee etc — might give us a dignified and intelligible point to divide on. The danger is that Fay might accept our policy and make it unworkable. I will see what can be done with the company and let you know.[2]

Yours sincerely

J. M. Synge

I think nothing can really be done till after Galway.[3]

MS fragment, Berg. *TB*, 263

1 Lady Gregory, who sent this letter on to Yeats after receiving it on 31 Dec 1907, has written 'mistake' above this quotation.

2 Yeats and Lady Gregory were advising JMS to encourage the Allgood sisters, Kerrigan, and any other malcontents to put their complaints against Fay's management in writing, perhaps even resigning in protest, as a basis for calling a meeting of enquiry (see *TB*, 261–3).

3 Dates for the performances at the Royal Court Theatre, Galway, were finally set for 6–10 Jan 1908.

To EDWARD M. SYNGE[1]

Glendalough House | Kings town

Dec 31st/07

Dear Edward

I've a piece of news *too*, I'm going to be married! but its more or less private still. Meanwhile let me congratulate you very heartily and wish you all good things, and many of them. I'm sure we'll find life more amusing when we are less solitary. When is it to be?[2] I've a new play to send you for a wedding present.

I've been very well indeed, on the whole, since the operation, but I am threatend with a renewal of same trouble in same place. I hope it may not come to anything. My future is the little lady who played 'Pegeen Mike' in the play-boy, and in her own way she is a very talented person indeed. She is partly of French Huguenot extraction, I believe, and is both Papist and Protestant, having been baptised into both churches in her infancy.

The worst of it is I dont quite know what we're going to live on. I think you'd better keep the matter to yourself for the present. It may come off very soon, but owing to my health and finances it is a little uncertain.

Much Good Luck again

Yours very cordially

J. M. Synge

MS, Synge

1 Edward Millington Synge (1860–1913; see I. 67), JMS's cousin, had spent

considerable time with JMS in Paris during the winter of 1901–2. After some years as a land agent, he was elected to the Royal Society of Painter-Etchers in 1898 and from 1901 devoted himself entirely to etching, travelling widely. He made his home in Surrey, where JMS visited him for two weeks in December 1906 (see I. 248–63), but he inherited 'Uplands' from his aunt Emily Synge and so visited Ireland regularly. According to his obituary in the *Guardian*, 27 June 1913, he had planned an illustrated edition of JMS's plays.

2 Mrs Synge wrote in her diary on 18 Dec 1907, 'Heard Edward Synge is going to be married to Freda Molony' (TCD); the marriage to his fellow artist took place in February 1908.

PART TWO
1908

*

Deidre of the Sorrows

To MOLLY ALLGOOD

Glendalough Hous[e] [Glenageary]
Jan 3rd 08

Dearest Child

I have come to the conclusion that you MUST[1] have warmer
clothes before you go away   You'll get some bad illness if you
dont. Please buy yourself some warm things tomorrow morning and
I'll lend you the price you can pay me off when you are clear of the
theatre. Shall I send you in my rug by the tram tomorrow. You
must have it. There were five degrees of frost outside my window
this morning so it is quite too cold for you to be dressed as you
are.[2]

Another thing⟨s⟩ can you lock up your picture *really safely*
before you go away or would it be safer with me? We must not
lose it.

Your old Tramp

I have been working at Kerry stuff today and found it a pleasant
change.

Remember this is quite serious you know what will *happen* next
week and if [you] get a chill you may get very seriously *ill*.

MS, Texas. *LM*, 236

1 Underlined four times.
2 Molly had been to tea at Glendalough House with Mrs Synge and JMS
on 2 Jan 1908.

To JOHN QUINN

Glendalough House | Kingstown | Co. Dublin
Jan 4th/08

My dear Quinn

I have been a disgraceful time about answering, and thanking
you for, your kind letter of Dec 11th, about Christmas over here,
some how, one finds it hard to find time for any thing. Even Dublin
seems to wake up a little though I suppose to you — with your
financial panics and big issues of every kind — we would seem like
the seven sleepers.[1] I am glad to say that since the operation I have
been as well as possible, walking a great deal, and very hard at
work. I dont know whether I told you that I am trying a three-Act
prose Deirdre — to change my hand. I am not sure yet whether
I shall be able to make a satisfactory play out of it — these saga

people when one comes to deal with them seem very remote; — one does not know what they thought or what they ate or where they went to sleep, so one is apt to fall into rhetoric. In any case I find it 'an interesting experiment,' full of new difficulties, and I shall be the better, I think, for the change. 'The Tinkers Wedding' was published two or three days before Christmas, if Roberts has not sent you a copy already I will send one next week.

I am extremely obliged to you for your proposal about publishing my plays in America. I, of course, will be very pleased if it can be managed and I am grateful for your kind offer to guarantee the cost of the plates. I think I told you how I stand as to the American rights of the plays. I do not know any thing about American publishing methods, it would be the best plan, I should think, to arrange matters so that the amount you guarantee should be cleared off before I get any royalties. I saw Roberts the other day but he was too busy to discus the matter. There is plenty of time however.

I am sending you the 'Playboy' Manuscript, such as it is, with this post. I do not think it is worth much, but I am glad that you should have it, if it interests you. Please do not value ⟨on⟩ it too highly.

There is nothing very interesting going on here at present; everything is flagging, I think, for the want of really strong personalities in Irish public life.

I hear Mr Yeats has gone — or is going — to New York, it sounds very enterprising.[2] As soon as I heard of it I went to his studio, but I did not find him, so I have heard no particulars.

Hugh Lane is to open his Municipal Gallery of Modern Art in Dublin in about a fortnight, I believe. I ran through the rooms a week or two ago and, as far as I could judge in the state of chaos that things were in, I thought the collection a really admirable one. Hugh Lane in his way is a strong personality if ever there was one, and it is extraordinary what he has managed to do ⟨almost⟩ against so much opposition.

That will be something new for you to see whenever we have the pleasure of having you in Dublin again.

Meanwhile believe me

Sincerely yours

J. M. Synge

P.S. I entirely agree with what you say [about] the Abbey company.[3]

MS, NYPL

---

1 Cf. John Donne, 'The Good Morrow': 'Or snorted we in the seven sleepers' den?' The legend of seven youths of Ephesus who hid in a cave from the persecutions of Decius and slept there for 187 years is a familiar one.

2 J. B. Yeats sailed with his daughter Lily on 21 Dec 1907 for New York, where Lily represented the Yeats branch of Dun Emer Industries at an Irish Exhibition in January 1908. Lily returned on 6 June 1908, but her father remained in New York for the rest of his life, despite arguments and pleas for his return from family and friends on both sides of the Atlantic (see Murphy, *Prodigal Father*, 324-33).

3 Concerning the Abbey's projected visit to America, Quinn had written on 11 Dec 1907:

> Personally I am against the plan of raising a fund. I think the matter ought to be taken up in a business way with some theatrical managers here. If they can be interested the question of a fund will disappear. It isn't so much the fund to bring the actors out, but it is their management after they get here. The key to the situation is a chain of theatres in the large cities, and that chain of theatres could only be secured if a regular theatrical manager was interested.
>
> (TCD)

To W. B. YEATS

[Glendalough House, Glenageary]
[6 January 1908]
         [p.] 2

Later - - -

I have been thinking over the matters you raise. Apart from my personal ⟨fell⟩ feelings I do not think your scheme — that I should draw up a statement and get it signed by company — is workable. They have all different grievances which would not go into any general statment. (2) the violent language was used in heated scenes that are now more or less forgotten or blurred. (3) I do not know how many of the company would be on our side in such a move --. it would soon be known that I (or we) were moving definitely in the matter -- O'Rourke, is on the Fay's side, Kerrigan is a very peacable creature, and Sara Allgood, as I said, is quiet uncertain.

Mac does not like Fay but I do not know that he has any particular grievance. I entirely agree as to the usefulness of the statement you propose,[1] but there is no ⟨use more, or less compromising ourselves by⟩ good trying to get it, if there is no likelihood of ⟨any⟩ getting what we need.

When I saw Fay after the tour his position was that he had sent in his proposals and that if they were not agreed to he would slip off to America and we should all part as the best of friends. That was probably the mood of an odd half hour only, but I think it is still possible to do things amicably, and it is greatly to be desired.
I

         Tuesday.

Sara Allgood has still sent me no statement, I am absolutely convinced that we cannot do much with the company and that the matter will have to be dealt with on Fay's proposals and our democratic scheme. We should keep Fay from getting the quarrel fixed on the Canavans² ⟨and then⟩ as in that case he would have the company and the public with him — I do not like the Canavans myself and I have not met anyone who does, except you⟨rself⟩.

If you still think any thing can ⟨still⟩ be done through the company you had better come over at the end of next week and call the meeting for a few days later, so that you can see them or write to them yourself, in the interval.

I see that we will have great difficulte in managing the meeting. We shall have to arrange some plan of action when you come over. If Fay wants to stay and is ready to meet our wishes the comittee sheme will have to be considered very carefully. Vaughan I think should go, whatever happens.³

I am sorry I cannot do what

TS (MS emendations), ('Later - - -'), MS fragment ('Tuesday'), Berg. *TB*, 267

1 Yeats had written on 30 Dec 1907, 'I have no doubt whatever that he [Fay] will make a case against us. I shall be in the chair. If I have a written statement before me of the company's grievance I can give it priority and force Fay to fight on that issue.' (*TB*, 266)

2 Yeats had written, 'So far as I can see we shall have to insist for one thing upon a return visit to Galway with Canavans.' *The Canavans*, a three-act comic folk-history play by Lady Gregory, first produced on 8 Dec 1906 (see I. 213), was particularly disliked by Frank Fay; Willie Fay had refused to perform the play in Galway or anywhere out of Dublin. In 1911 Yeats was still referring to *The Canavans* as one of his favourite plays (Lady Gregory, *Seventy Years*, ed. Colin Smythe [Gerrards Cross, 1974], 483).

3 The directors, Yeats had written, would have also to insist upon the dismissal of Ernest Vaughan, 'who is probably at the bottom of the whole mischief, and is in any case a bad actor'.

To MOLLY ALLGOOD

[Glendalough House, Glenageary]
Tuesday [7 January 1908]

Dearest Heart

I was surprised and delighted to get your little letter last night — I did not expect it till this morning — and to hear that you are down safe. The weather changed here too on Sunday evening and it has been very mild since, it will be cold again in a day or two. I heard from Mrs Cassidy on Sunday and I'm going out to see her rooms tomorrow I think, her house is in Upper Rathmines. That would be all right.¹

Sunday was a long day without you — I went for two little walks, and then wrote to Quinn and other letters in the evening. Yesterday Fraulein von Eicken[2] — the German lady — came to see us in the afternoon, so that made a little variety.

I am working at Deirdre again — I cant keep away from her, till I get her right. I have changed the first half of the first Act a good deal, by making Fergus go into the inner room instead of Conchubor, and giving C. an important scene with Lav. Then D. comes in and Lav goes out and D. and C. have an important scene together. That — when it is done — will make the whole thing drama instead of narrative, and there will be a good contrast between the scens of Deirdre and Conchubor, and Deirdre and Naisi. It is quite useless trying to rush it, I must take my time and let them all grow by degrees. I wonder have you seen Lady Gregory. Be very careful of yourself and dont go out in a boat with the company or do anything foolish. If all goes well I may move into Mrs Cassidy's next week. Wont that be fun.

Two pictures have come at last, but they are not well done and I am not happy about them. He has put the mounts too close in and I am afraid they are ruined *forever*   I have hung you up too oposite my table — where the pampooties were — you look very nice, but I get tired of your cigarette. Its a pity you're smoking. He has also put in your glasses and that makes you look as if you'd a black eye at a little distance.[3] However, you're charming all the same. Write me a long letter about every thing.

Your old

T.

MS, TCD. *LM*, 236

1 JMS and Molly planned to be married in the Rathmines church.

2 One of the von Eicken sisters (perhaps Claire) with whom JMS stayed in Germany in the 1890s; see I. 8.

3 The 'ruined' pictures were not, apparently, the ones by Jack Yeats and E. M. Synge, already framed and in place in JMS's study (see p. 93). E. M. Stephens, who helped his uncle move to Rathmines later in 1908, remembers a print of Giorgione's *The Concert* as also among his belongings (Stephens MS). The picture of Molly with glasses and a cigarette is also untraced.

To W. B. YEATS

Glendalough House | Kingstown
8.1.08

Dear Yeats

I got your letter this morning.[1] I may have been wrong in what I decided but in such things one has to follow one's instinct, and the many small considerations which effect one's view yet cannot be formulated.

If I am to tell the company of Fay's proposals and take their verdict on it that is another matter and I am quite willing to do so.[2] Shall I tell Mac, and O'Rourke and Kerrigan also, you only mention the Allgoods? I do not know whether Sara Allgood will do or say anything definite, it will not be easy to get ⟨anything⟩ a written statement from any of them. I think you ought to come over as soon as possible after Galway otherwise our whole season will be lost.

Fay seems to be very much on his good behaviour now with the company, and is treating them well. One does not know how long it will last.

Yours
J. M. Synge

P.S. I will try and get a formal demand for a meeting from them when they come back.

MS, Berg. *TB*, 269

¹ Yeats's letter has not survived.

[1] Yeats's letter has not survived.

[2] The players apparently did not see Fay's proposals of 1 Dec 1907 until much later, according to a letter signed by Sara Allgood, Arthur Sinclair, J. M. Kerrigan, and Maire O'Neill, and published in the Dublin *Evening Mail*, 21 May 1908 (see *TB*, 274).

To MOLLY ALLGOOD

G[lendalough] H[ouse] K[ingstown] 9.I.08

Dearest Heart

I got your two letters all right thanks. I'm sorry to hear you've been coughing. Tomorrow night you'll be done with Galway, I suppose, so you'll be home on Saturday, and we'll meet on Sunday. Tell me what time you leave on Saturday, but I suppose in any case there will not be time for me to write to you again. I didn't go to Mrs Cassidy yesterday as it was a very bad day, but I'm going this afternoon as it is finer again. I'm sure I told you about the German Lady. She is an elder sister of the mug one[1] — and she called here to see me weeks ago but I was out, then I called on her but she was out, so at last we invited her here to tea. She is going away again in a few days! and she's about 50.

The blotting paper was a feeble attempt to make your letter 'fat', but evidently i[t] didn't serve its purpose. I think you're losing your sense of humour. Nish! You've written me very nice letters this tour I hope I'll have another tonight.

It is queer that Lady G. hasn't turned up. I wonder if her son is at home I haven't heard. I had a letter from Yeats yesterday he'll be over soon. I dont seem to have much to tell you today — it has been so wild I haven't been doing anything. Florence Ross is in town today getting lodgings for herself I wonder how she'll get on. I sent the P.B. MS. to Quinn yesterday — that is private remember — I wonder what he'll send me for it. I am working quietly and slowly at Deirdre and gradually improving her, I think. There is no use doing much at her now at a time, as what I have to do can only be done when I am fresh and clear.

I wonder what I'll think of Mrs Cassidy and her place. I feel in a fuss, as it is a difficult bargain to make. I wish you could do it for me In future that'll be your — *one of your* — little jobs. Let me know when you are to be home dear Heart and leave your address behind you in case I write again and the letter does not catch you.

Your old

T.

I am *very glad* your flannels are comfortable.

MS, TCD. *LM*, 237

1 A shaving mug decorated with a violin and scroll of music was given to JMS while he was with the von Eickens — probably by Valeska (see I. 10), his closest friend in the family.

To JOHN MARTIN HARVEY[1]

Glendalough House | Kingstown | Co Dublin

Jan 10th/08

Dear Mr Harvey

I have been a disgraceful time about thanking you for your kind letter when you were leaving Dublin I wanted to send you the 'Tinkers Wedding' and it was delayed and delayed in the press so I delayed also — that is my excuse.

As you will see the Tinkers Wedding is rather impossible for our audiences, so I fear we shall never be able to put it on.[2]

I do not know yet when I am likely to be in London again I hope it may be some time when you are there also and that I may have the pleasure of seeing you.[3] Please remember me to Mrs Harvey and believe me with many good wishes for the season

Yours sincerely

J. M. Synge

MS, NLI

1 John (later Sir John) Martin Harvey (1863–1944), actor-manager (see I. 235), knighted in 1921, whose career as a romantic actor was permanently linked with his performance of Sidney Carton in *The Only Way* (a dramatization of Dickens's *A Tale of Two Cities*) with which he began his management of the Lyceum Theatre, London, in 1899. He had written to JMS on 17 Nov 1907 (TCD); see above, pp. 93–4.

2 *The Tinker's Wedding* was finally produced in Dublin at the Pike Theatre on 24 Sept 1963, directed by Liam Miller.

3 Martin Harvey replied on 23 Jan 1908, renewing an invitation to visit them in London, and adding, 'I need not tell you how delighted my wife and I were with your kind remembrance, or how we shall treasure a work of yours given to us by yourself. I wish I could describe to you the perfect delight your "Playboy" gave me! What would I give to be able to play him! . . . I saw an excellent likeness of you by a man whose work I greatly admire — James Paterson.' (TCD)

To MOLLY ALLGOOD

[Glendalough House, Glenageary]
Jan 10th 08

Dearest Heart

I'm not sure that this will find you, as you didn't tell me when you leave, so I'll send a line only to show that I'm dutiful![1] I got your letter last night, and I'm sorry to hear of bad houses. I went to Mrs Cassidy's yesterday but she was out and had left a message that I was to wait for her for an hour. I went over the house with a small boy who let me in, and then I went off. I dont much like either the house or neighbourhood — Upper Rathmines — so I'm putting an Add. in the Times tomorrow, and writting to another place besides. Florence Ross has given — or at least lent the bed[2] — so that's all right, but there's no use draging one's things into a dreary house where one would not be cheerful. I'm just off for my walk, it is very cold I've written 5 letters and a card this morning.[3]

Your o T.

MS, TCD. *LM*, 238

1 On the back of the envelope, addressed to 'Miss O'Neill the Royal Hotel Galway', JMS has written, 'If not found please forward to the Abbey Theatre, Dublin'.

2 A double bed which had belonged to her mother, lent to the couple for the new lodgings.

3 The preceding letter, to Martin Harvey, was evidently one of these. Another was apparently to C. P. Scott of the *Manchester Guardian*, offering to write an article on the opening of the Municipal Gallery; Scott replied on 13 Jan 1908 (TCD), reminding JMS of his eagerness to see the article on 'Irish Types'. A third letter was doubtless in reply to Hugh Lane's of 25 Dec 1907 (TCD), apologizing for having missed him and promising to show him over the Gallery whenever convenient.

To MOLLY ALLGOOD

Glendalough [House, Glenageary]
11.1.08

Dearest Heart

I didn't write to you this morning as Yeats was in town and I had to see him. I'm in great spirits and joy to think I'll see you tomorrow come by the quarter to two as you say. Did you get my letter this morning in Galway? I'm writing this in a hurry I've been in town with Yeats and Lady G. all the afternoon, and just got home to supper.

L.G. told me how bad the House was on Friday, you seem to have had ill luck.[1]

I had another good go at Deirdre this morning I think she's coming on. Yeats says Masefield has written a wonderful play[2] — the best English play since the Elizabethans so I'll have to look out, but perhaps he excepts me because I'm Irish.

Dont miss your train tomorrow and be in a very good humour. My add is in the Irish Times.[3] I wonder what answers I'll get

Your old T.

MS, TCD. *LM*, 239

1 Having delayed attending the performances in Galway 'because it is such a nationalist programme' and to avoid a confrontation without her fellow directors present, Lady Gregory finally precipitated a discussion with Willie Fay on the 10th, when the poor business was evidently 'the last straw'. She wrote to Yeats that night suggesting a meeting with JMS in the afternoon of the next day; Yeats was then to see Fay privately in the evening to discuss the Fays' resignation (*TB*, 269–70).

2 *The Tragedy of Nan*, published in 1909.

3 'Unfurnished — Two Rooms Wanted, Rathgar or neighbourhood. Address "Z 1891, Rooms," this office' (*Irish Times*, 'Apartments Wanted', 11 Jan 1908, 3).

To W. B. YEATS

Glendalough House | Kingstown
12.1.08

Dear Yeats

I have not much cold but I have a bit of a headache and I'm rather worn out as a hot bottle came open in my bed last night — is that an effect of the stars which are against me? — so that I didn't get much sleep. It is very important for me to keep well at present so I think I'd better stay at home tonight. Please do not make any statement to the company without seeing me, I can go up any hour tomorrow if you will *kindly wire to me early*.

Although I did not say much yesterday you will understand that I was not quite in agreement with a good deal of what Lady Gregory said.[1] I do not think the company had acted 'disgracefully'. They have simply done as any other young undisciplined people would have done under management as faulty as we know Fay's to have been. If he had been a good manager we could have agreed to his proposals, if he has been a bad manager why should we talk of dismissing the company, or of making any hostile demonstration against them, because his management has failed? I *know* there has been no idea of getting Fay out, and I believe there will be a feeling of depression when he goes rather than a desire to "crow". When we know how utterly unfounded his charges against us, the directors, are, as to interference, plotting with Vaughan etc, it is not fair to take action on the ground of his complaints against the company without investigating the complaints ⟨he makes⟩ and giving the company an oportunity of answering. That is highly undesirable, therefore his complaints must be ignored — there is no other honorable course.

I am still in favour of some democratic method with the company — Payne said to me last year that discipline would never be got in the Abbey unless we organise the public spirit of the company. I entirely agree with him; coertion has never been a success in Ireland, and it is rather doubtful to try and make examples of the company by dismissal when most of them believe — rightly or wrongly — that they would get on better somewhere else.

I see no reason why we should not have a spirit of co-operation between ourselves and the company — as we had at one time — instead of a spirit of hostility. However this letter has become far longer than I intended needlessly so as I'm to see you tomorrow I suppose

Yours sincerely
J. M. Synge

MS, Berg. *TB*, 270

1 Evidently Lady Gregory was sufficiently angered by the situation in the company, with the Fays' impending departure, that she was prepared to sacrifice the present organization completely and start afresh (*TB*, 264–7). She was also less than happy with JMS's defence of Molly, having written to Yeats on 22 Dec 1907, 'If Molly Allgood "cant be in time for anything" I dont see how we can keep her on' (Berg).

To MOLLY ALLGOOD

[Glendalough House, Glenageary]

13.I.08

Dearest Child

It has occured to me that the best thing you could do — *much* the best thing I think for many reasons — would be to take a room on business footing, paying usual rent, from your brother-in-law T. Callender,[1] for the few weeks till we can finish our arrangements. It would simplify matters in several ways — I feel strongly so — and it would be convenient as we would then, I think, be in range of Peter's Church where the curate is an old friend of mine.[2]

I am writing this in a hurry to catch you in the morning.

Your old T.

MS, TCD. *LM*, 240

[1] Tom Callender, husband of Molly's sister Peggy, with whom Molly had stayed for a while at Park Chambers, 13 Stephens Green North, in the summer of 1906; see I. 192. Molly does not appear to have returned to them at this time. Thom's Directory for 1908 gives an address for a T. Callender in Fairview.

[2] The Revd Stanford F. H. Robinson MA, with whom JMS had studied music at the Royal Academy of Music during the 1890s and who was a regular visitor to the theatre, was senior curate of St. Peter's Church of Ireland, Aungier Street.

To MOLLY ALLGOOD

Glendalough Ho [Glenageary]

Jan 14th

Dearest Heart

I was greatly relieved to get your note yesterday to say that all was quiet — keep it so at any cost, for the present.

I hoped for a note this morning to tell me what had happened last night — you have heard the great news of course about the Fays[1] — perhaps I shall hear by the middle of the day post. I am going to the doctor this afternoon, and then to the directors, and tomorrow morning I am to see Lane at his gallery as I am to do an article on it for the Manchester Guardian so I dont know when I'll be free I may wire to you about the middle of the day to make an appointment somewhere. I have had an answer to my advertisement that seems very promising indeed in Rathgar — I'll have to go out to it, too, sometime. It is a thousand pities I am so busy this week as you are free on the three latter days I hope we may be together. This is all I can write now till I see if a letter comes.

No letter — I am a little uneasy please write at once and fully
Your old T.

I was in with the directors yesterday they wired for me.[2]

J.M.

MS, TCD. *LM*, 240

    1 On 13 Jan 1908 Willie Fay submitted his resignation to Yeats as managing director, giving one month's notice; Brigit O'Dempsey (Mrs W. G. Fay) and Frank Fay followed suit the same day, the latter having the foresight to make clear (NLI) that he was resigning his engagement with the National Theatre Society Ltd. and not his membership in either the Irish National Theatre Society or the National Theatre Society Ltd. Yeats wrote to Bernard Shaw on the Fays' behalf and gave Willie and Brigit the use of his London flat in Woburn Buildings. By early February the three Fays were on their way to New York under Frohman's management with permission to produce *The Rising of the Moon*, *The Pot of Broth*, and AE's *Deirdre*.

    2 Probably to discuss the attack by 'W' [W. J. Lawrence] in the *Evening Mail*, 13 Jan 1908, using the news of the Fays' resignation to charge the directors with 'shelving plays that drew audiences, and . . . insisting upon the performance of others towards which the public evinced no great liking'. Yeats replied the next day challenging the editor of the *Evening Mail* and 'W' to appoint a committee of three to 'invite rejected dramatists to send them their plays', and enclosing a paragraph written for the next *Samhain* praising the Fays and regretting their departure. The correspondence between Yeats and 'W' continued for five days before frittering away, Yeats, predictably, having the last word.

To MOLLY ALLGOOD

[Glendalough House, Glenageary]
Jan 15/08

Dearest Nish

    I'm a sorry as you are. for difficulty in seeing you — I will *wire* to you today to come down if I am free in the afternoon. I'm just off to town now.

    We feel very confident about the Abbey now — I have some things to tell you that will interest you.[1] I wonder what F.J.F wants to do with Sally

    I dont think you're at all fair in calling yourself a *little* ass — I think you're a <u>BIG</u>[2] one. Nish! — I write to you to say I am going to be with [you] the three last days of the week, in any case, and you write a hullabuloo about the *whole* dreary week! Nish.

    Please Heaven I'll have you today we might have a good walk somewhere be ready for your wire. Though I cannot be sure yet — tomorrow *I am* sure of. Now I've just time for my train.

J.M.S.T.

The doctor says I'm 'grand'

MS, TCD. *LM*, 241

1 Among them, perhaps, that Kerrigan, to whom he had written reinstating him in the company, had replied on 15 Jan 1908 (TCD).

2 Underlined six times.

To MOLLY ALLGOOD

Glendalough Ho [Glenageary]
Jan 15th /08

My dearest Little Treasure

I am very lonely tonight, and I am longing to have you here to rest and comfort me. I was at business of various kinds all day and I am giddy with weariness. I could not go out to Rathgar so I am writing to the people to say I'll go tomorrow. Dont be annoyed about it — it was quite impossible for me to go. The day was extraordinarily close and heavy and I feel utterly fagged — that'll pass of course.

There is the usual treasury call tomorrow morning you'll find Yeats and J. M. Synge doling out the money.[1] Afterwards we W.B.Y. and I have newspaper men to see so I wont be free for you. Please dont be unreasonable or annoyed, I may see you in the evening though it's not very likely — and I'll see [you] on Saturday I hope and of course on Sunday. Dont be depressed about it, I'll soon have you always.

It's out about Sally and Tree — The Editor of the Mail told Yeats and me about it at 1.30, and another man — who is a secret told *us* at 2.15 — that's the way secrets are kept in this country.[2] I'm glad it's known. I thought I would have had a letter from you today perhaps one will come tonight I hope you weren't too tired. Be nice and helpful tomorrow and believe I'm dying down dead to be with you. I feel as if I hadn't been nice enough to you yesterday. Was I?

Your old T.

MS, TCD. *LM*, 241

1 Ernest Vaughan had also resigned, and JMS was looking after the business management of the company, although Vaughan appears to have stayed on until the end of the season.

2 Beerbohm Tree had asked the directors to release Sara Allgood for performance in one of his Shakespeare productions in February, but because of the additional responsibilities for stage management which she shared with Yeats, JMS, and Lady Gregory, this request was not granted. She was given permission to play Isabella in William Poel's production of *Measure for Measure* in April 1908 (see p. 82 and *TB*, 274). The editor of the Dublin *Evening Mail* was perhaps James Y. McPeake, frequently mentioned in Holloway's diaries (NLI) in connection with the paper.

To MOLLY ALLGOOD

[Glendalough House, Glenageary]
Friday night. [17] Jan [1908]

Dearest Heart

I saw the rooms today three — one with place for gas-cooker — *with attendance* and cooking for 12/6 a week. I dont *very* much like the house and the landlady has a sore nose — those are the drawbacks — I wish you'd come down tomorrow and talk it over with me. Come by the quarter to two unless I wire some other hour — If you cant come send me a card

In haste your old T.

MS, TCD. *LM*, 242

To MOLLY ALLGOOD

Glendalough House [Glenageary]
Jan 21st [1908][1]

Dearest Love

I got a cheque for £6. last night — returned income Tax — and I want you to make out a list of what we want most up to that amount. I suppose you could get some of the things for us, I expect you're a better hand than I am. I feel in great spirits today. It's funny the qualms we get but natural enough I suppose

I believe I'm to go to a supper at the Nassau tonight in honour of Hugh Lane, and I'll probably be in the Abbey tomorrow morning. On Thursday evening we must meet and talk over our affairs. I wish you'd get Whittaker![2]

Now I must write to Mme M[*illegible*][3] I was too late and too tired last night — and then I have my article to write and post today — God help me —

Your old T——

MS, TCD. *LM*, 243

1 '1908' is added in Molly's hand.
2 Probably *Whitaker's Almanack*, which would give information about the publication of banns, etc.
 3 The illegible name is probably 'MacClinchie' — i.e. Mrs McClinchie, of 47 York Road, Upper Rathmines, subsequently JMS's landlady.

To MOLLY ALLGOOD

[Glendalough House, Glenageary]
Wednesday Jan 22nd [1908] *3 P.M.*

My own dearest Child

I'm sure you thought I was 'horrid' today, there were many things to think of so I couldn't well help it. I got away just before two and slipped down here by the 2 train. You looked very nice and quiet and pretty this morning I felt proud of you though you didn't guess it! Isn't it a pity, though, to wear out your nice new dress by hacking it down at the theatre. It'll be shabby in a week! It is trying for both of us to be half seeing ourselves, and not able to talk, next week when I move it will be better I hope. Poor Yeats with his bad sight and everything is very helpless, and I have to look after him a bit.[1] The question you spoke of about 'Stage-Management' is serious enough, we'll feel our way for a day or two and see what can be done. Casey is a nice fellow I think, like you I'm not quite sure how much I like his play, it has good scenes especially in the first act.[2] I suppose I shall go in tomorrow again but I'm afraid I wont be able to get away with you — it is just possible however — perhaps on Friday afternoon I might get you down here.

I dont know what I am going to do about moving,[3] I must get your advice. I wonder if you're depressed, my poor changling, because I ran away from you today, if you could look into my little bosom and see how I am yearning for you, you'd forgive me write me a nice letter

Your old T.

I have just finished my article[4] and I am posting it with this that is some thing done.

MS, TCD. *LM*, 243

1 Stephen MacKenna recalled, in a letter dated 'Oct Nov '28' to Arthur Lynch, that JMS 'had . . . a curious admiration for Yeats on the practical side of things; he said once Yeats is a genius in bossing carpenters and judging the good qualities of nails and the price of a wooden platform; S. pined for these powers' (TS with MS additions, TCD).

2 *The Man Who Missed the Tide*, by W. F. Casey.

3 JMS had taken the three rooms at 47 York Road, Rathmines, in the house of Mrs McClinchie.

4 The article, 'Good Pictures in Dublin. The New Municipal Gallery', *Manchester Guardian*, 24 Jan 1908, opened somewhat politically with a reference to the need still for leaders in the arts, and after a brief description of the building, formerly the town house of Lord Clonmel, singled out paintings by Manet, Puvis de Chavannes, and Corot for special comment: 'Perhaps no one but Dublin men who have lived abroad also can quite realise the strange thrill it gave me to turn in from Harcourt-street — where I passed by to school long ago — and to

find myself among Monets, and Manets and Renoirs, things I connect so directly with the life of Paris' (*Prose*, 391).

To MOLLY ALLGOOD

Glendalough Ho [Glenageary]
Jan 28th '08

Dearest Heart

Will you please send me your basket tomorrow morning. I think I will not be able to get on without it. I am having the cart on Thursday and I suppose I'll get over myself on Friday or Saturday or Monday at the latest. Did you get Whitaker?

By the way I've a crow to pluck with you about today. Why didn't you come with me? I waited as long as I could at the scenery room door then I streeled along half thinking you might come after me. Then I saw you and when I went back to meet you, you ran away. I felt upset for the moment, and I couldn't eat my dinner when I got home. Somehow, changling, you dont try and make things easy for us — for you and me, I mean — at the Theatre. It is a difficult position for the moment, and — well there's no good bothering about it now.

I dont know where to begin my packing it's a rather ghastly job. I think I'll [go] out and see Mme MacC[linchie] tomorrow,[1] I may not, however and I may wire to your house to ask you down, but I am not sure. There is a lecture in town in the afternoon I rather want to go to.[2]

I am sad somehow today. Why do you tease me so much? It is easy to give me pain. Your old

Tramp

MS, TCD. *LM*, 244

1 According to Mrs Synge's letters to her son Robert, who was in South America during the first part of 1908, the upper rooms at 47 York Road were very sparsely furnished. She gave JMS some old furniture, and on 14 Apr 1908 when marriage was apparently imminent his mother urged Robert — the most sympathetic of the family towards JMS — to give him a wedding present: 'You can afford it and he has so little furniture for his sitting room he ought to buy a few little things. I am going to give them some money as soon as they are married as a wedding gift. I have not much to give at present I have had so much to pay.' (TCD)

2 Probably the lecture by Frank Rutter on 'The French Impressionist School' given at the Municipal Gallery of Modern Art at 4 p.m. on 29 Jan 1908.

To EDWARD M. SYNGE

Glendalough House | Kings town
February 1st 08

Dear Edward

I believe this is your eventful day so I send you my 'Tinkers Wedding' as a token, and many good wishes.

My own day may come very soon now, if nothing untoward happens — we're going to risk penury I believe, ⟨and⟩ so I've taken rooms (near where you saw Stopford,)[1] and moved some of my books and trifles into them, to follow myself in a few days. We are in a commotion in the Abbey as Fay — our Stage-manager etc — has left us, and we have to do everything ourselves. I'm managing the finance God help me and it!

Let us hear of you some time

Yours cordially
J. M. Synge

MS, Synge

1 E. A. Stopford lived at no. 1 Frankfort Avenue, Rathgar, in the house belonging to Count Markiewicz, just round the corner from York Road.

To W. A. HENDERSON[1]

IRISH PLAYS
PRESENTED BY THE NATIONAL THEATRE SOCIETY
FROM THE ABBEY THEATRE DUBLIN
TOURED UNDER THE DIRECTION OF A. WAREING[2]

WEEK BEGINNING
MAY 28TH· CARDIFF THEATRE ROYAL
JUNE 4TH·GLASGOW KINGS THEATRE

Feb 3rd/08

My dear Henderson

I dare say you have heard of the changes we have had here in the Abbey.

We are opening with two new⟨s⟩ plays next week[3] and every thing is going well ⟨with⟩ I wonder if you are still disengaged and if you would care to come on with us in your old position and at former salary. For the moment I am looking after the money matters and I suppose between us we could get some system of book-keeping that we could work.

As you know our arrangements are always liable to change from one reason⟨s⟩ or other, but if you come back we could offer you the post ⟨at this⟩ for certain till the autumn, if that would suit you,

Excuse this line I am very busy getting through everything. Please let me know what you think of what I propose, and when I could see you

Yours sincerely

J. M. Synge

P.S. Feb *8th*   This was sent to a wrong Belfast address and returned here. I hope it will find you. Please [?wire][4]

MS, NLI

1 William A. Henderson (1863–1927), secretary of the National Literary Society of Dublin from 1898, had been business manager of the Abbey Theatre from August 1906 to July 1907; see I. 188. His 1913 character sketches of J. M. Kerrigan and Arthur Sinclair, published in the *Evening Herald*, have been reprinted in *The Abbey Theatre: The Rise of the Realists 1910–1915*, comp. Robert Hogan with Richard Burnham and Daniel P. Poteet (Dublin, 1979), 264–9.

2 On old company touring stationery of 1906, with the theatre emblem in the left-hand corner.

3 *The Man Who Missed the Tide* (Casey), stage-managed (i.e. directed) by Sara Allgood, and *The Piper* (O'Riordan), stage-managed by the author, first produced on 13 Feb 1908.

4 The last word is almost illegible. Henderson replied from his sister's home in Belfast on 9 Feb 1908 (TCD), saying that he would come to Dublin on Thursday to discuss the matter before definitely deciding.

To W. A. HENDERSON

[Post Office] Highfield Road Dublin

Feb 10/08

Henderson Ferndale St James Park Donegall Road Belfast   Can you in any case take front of house this week[1]

Synge

Telegram, NLI

1 Henderson accepted the appointment and remained with the company until September 1911, but JMS worked closely with him, retaining most of the responsibilities of business manager. On 14 Feb 1908 new agreements (Gregory) were drawn up between the actors and the National Theatre Society Ltd. for the duration of one year: Sara Allgood received £2.0.0 a week, Molly £1.5.0. JMS was also responsible for augmenting the company: J. H. Dunne and Maire nic Shiublaigh returned at JMS's request about mid-March; and Ambrose Power was back by early April 1908.

To JOSEPH HONE

47 York Rd | Rathmines
Feb 20th [1908]

When do you want Article on Kerry?[1] Please give me a day or two to get it ready

Yrs
J. M. Synge

MS postcard, Blackwell

[1] Although JMS completed the first draft of 'In West Kerry. To Puck Fair' before 4 Nov 1907 (the date stamped on the galleys, TCD), the Winter 1907 issue of *The Shanachie*, in which it was published, did not appear until 1908; the NLI copy of that issue has an accession date of 26 Feb 1908.

To HOLBROOK JACKSON[1]

Abbey Theatre | Dublin
Feb 22nd/08

Dear Holbrook Jackson

I was very glad to get your letter a couple of weeks ago, and hear your news. Your view of my 'Tinkers' is quite the same as my own, which shows I suppose that we are both wise men.[2]

It is quite true that I am doing a play on the Deirdre Story, but everything is too vague ⟨yet it is still rather vague⟩ to put into paragraphs; I will let you know about it later on.

March 15th

Excuse this disconnected scrawl — I daresay you have heard that the Fays left us early in the year, and since then Yeats and I have been running the Abbey so that we have had no time to draw our breath. Everything, luckily, is going very well so we are pleased with ourselves and the world.

I dont know when I shall get over to London again, I generally go over in the spring or early summer, but this year I cannot say. Whenever it is I shall hope to see you. I am glad to say I am very well now — I hope you're the same. Come over and see Ireland some time.

Yours cordially
J. M. Synge

MS, AS

[1] Holbrook Jackson (1874–1948; see I. 336), essayist, bibliophile, and at this time co-editor of the *New Age*; he and JMS first met in Leeds when the company was on tour in 1906.

2 Jackson's letter is missing. An unsigned review of the Maunsel edition of *The Tinker's Wedding*, almost certainly by Jackson, appeared in the *New Age*, 29 Feb 1908, 353-4:

it does not quite attain to that fullness of imaginative conception which is so notable a feature of the other plays. Throughout both acts the humour is broader, and it lacks at times the essential note of comedy. But it is rich in that beauty of language . . . he has succeeded in achieving something very like comedy with a theme that would have lent itself more readily to farcical treatment . . . . It is a slight enough theme, but Mr. Synge shows genius in his handling of it, and in the way in which he displays the simple natures of these vagabonds, with their cunning and superstition, their greed and com-radeship — so little different, yet often so superior to similar characteristics in the priest.

To STEPHEN MacKENNA

47 York Road | Rathmines
Feb 23rd [1908]

My dear MacKenna

I feel it is a sin and a shame to have left your letter[1] so long without an answer, but our Abbey affairs have been in such a state of turmoil these last two months, I have not had a moment's peace. You know of course that the Fays left us early in Jan. and since then Yeats and I have been running the show i.e. Yeats looks after the stars,[2] and I do the rest. Everything luckily has gone well and I think we have pulled through the crisis, but it might have meant anytime the breaking up of our whole movement.

As you see I am in Rathmines[3] now — but I am not married yet — things have been too uncertain. I am writing this without your letter which is in Kingstown, so that I can only answer the bigger points in it. I liked your article that you sent me in the way you expected me to like it. It seemed sound and simple and direct, — though, perhaps (if I may risk a criticism on what I remember only vaguely) your children are too often "little children," and their brothers, "little brothers," — such adjectives are well enough in one sentence but they make one's stuff soft if too frequent.[4]

I am very interested in the Plotinus. I have not seen Maunsel — at any leisure — since I heard from you, but I'll sound him on subject in a day or two. It would be a mistake to send your MS. to Yeats and A.E., as what one likes the other hates — that is sad but true. "Tantane something in celestial minds" *Virgil!*[5]

If you are coming over soon bring us your script or send me a chunk any time, — to Glendalough House is safest I think. It will probably take time to arrange anything, but I should think if you make your successful version it is bound to get a place somewhere.

How about your coming over? I have been here for two or three weeks — I have the top of a little house and attendance — of a kind — for 12/6 a week. I have to be at the Abbey so much I could not possibly stay on in Kingstown. I may get married very soon now, if all continues to go well. My work has been thrown back very much by all these theatrical worries. That is the worst of it all, but it cannot be helped.

Will you make my compliments to Madame, and let me know very soon what you [are] doing and going to do.

Yours cordially

J. M. Synge

MS, TCD

  1 MacKenna's letter (TCD) is undated.

  2 Like Miss Horniman, Yeats was an accomplished astrologer (see I. 89 and above, p. 95).

  3 MacKenna's reply, also undated, speaks of his and his wife's wish to move to Dublin, and continues, 'It is hard to think of you as a citizen of RATH-MINES? DOES RATHMINES LIKE YOU? DO YOU LIKE IT? You will see you will be opening a bank-account at the Bank of Ireland one of these days soon: you will belong to Greene's library; it may be you will join the Y.M.C.A.; there is danger in RATHMINES.' (TCD)

  4 MacKenna had enclosed 'a little thing by Fear Dorcha [the blind or 'dark' man] which perhaps you might some time, of idleness, read and tell him whether the style of it is anything better'; the enclosure is missing.

  5 'Since seeing you I have fallen again under the unconquerable spell of my old friend PLOTINUS,' MacKenna wrote (TCD), asking JMS to help him persuade Maunsel to publish the *Enneads* 'in six cheapish paper "volumets" one each year or so', and considering sending copies of the first *Ennead* to JMS, Yeats, and George Russell (AE). JMS is quoting from the opening of Virgil's *Aeneid*, 'Tantaene animis caelestibus irae?' (Can there be such anger in celestial hearts?).

To MOLLY ALLGOOD

[47 York Road | Rathmines
[? late February 1908]

Dear Little Heart

Come to tea, and bring eggs with you I was *overjoyed* to get your note this morning —

My poor pet!

No time for more[1]

Your old T.

MS (photo), NLI. *LM*, 245

  1 JMS was directing Lady Gregory's translation of Sudermann's *Teja*, first produced 19 Mar 1908; he was also involved with rehearsing the new casts

for the 7 Mar bill (*The Gaol Gate*, *The Shadow of the Glen*, *The Hour Glass*, and *The Rising of the Moon*).

To ROBERT HEALY[1]

[47 York Road, Rathmines]
[9 March 1908]
Copy of answer March 9th

Dear Sir

I beg to acknowledge your letter of March 4th which informs me that Mr Lingard purposes to pay off my mortgage of Eight Hundred pounds.

I am willing to accept payment with interest to date before the First of October if you will be good enough to give me notice that you intend to do so at least a month beforehand.[2]

I shall be much obliged if you can let me have the half yearly interest by first of April next as soon as you

Yours
J. M. Synge

MS (draft), TCD

[1] Robert Healy, house and land agent, 6 Bachelor's Walk, Dublin, had written on 4 Mar 1908 (TCD) on behalf of Mr Mark Lingard of Fort Eyre, Galway, who wished to pay off his mortgage earlier than due date with interest. JMS has copied his reply on the back of the letter.

[2] This investment of £800 had yielded JMS the '£40 and a new suit' he used to claim as annual income (Lady Gregory, *Our Irish Theatre*, Coole edn. [Gerrards Cross, 1972], 77). The payment was made and JMS apparently consulted his brother-in-law, Harry Stephens, of Fred Sutton & Co., solicitors, concerning further investments (27 Mar and 8 Apr 1908, TCD).

To BEN IDEN PAYNE[1]

47 York Road | Rathmines
Thursday [12 March 1908]

I am too tired out to go out to see you tonight, so I'll turn up at Matinee[2] on Saturday, and I'll see you then

Yours
J. M. Synge

MS postcard, Langmuir

[1] Ben Iden Payne (1881–1976; see I. 299), English actor and director who served as manager of the company from February to June 1907, before resigning to become manager of Miss Horniman's new Manchester Playgoers Club, where

he remained until he went to America in 1913. See I. 370 and *TB*, 163–201 and 223–8, for the complexities surrounding his appointment to and resignation from the Irish National Theatre Society Ltd.

2 Miss Horniman's company, under Payne's management, was performing at the Gaiety Theatre, Dublin, 'direct from the Royal Court Theatre London', for the week of 9 Mar 1908 in a programme of Shaw's *Candida*, preceded by *The Subjection of Kezia* by Mrs Havelock Ellis, and Shaw's *Widowers' Houses*, preceded by *A Question of Property* by J. Sackville Martin.

To MOLLY ALLGOOD

[47 York Road, Rathmines]
[? late March 1908]

My Dearest Love

Henderson kept me so long today that I am only getting down[1] by the quarter to one. I will come back as soon as ever I can, but I may not be back till five. Type and amuse yourself, my poor heart, till I come, perhaps I'll be back at four.

Your old T. − (Its a long time since I've written that.)

MS, AS. *LM*, 245

1 Probably to see his mother, who returned to Glendalough House on 29 Feb 1908 after an operation at Elpis on 18 Feb to remove a lump from her leg.

To MRS W. G. FAY[1]

Abbey Theatre | Dublin
[late March 1908][2]

To Mrs W. G. Fay
Dear Mrs Fay

At a meeting of the committee of the Irish National Theatre Society held March 18th 1908 present Messrs W B Yeats, U. Wright, J. M. Synge, you were suspended from membership of the Society for breach of, and under, Rule V.(K)[p][3]

Yours faithfully
J. M. Synge[4]

MS, NLI

1 Anna Bridget O'Dempsey ('Brigit O'Dempsey'; see I. 171–3) married W. G. Fay on 29 Oct 1906 and resigned from the company with him on 13 Jan 1908.

2 The letters of suspension were received by the Fays in New York on 9 Apr 1908.

3 The clause, which was invoked in 1904 to suspend P. J. Kelly (see I. 154),

stipulates that if an acting member takes part in a performance, other than those given by the Society, which the Committee judges 'prejudicial to the interests of the Society', that member shall be suspended from membership (NLI). The formal letter to Mrs Fay ends here; that to Frank Fay (and presumably to W. G. Fay), as quoted by Frank Fay to W. J. Lawrence (7-10 Apr 1908, NLI) adds the following sentence: 'Your breach of this rule might under different circumstances have been merely technical but recent misunderstandings and misrepresentations have made the step necessary in interests of the Society.' The 'misrepresentations' referred to the billing by Frohman's agents of the Fays as the 'Irish National Theatre Company' despite repeated protestations by John Quinn on behalf of the Abbey Theatre (see *TB*, 273-4). According to a letter from Lady Gregory to W. G. Fay, mentioned in Frank Fay's letter to Lawrence, the directors had at first considered this a temporary suspension only, 'to cut Frohman's claws'.

4 JMS signed the letter to Frank Fay as Secretary of the Society.

To MOLLY ALLGOOD

[47 York Road, Rathmines]
Tuesday [24 March 1908]

Dearest

I have developed a big cold in my head. Will you bring me some eggs, butter and marmalade if you can, and the Molière script[1]   I'll be here all day. I'm not very bad.

Come early

Yours *affecionately*
J.M.S.

MS, TCD. *LM*, 246

1 Lady Gregory's Molière translation, *The Rogueries of Scapin*, was first produced under JMS's direction on 4 Apr 1908, Molly playing Zerbinette. Joseph Holloway noted in his diary for 1 Apr 1908, 'Called in at the Abbey and saw Mr Synge in the Manager's room and he showed me the French version of "The Rogueries of Scapin" with all the stage directions inserted in little slips of paper between the pages' (NLI).

To JAMES PATERSON

Glendalough House | Kingstown | Dublin
March 27th/08

My dear Paterson

I have just received your portrait of me[1] and hung it up on my wall. I am delighted to have it — for itself, and as a remembrance of our pleasant talks in Edinburgh. It has come at a good time as I have just set up in little rooms of my own — 47 York Road Rathmines Dublin— though my permanent address remains as before — and your picture on my wall makes me feel at home. I have moved in nearer Dublin so that I may be in reach of the Theatre. I dare say you have heard that the Fays have left us, and that Yeats and I are looking after everything now. The Fays are a great loss in some ways, yet in other ways we get on better without them as we have more direct control.

I am sending you a little play which I wrote some years ago but did not publish till the other day — The Tinkers Wedding — as you will understand we think it too dangerous to put on in the Abbey — it is founded on a real incident that happened in Wicklow a few years ago.

I hope you and Mrs Paterson and all your party are keeping well. I am glad to say that I am in very good health this year[2] and nearly through another play. When are you coming over to see Ireland.

Please remember me to Mrs Paterson and believe with *very many thanks* for your charming picture

Yours cordially
J. M. Synge

MS copy, TCD

1 Mrs Synge wrote to her son Robert on 30 or 31 Mar 1908, 'Johnnie was here on Friday . . . It came on a terribly wet evening I lent him my water proof cape as he was taking away a picture, a portrait of himself done in crayons by some artist in Edinburgh when J. was over there. It is like in some respects but none of them catch his expression' (TCD). The drawing (see I. 277) was reproduced in the 1910 *Collected Works*, and as frontispiece to Stephens, *My Uncle John*.
2 In the same letter to Robert Mrs Synge reported that JMS 'is still suffering from the ailment and talks of an operation as the only hope of a cure! I told him I could not pay for another and I did not think it was necessary — he has not been to Dr Parsons about it at all and is eating a great deal of fruit which he hopes will cure him but it does not do so.'

To THOMAS MacDONAGH[1]

[Abbey Theatre, Dublin]
[30 March 1908]

. . . I am very sorry for long delay in answering your letter[2] — there was no good writing till I could tell you something definite, and (owing to influenza and great pressure of work) Mr. Yeats has only just been able to give me his final opinion of your work — with which I agree.

We would like to produce your play — possibly this season possibly in the autumn — but we must be permitted to cut certain passages here and there (not a great deal) according as we feel the necessities of the stage may require. The hero's references to poetry, for instance, would, we think, have to be left out, wholly, or in great part. I see by your letter that you are going to be in Dublin at Easter, so perhaps you could meet me then and I could talk the matter over with you.[3]

I trust you will forgive the long delay there has been — your play required a great deal of consideration and our hands have been very full. Mr. Yeats is going to London today so he asked me to write you our opinion, as he could not write himself.

Fragment, as published in Parks, *Thomas MacDonagh*, 102

1 Thomas MacDonagh (1878–1916), poet and essayist, one of the founders in 1908 with Padraic Pearse of St. Enda's College, co-founder in 1914 with Edward Martyn and Joseph Plunkett of the Irish Theatre, a signatory of the Proclamation of the Irish Republic and one of its victims. 'A Fragment', later entitled *When the Dawn Is Come* (see p. 91), was his first completed play.

2 MacDonagh's letter is missing, but it presumably followed his visit to the directors after receiving encouragement from Yeats to revise and resubmit his play; he wrote to J. Dominick Hackett on 27 Feb 1908,

> I went up to Dublin this day week and that evening saw Yeats at the Abbey. He was bad with influenza and could not talk business or anything else. Later I saw Lady Gregory who is tremendously impressed with the play and almost knows it by heart; she wants it to go on at once. Then Yeats again when he is better. He wants it to go on, too, but meantime wants me to write other plays; they think I can be best as a dramatist. Then Synge, who is now running the Abbey. He said better things of praise than the others but sees difficulties on account of the unusual nature of the play and does not think they can put it on until I am there for rehearsal. I am less anxious than anybody, I think about my work at present, and told him to hold it till the Autumn or so. But he is to see Lady Gregory and Yeats about it one of these days and see if they can put it on at once.   (NLI)

3 On 10 Apr 1908 MacDonagh reported to Hackett, 'I am to go into it with Synge and fit it for the stage. It requires very little alteration.' Finally, on 5 May 1908, after JMS went into hospital, he wrote, 'I had talked the whole thing out with him so fully that he would have carried out all my ideas. I hope his illness is not serious; he is a fine fellow.' (Both NLI). When the play was finally produced at the Abbey, in the autumn of 1908, it was not a success. MacDonagh's memories of JMS were published in *T.P.'s Weekly*, 9 Apr 1909, 469.

To ELIZABETH CORBET YEATS[1]

[47 York Road, Rathmines]
[2 April 1908]

. . . Thanks for your letter. I feel in a difficulty about this Deirdre book as it is not finished and at present I have hardly any time to work at it . . . . I do not know how long the play will run with your pages, it will have three acts — each about 23 pages of typewritten ms. I propose to call it 'Deirdre of the Sorrows' a Play in three Acts. That is about all there is to say about it I think . . . .[2]

MS fragment, Healy

1 Elizabeth Corbet (Lolly) Yeats, younger sister of the poet, was founder of the Dun Emer Press, later the Cuala Press. On the invitation of Evelyn Gleeson she and her sister Lily joined the Dun Emer Industries in the winter of 1902–3 to establish an embroidery division and printing press. The partnership was somewhat turbulent, and so some time in June 1908 the sisters moved the press to Churchtown, near Gurteen Dhas, and re-established as the Cuala Industries. W. B. Yeats served as literary adviser and editor to the press, first publishing some of his own works there.
2 Although preliminary discussions took place about the publication by the Dun Emer/Cuala Press of JMS's next play, *Deirdre of the Sorrows* did not appear under that imprint until 1910, after the publication of his *Poems and Translations* (1909).

To [?] FRED SUTTON & CO.[1]

[Glendalough House] Kingstown
[9 April 1908]

Dear Sir

I have just received yours of ⟨the⟩ 8th inst. ⟨I am and⟩ I ⟨quite willing that⟩ have no objection to the £1530 being divided in the way you suggest — giving Miss Fitzgerald as you say about £50 — provided of course that ⟨the⟩ the arrangements you are making do not interfere with the pro payment⟨s⟩ of the interest due to me.

Yours faithfully
John M Synge

MS (draft), TCD

1 This draft, scribbled on the back of an early TS of the article 'In A Landlord's Garden', which JMS was revising for his projected book of essays on Wicklow and West Kerry, was apparently addressed to Fred Sutton & Co., 52 Dame Street, the solicitors who looked after the Synge estates. JMS's brother-in-in law, Harry Stephens, was a member of the firm, in which his nephew, Francis Edmund Stephens, also worked. Miss Fitzgerald is unidentified.

To ROBERT GREGORY[1]

THE NATIONAL THEATRE SOCIETY, LTD. | ABBEY THEATRE, DUBLIN
April 21st/08

My dear Gregory

I do not know if you ever got my letter — written about a fortnight ago — about the designs. In any case time has run so short that Yeats has got designs from Rickets and we are going on with them.[2] It was not possible to wait any longer. I hope you have not been giving time to them, ⟨also⟩. If you have done the designs — the back cloth at least may come in handy for my Deirdre which is to be ready in autumn,

Forgive this line and believe that I'm very grateful for your offor for the design although it has not come off. I suppose you're very busy, — as we are here

Ever very sincerely yours
J. M. Synge

MS, Gregory

1 William Robert Gregory (1881–1918; see I. 71) was at this time studying art in Paris. He designed various productions for the Abbey, notably *The Hour Glass*, *Kincora*, *The Shadowy Waters*, *The White Cockade*, *The Image*, *Dervorgilla*, *On Baile's Strand*, *Deirdre* (Yeats), and *Deirdre of the Sorrows*.

2 The designs were for a revised production of *The Well of the Saints*, projected for 14 May 1908. Charles de Sousy Ricketts (1866–1931), designer, painter, sculptor, author, and collector, was co-founder and designer of the Vale Press and editor with Charles Shannon of *The Dial*. He was closely associated with the first productions of many of Shaw's plays, including *Saint Joan*, and with the Literary Theatre Society in London, and frequently advised Yeats on Abbey Theatre productions, although apparently he never visited Dublin. See *TB*, 275–7 for his work on *The Well of the Saints*, the designs transmitted by letter to Seaghan Barlow for execution. His *Self-Portrait*, a compilation by T. Sturge Moore of Ricketts's letters and journals, ed. Cecil Lewis (1939), includes several descriptions of meetings with JMS.

To MOLLY ALLGOOD

[47 York Road, Rathmines]
[24 April 1908]

Dearest

Dont be uneasy about me   Henderson told *me* about six times that I had a tumour, but he knows about as much about it as a tom cat. I'm to see Ball on Monday I believe and we wont know much till then.

I'm going out now three o'clock its a pity I cant meet you. Wait for me tomorrow Saturday between 3[1] and four at the Abby and I'll come over if I can and we can go to the Park. Nish[2]

Your old T

MS, Texas. *LM*, 246

1 Underlined three times.

2 Mrs Synge had reported to her son Robert on 14 Apr 1908, 'Johnnie came to see me on Friday last he is seriously thinking of been soon married; his money is wasted I fear by his landlady buying inferior beef etc., he thinks she drinks and does not like her and says he wants Mollie to look after him as he is determined to marry it is no use opposing him any more and we must only trust that he may get on' (TCD).

To LADY GREGORY

47 York Road | Rathmines | Dublin
April 27/08

Dear Lady Gregory

I have been waiting from day to day to write so that I might say something definite about my 'tin-tacks'[1] and possible plans. I was with the doctor again today, and he thinks I may have to go in to hospital again, and perhaps have an operation — but things are uncertain for a day or two. I am to go to him again tomorrow and I will let you know, then what is decided. For the moment I am leaving everything to Miss Allgood — but that should not go on too long. This week we are playing 'Casey' and the 'Workhouse Ward' for three nights.[2] I am not sure that it is wise, but it seemed to expensive and troublesome to give the furniture for 'Casy' for one night only. (We had to put off the Well of the Saints as the scenery could not be got ready in time) I fear there is little possib[il]ity of my being able to go [to] the shows this week, so I do not know if you ought to come up, if you can without inconvenience. I am rather afraid of slovenly shows if there are poor houses and no one there to supervise. It is very trying having to drop my rehearsals of the Well of the Saints — in fact this unlooked for complaint is a terrible upset every way — I have so much to do.

I got one design from your son yesterday, and of course the one you kindly sent from Coole,[3] but Ricketts were already on hand as promised and I could not change. There will not be too much time as it is to have things ready for next week.

I will report things to you again tomorrow or next day.

Yours sincerely
J. M. Synge

MS, Berg. *TB*, 278

1 'An allusion to the old man in *Workhouse Ward* who has pains like tin-tacks in his side' (*Our Irish Theatre*, 81).

2 *The Workhouse Ward*, a complete rewriting of *The Poorhouse* (Gregory and Hyde, 1903), received its first production on 20 Apr 1908; *The Gaol Gate* (Gregory) was added to the bill with *The Man Who Missed the Tide* (Casey)

on 30 Apr to allow Sara Allgood, fresh from her triumph as Isabella in William Poel's Manchester production of *Measure for Measure*, an opportunity to receive applause (*TB*, 279). Hereafter she was to take on much of the responsibility for the productions.

3 On 19 Apr 1908 Lady Gregory had sent a sketch (TCD) of a side wing adapted from Aubrey Beardsley's *Perseus*, in case Robert Gregory's designs had not turned up.

To W. B. YEATS

47 York Road | Rathmines
April 28th/08

Dear Yeats

I got your note this morning I am sorry I have been too ill all this week to attend to the audit matter. Swain said to me at the time⟨s⟩ that he could not make out Vaughan's accounts to his satisfaction, but that there was no deficit so that it was merely a matter of book-keeping. There were initial expenditures of printing etc, which he puts down as tour expenses and Vaughan did not, which makes some of the differences. The subsidy salaries make confusion also.

Vaughan cannot get hold of Swain for the moment as, he is nearly always away.[1]

Now for a serious matter. I have just been with my doctor again and he has found a lump in my side so that it is necessary for me to go into a private hospital again — first of all to let them diagnose me, and then, probably, for an operation. So I can do no more at the Abbey for the present — a bad look out for the Well of the Saints! I do not know if Lady Gregory will come up ⟨I asked them⟩ I wrote to her yesterday to say that I was seriously unwell, and I am writing again now with particulars. I fear everything is more or less standing still about costumes etc. I have not been in for three or four days   Have you made any further steps about bringing Poel over in June?[2]

Yours sincerely
J. M. Synge

MS, TCD. *TB*, 279

1 Yeats had written from Stratford-upon-Avon on 22 Apr 1908 to praise Sara Allgood's Isabella and to question the auditors' account (*TB*, 277). W. Swayne Little, Seafield House, 5 Janeville, Merrion, Dublin, was the theatre's accountant.

2 At JMS's urging, William Poel was being invited to instruct the company in verse-speaking, as a replacement for Frank Fay's tuition.

To LADY GREGORY

> 47 York Road | Rathmines
> Tuesday [28 April 1908]

Dear Lady Gregory

I have just been with my doctor again, and I am to go into hospital the day after tomorrow, so I can do no more at the Abbey for the present. I am uneasy about the costumes and every-thing for the Well of the Saints as there is no one to see to them.

In haste

> Yours sincerely
> J. M. Synge

MS, Berg. *TB*, 280

To W. B. YEATS

> 47 York Rd [Rathmines]
> [29 April 1908]

Dear Yeats

Your typed letter came too late for me to answer last night, but I wrote for Henderson to come round and I will give him your directions as to sending accounts.[1] REMEMBER, by the way, that it is important that the books should not be kept away for any length of ⟨long⟩ time or the current accounts which should go into them daily will get mixed again, also the Deposit Receipt which you ask me to send you must be taken care of, as it *is required* in order to get out the money when we need it. The cheque you wrote out last winter on the Deposit, was no value, — cheques do not apply it seems to sums in Deposit. ⟨I am writing⟩ The receipt is now in our Safe — I put it in there a day or two ago — so Henderson can send it to you.

I fear you will not make anything of the accounts — they seem to be in great confusion, some things entered in two books others, of same nature, in one only; ⟨things cheque⟩ sums put as scenery and stage, which turn out to be coal and gas, and the the sub — advances also — However it is certainly desirable to do what can be done.

It will take a day or two I suppose to get the bank books made up — write any further direction to Henderson as I go to hospital tomorrow. By the way if my ailments turn out to be serious — I have a nasty lump in my side[2] — I will not be able to have Deirdri for your sister. I have written to tell her.

> Yours J. M. Synge

Dear Yeats

Your typed letter came too late for me to answer last night, but I wrote for Henderson to come round and I will give him your directions as to sending accounts. Remember, by the way, that it is important that the books should not be kept away for any length of time or the current accounts which should go into them daily will get mixed again, also the Deposit Receipt which you ask me to send you must be take care of, as it is required in order to get out the money when we need it. The cheque you

To W. B. Yeats, 29 April 1908

P.S. I have seen Henderson and given him directions. I am not sure where the bank Book of the I.N.T.S. is it may be in Directors Box but I dont quite like setting Henderson to rummage there, where there is so much various correspondence. ⟨Shall I⟩   Postscript

I hear the Well of Saints scenery will *not* be ready even for next week. I think you or Lady Gregory will have to come to Dublin. MacDonagh play will be in in a day or two and I dont know [who] will stage manage it.[3]

                                                                J.M.S.

MS, TCD. *TB*, 281

1 Neither letter survives.
2 On 3 May 1908 Mrs Synge wrote to Robert Synge,
how little you know all we are going through over here and how much I want you. Johnnie came on Wednesday . . . he was later than I expected and we had begun dinner I went out to the hall to see him and was quite shocked to see him looking so ill and so changed since I saw him over 3 weeks ago — he is thin and white, a pallor I do not like to see, it gave me quite a turn, as he had not told me how much he had been suffering, I fortunately had a chicken for he told me he could not eat chops! he had been getting steadily worse and lying awake till 3 with pains in his stomach and back he had been twice to Dr Parsons, but he bore it a great deal too long in that lonely lodging and no proper food. He did not tell me how bad he was for fear of upsetting me as I was so ill myself with this neuritis — after dinner he came upstairs to my room and we talked I felt so much I could not help showing it, there is a small lump somewhere in his side, but the pain does not seem to be connected with it, he left by 3.15 train as he said he got worse in the evenings — he went in to Elpis next day Thursday.   (TCD)
3 Lady Gregory arrived in Dublin on 30 Apr 1908, the day JMS entered Elpis; Yeats arrived a day or so later. *When the Dawn Is Come*, postponed until 15 Oct 1908, was staged by the author.

To MOLLY ALLGOOD

                                        [Elpis Nursing Home, Dublin]
                                                        [4 May 1908]
Dearest
    Will you come and see me here at four today as I am not to go out. The operation is to be tomorrow,
                                                        Your old T

MS, TCD. *LM*, 246

To MOLLY ALLGOOD[1]

                                        [Elpis Nursing Home, Dublin]
                                                    May 4th [1908][2]
My Dearest Love
    This is a mere line for you, my poor child, ⟨if⟩ in case anything

goes wrong with me tomorrow, to bid you good-bye and ask you to be brave and good, and not to forget the good times we've had and the beautiful things we've seen togethe[r]

Your old Friend.

MS, TCD. *LM*, 317

¹ JMS addressed this letter to Molly at the Abbey Theatre and wrote on the envelope '(to be sent in cover in case of death)' (TCD); she received it some time after 24 Mar 1909.
² Molly has written 'Elpis' and the year in ink.

To LADY GREGORY

Elpis [Nursing Home] | Lower Mount St
[4 May 1908]

Dear Lady Gregory

I am to have the operation tomorrow at eleven so I am not allowed out today. Sir Charles Ball would not say what he thought my trouble was, but he looked glum enough over me this morning. They do not really know of course what they may find when they go to work.

I feel this break down peculiarly as I had intended to get married to Miss M. Allgood about Easter though I said nothing about it to avoid gossip or advice. I am sure you will do what you can for her if anything should go wrong with me in this 'gallère'.¹

By the way the General Meeting of the *I.*N.T.S, must be held this month so the notices should soon go out, will [you] get someone to see to it, please, as I — the Secretary — cannot do anything.²

Yours sincerely
J. M. Synge

MS, Berg. *TB*, 282

¹ Lady Gregory wrote to Molly from Italy, 22 May 1909: 'I have just been sent a letter written to me by Mr. Synge just before the operation last year. He tells me of his having hoped to marry at Easter, and asking me in case of his death to do what I could for you — I know you will be touched by this proof of his thought for you, as I am touched by his having written as it were a farewell to me . . . . I hope you are keeping well, and keeping your courage, as he would have wished you to do.' (Coxhead)
² At this general meeting of the Irish National Theatre Society Ltd., the suspension of the Fays was to come up for ratification or review; it seems likely that the meeting was held before 21 May 1908 (*TB*, 274, 278).

To W. B. YEATS

[Elpis Nursing Home, Dublin]
May 4th/08

W. B. Yeats Esq
Nassau Hotel
Dublin
Dear Yeats

This is only to go to you if any thing should go wrong with me under the operation or after it,[1]

I am a little bothered about my 'papers'   I have a certain amount of verse that I think would be worth preserving, possibly also the I and III acts of Deirdre, and then I have a lot of Kerry and Wicklow articles that would go together into a book,[2] the other early stuff I wrote, I have kept as a sort of curiosity but I am ⟨not⟩ anxious that it should *not* get into print.

I wonder could you get someone — say MacKenna who is now in Dublin — to go through them for you and do whatever you and Lady Gregory think desirable.

It is rather a hard thing to ask you, but I do not want my good things destroyed, or my bad things printed rashly, — especially a morbid thing about a mad fiddler in Paris, which I hate.[3] Do what you can

Good Luck

J. M. Synge.

MS, NLI. *TB*, 299

1 Yeats received this letter sometime in May 1909, and published it — omitting MacKenna's name — in *Synge and the Ireland of his Time, With a Note Concerning a Walk Through Connemara with Him* by Jack Butler Yeats (Dublin: Cuala Press, 1911).

2 Because Yeats did not feel the Kerry and Wicklow articles were of the same standard as JMS's other prose work, he withdrew his support of the *Collected Works* published by Maunsel in 1910, and published his Introduction in *Synge and the Ireland of his Time*.

3 *Etude Morbide*, finally published in *Prose*, 25–36.

To MOLLY ALLGOOD

[Elpis Nursing Home, Dublin]
[*c*. 11 May 1908]

Dearest Heart

Sorry to hear you are not well, I hope you will get all right soon.

I have been *very bad* for last 24 hours with my stomach, but I am a little easier to night though still in bed with a poultice all over me. I am afraid, Dear Heart, we must put off your visit again for a day or two. I shall be in bed tomorrow again, and in this state we could get no good of a visit. Dont be uneasy about me, I think I am over the worst now, but I have to stay very quiet indeed.[1] Write plenty of nice letters to me to keep me going

With endless love
Your old Tramp.

MS, TCD. *LM*, 247

1 Mrs Synge had heard confidentially from Dr Parsons on 5 May 1908 that a tumour was discovered '10 or 11 days ago'; he wrote again after the operation to report that the tumour 'was adherent . . . and it would not have been desirable to have attempted its removal'; the surgeon 'made another passage by short curtailing.' JMS (as she reported to her son Robert on 5–6 May) 'bore the operation well', but when the surgeon removed his stitches, the bowel drained and continued to drain. On 12 May 1908 Mrs Synge wrote again to Robert, 'Ball had no hope of our dear boy's life . . . . the tumour or abscess is still there as it cannot be removed . . . . He has no idea he was in danger — the Drs. hid it from him completely.' (Both TCD)

To MOLLY ALLGOOD

Elpis [Nursing Home, Dublin]
Thursday [11 June 1908]

Dearest

This is a line only (as I'm rather tired from one thing or other) to tell you I'm getting on very well.[1] I've been up since 12.45 and it's 7 now.

I got your note last night and I hope I'll have a longer one this evening. I'm sorry your weather is so bad.[2] I haven't many visitors now, F Ross today and my younger nephew. S. Gwynne called this morning but I didn't see him as I was in bed. He wrote me a very kind note.[3] Lady G. is gone, I haven't seen Henderson yet.

Goodby Dear Heart,

J.M.S.

MS, TCD. *LM*, 247

1 Mrs Synge wrote to her son Robert on 1 June 1908: 'We hear he is better and looks better and he says the wound is healing but Annie [Stephens] says Miss Huxley seemed anxious last week when she saw her, as they dont know if the bowel has healed properly, it has done so to a certain extent — so we are kept very anxious but *he* does not know anything of this I suppose as Annie says he seems cheerful' (TCD).

2 Molly and Sally Allgood had gone to Balbriggan until 16 June for a brief holiday after the theatre closed for the season.

3 The novelist and travel writer Stephen Lucius Gwynn MP (1864–1950; see I. 131) was a co-director of Maunsel & Co. Gwynn had written, on Elpis note-

paper, 'I hope from my heart that you may soon be out and as well and strong after your operation as various of my near kin are today after the gravest possible experiences of the kind' (TCD).

To MOLLY ALLGOOD

[Elpis Nursing Home, Dublin]
Saturday [13 June 1908]

Dearest

I have had two more *little* notes from you — one without a stamp but I only smiled — why dont you write me a good long letter, as I thought you promised, of three or four sheets? I hope you haven't made yourself ill doing too much rowing or anything. Why do you go to the W[1] so often, that sort of thing gets a great nuisance after a day or two. Are you coming home on Tuesday? I had a visit from my mother yesterday[2] and then Henderson came, and nearly wept over me when he talked [of] my bad times. I got him to lend me a book "Tristram and Iseult" that I wanted very much to read,[3] so he left it round this morning and I am happy with it for the day.

I seem to have lots of things to write to you, but I wont write them as you are treating me so shabbily. Nish. Are you ashamed of yourself! Sirrah! d—— little b.

My gap is still closing slowly but nothing is settled about going away[4]

Give my love to Sally

Your old
T.

MS, TCD. *LM*, 248

1 Relatives of Dossie Wright who lived in Balbriggan.

2 Mrs Synge wrote to Robert on 16 June 1908, 'I saw dear Johnnie on Friday last he was up and dressed sitting in his chair   He had shaved and looked more natural but I hear he had the hair dresser yesterday so I suppose he got a general trimming up, his hair was very long . . . .' (TCD)

3 Probably *The Story of Tristan and Iseult*, rendered into English from the German of Gottfried von Strassburg by Jessie L. Weston (1899).

4 In the same letter of 16 June to Robert Mrs Synge reported: 'Johnnie does not seem anxious to make any move out of that; the wound is not yet closed so if he came here we should have to get a nurse to come every day and dress it . . . . Sir Charles Ball only sees him twice a week now. He had not said anything about his going out to us so every thing remains very unsettled.' (TCD)

To MOLLY ALLGOOD

[Elpis Nursing Home, Dublin]
Sunday | June 14/08

Dearest Child

I got your note this morning and I nearly got tears in my eyes —
you know I'm shaky still — it was so short and scrappy and external.

I'm very sorry you are feeling so unwell, I hope you're taking care
of yourself. You needn't have taken the stampless letter so much
to heart, you poor child, I'm afraid I'm a great tyrant, you are in
such awe of me. I dont mind that sort of thing a bit.

I suppose you ought to stay on longer if you feel inclined   It is a
pity to have had such a poor holiday

I am much the same, but I've got my beard off

Your old
T.

MS, TCD. *LM*, 249

To MOLLY ALLGOOD

[Elpis Nursing Home, Dublin]
June 16 [1908]

Dearest

I got your letter last night — a much longer and better one. As
usual however you dont tell me where to write today so I must send
this to you[r] old address on chance. There is nothing very new to
tell you here. I heard from Q[uinn] in New York the other day with
£20 for the MS. It is cruel that it will all be lost in the expenses of
this present business. He also invites me to go to New York for a
fortnight and offers to pay my way out and back. I dont think I'll
go however.

I go for a walk down the passage every day now and look out of
the window.

Later

Henderson has been to see me again. He tells me U. Wright has
been staying in Balbriggan too. Is that true?

It makes me feel — I do not know how. Your

T.

Please answer question at end <u>BY RETURN</u>[1]   I feel queer and
shaky

MS, TCD. *LM*, 249

---

1 Underlined three times.

To JOHN QUINN

Elpis Hospital [Dublin]
June 16/08

My dear Quinn

I am glad to be able to answer your letter[1] myself — sitting in an arm-chair — the stage I have reached now. I hope to move out of this place somewhere into the country in a week or so,[2] and then gradually to pick up my strength. All my doctors and nurses say I have made a very exceptionally quick recovery since I once began to mend, that, I suppose, is a good thing.

I am greatly obliged for your very kind invitation to New York, but I'm afraid it would be hardly the thing for me. I am not always a good sailor and with this recent and deep wound in my stomach the strain of being sick might do me harm. At any rate I could not go for a long time still.

I will be very glad that you should have the MS of Deirdre when ever it is finished to my satisfaction[3] — I suppose after the summer I'll get to work on it again. It is difficult picking up work ⟨again⟩ after such a complete break in one's ideas but in the end one often gains in richness. Many thanks for your cheque for the P.B. MS. — there was of course no hurry about it.

I am very pleased to hear of proposed American edition of my plays — and again very grateful for your kind offer as to plates, — the arrangement you tell me of with Dutton seems, I think, quite satisfactory.[4] Of course if I give the right of the book for the whole copyright, I suppose ⟨on⟩ as the various publishers Mathews etc rights expire the full royalty will become payable to me.

It would be a great thing ⟨for⟩ if W.B.Y. could write the introduction I wonder how he would feel about writing on my plays again, as most of the ground was covered by his introduction to Well of the Saints.[5] I wonder if he could retouch that preface so as to make it fit the whole book — we know he has a passion for re-writing!

Now I'm getting weary so with many thanks I remain

very cordially yours
J. M. Synge

Address
⟨Glenalough⟩ Glendalough House   Kingstown   Co Dublin

MS, NYPL

[1] Quinn's letter of 5 June 1908 is in TCD.
[2] Mrs Synge wrote to her son Sam in China on 11 June 1908 (TCD) that Dr Parsons had arranged for JMS to go to Bell View in Delgany, former residence

of the La Touches, now a recovery home for invalids, as she was going to Tomri-
land, Co. Wicklow, for the summer; instead, JMS went to his sister's house in
Kingstown.

3 An acting text of the unfinished play was assembled by Yeats and Lady
Gregory, with Molly's help, after JMS's death. The MS was then sent to Quinn
by the executors, as promised; Quinn had a copyright edition printed in
1910.

4 'Young [George] Roberts has been here arranging about books,' wrote
Quinn on 5 June.

> He was just in at noon and told me that he had arranged with Dutton & Co.,
> a very responsible firm in this City and a large firm, for the publication of
> a volume of your plays . . . with a possible introduction by W. B. Yeats,
> retaining your prefaces before each individual play. or in an appendix . . . .
> Dutton's would be willing to get out an issue of 5,000 copies to be printed
> from plates, provided Roberts would agree to take the plates at their cost,
> which they estimate at about £30. I told Roberts that I would underwrite
> that cost, so that I would advance to Roberts the £30 necessary to purchase
> the plates from Duttons. The plates will then be sent to Dublin and Roberts
> can print up his edition from these plates, Roberts returning to me the £30
> from his first sales. Dutton insisted upon having the right to the book for the
> period of the copyright . . . . it is not an uncommon arrangement here. Yeats
> had to give all his plays to Brett of the Macmillan Company here for the
> period of the copyright.   (TCD)

5 The suggestion of an introduction by John Butler Yeats (see p. 49, n. 6)
seems to have been forgotten, and evidently JMS was not distressed by the
touches of romanticism W. B. Yeats had added to his 1905 *Well of the Saints*
preface ('He had wandered among people whose life is as picturesque as the
Middle Ages, playing his fiddle to Italian sailors, and listening to stories in
Bavarian woods'); 'That's the way Yeats writes', JMS laughingly told his nephew
(Stephens MS).

To LADY GREGORY

Elpis [Nursing Home, Dublin]
June ? 18 [1908]

Dear Lady Gregory

Thanks for your letter which came yesterday, and the enclosure
from the I.S.Society.[1] Their apology is rather lame.

I hope your son and Mrs Gregory have got safe home to you
by this time, after all your anxiety.[2] I am getting ahead rather slowly
now — they warned me all the time that the last stage of closing
of the wound would be the most tedious — but I am gaining strenght
and I talk walks up and down the passages. I do not know when I
shall be sent home — I dont think I would gain much by trying
to rush things, though I am getting very weary of this room.

I have just had a visit from Quinn's clerk who is on a visit here,
and was sent to get news of me.[3] Roberts was in here yesterday in

great spirits after his trip   He has arranged I belive for an American edition of my plays.

Yours sincerely
J.M.S.

MS, Berg. *TB*, 284

1 Lady Gregory's letter of 16 June 1908 from Coole (*TB*, 283) enclosed a letter dated 12 June from the Hon. Sec. of the Irish Literary Society of London assuring her that *Riders to the Sea* would not be produced by the Irish Stage Society at the Court Theatre as announced in certain newspapers.

2 The illness of Robert Gregory's wife Margaret, expecting her first child, had delayed them in London *en route* from Paris.

3 Quinn's secretary Freddy White, D. J. O'Donoghue's brother-in-law, had tried several times to see JMS. J. B. Yeats had reported to his son W.B. on 1 July 1908, 'When Quinn heard of Synge's illness he was like a raging lunatic. He inveighed against you, Russel and myself and all Ireland. He seemed to think that no one cared whether Synge lived or died.' (*Letters to His Son*, 109)

To MRS KATHLEEN SYNGE[1]

Elpis [Nursing Home, Dublin]
Saturday [4 July 1908]

My dearest Mother

I got your letter this morning, and I am sorry to hear you were so tired on the way up. It is hardly to be wondered at, you have been unwell so long, and the journey is so tedious.[2] I hope you are better by this time.

I am going out to Silchester[3] on Monday. Ball came up the other day and said I might go whenever I liked but I have waited a few days to get into the way of walking up and down stairs and dressing the wound. I think I'll go by tram to Sandycove and then take a ⟨han⟩ cab up, that will be the quickest and cheapest way.

In the hurry the other evening when I was writing to you I forgot to mention the money, it was very kind of Robert[4] to think of sending it so immediately. Please thank him heartily when you write. I had another drive on Wednesday out by Stillorgan and Dundrum It is cool and pleasant on the shady roads near Merville.[5] Yesterday I went to Blackrock Park with Molly but the trams were very hot and crowded part of the way. Today it is like a change and there is thunder in the distance — I dare say you will get it in the hills. I hope to hear of you soon again.

Your aff son
J. M. Synge

MS, TCD

1 Mrs John Hatch Synge (1830-1908), widowed when JMS was a baby; see I. 49.

2 Mrs Synge had been ill with neuritis since the operation on her leg in February; the journey to Tomrilands by cart took several hours from Kingstown.

3 Silchester House, the home of JMS's sister Annie Stephens, was round the corner from Glendalough House, in Silchester Road, Glenageary, Kingstown.

4 Robert A. Synge (1858-1953), JMS's eldest brother, an engineer, had been in the Argentine on business since 24 Jan 1908.

5 An estate at the corner of Foster's Avenue and Stillorgan Road, Booterstown, owned by J. Hume Dudgeon, stockbroker.

To MOLLY ALLGOOD

[Silchester House, Glenageary]
[7 July 1908][1]

Dearest Pet

I got your note this morning all right.

I got down here last night, and I am rather knocked up by the fatigue so I am staying in bed and may not write.

A thousand blessings   Dont be uneasy.

Your old T.

MS, TCD. *LM*, 250

1 Molly has added the date.

To MOLLY ALLGOOD

[Silchester House, Glenageary]
Wednesday [8 July 1908][1]

Dearest Love

I am better again today, but I'm still in bed. I was so feverish yesterday my sister[2] went in and told Sir Charles Ball and he came down to see me in his motor. He couldn't find anything wrong so I hope it was only the fatigue. I slept like a top last night, and I feel "grand" today, perhaps I'll get up this evening. I am dying to see you but I'll have to be up and about first I'm afraid. I meant to have you down for this afternoon but now that cant be done

How are you? You dont tell me if your back is all right. I hope you *aren't* going to Miss Dickinson[3] today.

This is a stupid letter my poor love, but I cant manage much while I'm stretched here. Be good and be happy and go to your picture gallerie and write me nice *long* letters

Your old T

MS, TCD. *LM*, 250

¹ Molly has added the date.

² Annie Isabella Stephens (1863–1944), JMS's only sister, whose disapproval of the match with Molly had dissipated during his illness.

³ Mabel Dickinson, sister of the artist Page L. Dickinson; Thom's *Directory* lists her as 'medical gymnast and masseuse'.

To MOLLY ALLGOOD

Silchester [House, Glenageary]
Thursday [9 July 1908]

Dearest Love

I got two notes from you yesterday as your morning's note came at midday, and so I had none this morning.

I got up yesterday about 4.30 and went into my nephews room to sit there for a while. Five minutes afterwards my sister came up to say that two nurses had come down from Elpis¹ to see how I was as they had heard I was ill. They came up and brought me down-stairs and stayed with us for a good while. Then they went away and I went back to my bed. Today I am better, but I'm still "a bit" shaky. I wanted to wire for you this morning, but my sister thought it would be better to have you tomorrow when I'm stronger. So come down tomorrow by the quarter *to* 2 unless we wire to the contrary. You can go back by the ¼ past five. I hope it'll be fine so that we may sit out in the garden but in any case I've a quiet little corner where we can be for part of the time any how. I wonder how you are today. It is beautiful weather as far as I can see I haven't been out yet. I have no further news.

Your old T.

I heard from Agnes² the other day, and from Quin again.

P.S. Your letter of today has just come. I suppose you'll be well enough to come tomorrow if not send me a line. Dont let Miss D[ickinson] talk you over into doing anything foolish. If you do not need the drill as she says, and if it hurts you, why do it? Has your back recovered?

I feel "mighty flat" today, sitting here by myself in silence and solitude. Aren't [you] glad you weren't Kerrigan?

T.

Blessings as usual.

MS, TCD. *LM*, 251

¹ JMS corresponded (TCD) with four nursing sisters, A. Whitford, Mollie Mullen, Esther Grierson and G. Thornton after he left Elpis.

² Agnes Tobin wrote from San Francisco on 21 June 1908 (TCD), enquiring about JMS's health, the fate of *Deirdre*, and an unidentified 'Miracle Play'.

To LADY GREGORY
        c/o Mrs Stephens | Silchester House | Glenageary | Kingstown
                                                        July 11th/08
My dear Lady Gregory
    I am out of Hospital at last! I am staying with my sister, who has
a large garden, so that I am able to lounge about and pick up my
strength. I do not know how long I shall be here. I meant ⟨but⟩ to
move on to some more bracing place pretty soon, but I feel rather
shaky about starting off just yet.
    I saw Yeats as you will have heard on his way through, and since
then I do not think I have had news of anything striking. F. Fay is
still in Dublin I believe but he seems to have quieted down.
    I hear they begin again at the Abbey on Monday.
    I hope you and your party — and the puppies[1] — are well.
                                                Yours sincerely
                                                J. M. Synge

MS, Berg. *TB*, 285

    1 'Simple things always pleased him. In his long illness, at a Dublin hospital
where I went to see him every day, he would ask for every detail of a search
I was making for a couple of Irish terrier puppies to bring here, and laugh at
my adventures again and again.' (Lady Gregory, 'J. M. Synge', *The English
Review*, March 1913)

To JOHN QUINN
                                        Silchester [House] | Glenageary
                                                        July 11th/08

My dear Quinn
    This is just a line to thank you for your letter of June 25th which
I found waiting for me when I came out of the hospital five or six
days ago. For the time being I am staying with a married sister who
has a large quiet garden where I can lounge about and pick up my
acquaintance with things again — a heavy illness, and two months
confinement make a curious break in one's life.
    I saw Yeats the other day on his way from Paris to Coole, and he
very kindly agrees to do the Introduction to the plays — or, at least,
to expand what he wrote for the Well of the Saints, into a general
Introduction.[1] I will be very much obliged if you can have a look
at the contracts with Dutton as you kindly suggest.

In a few weeks when I am stronger I hope to move on to some bracing place on the Northern coast to pick up more thoroughly.

Very cordially yours
J. M. Synge

Address Glendalough House | Kingstown

MS, NYPL

1 Yeats wrote to his father on 7 Aug 1908 'I have written half an elaborate essay on Synge, an analysis of Irish public opinion and the reason why his work is so much hated in Ireland' (*Letters*, ed. Wade, 533, where it is misdated 1909).

To MOLLY ALLGOOD

Silchester [House, Glenageary]
July 11th/08

My dearest Love

I meant to write you a particularly intimate and tender note today — because you were so good yesterday — but now I have been writing semi-business letters till I am tired out so I can only send you a line, to say that I think you are very nice — when you like.

I have written to Quinn and Lady G. and I have 21 more letters to write but I cant do them. (sings) Oh K.H.

Oh " "
Oh " "
etc.[1]

How are you today I hope the gooseberry didn't disagree? I wonder if Sally will get down today. There is supposed to be a tennis-party here today — T[ramp] of course not visable — but [it] is half wet and they dont know what to do.

Oh — —

Your O.T.

MS, TCD. *LM*, 251

1 Probably a refrain from a lament such as 'Och, Och, Eire, O!' (Sam Henry collection of Songs of the People, NLI):

For och, och Eire, O!
Lone is the exile from Eire, O!
'Tis my heart that is heavy and weary . . .

To MOLLY ALLGOOD

[Silchester House, Glenageary]
July 12th/08

Dearest Love

This is a short line only to thank you for your charming — Nish — letter that I got this morning, and to tell [you] I'm going on well. I've been out in the garden all day from 11 to 7 except for my meals so I'm "a bit" tired now and I'm going to bed. I wish you'd always write as fetchingly as you did yesterday — if you did I'd have to buck up or you'd beat me at letter-writing and that wouldn't do, would it?

It has been a lovely day here in the garden with the birds and Brunettes[1] it is a pity you weren't here.

God help me I've wind enough in my poor belly — saving your presence — this evening, to drive a mill.

Be good and let me know all about your arrangement with Powell.[2]

Your old T.

MS, TCD. *LM,* 252

---

1 The Stephens family dog was named Bruno.
2 William Poel, for his classes in verse-speaking; see p. 150. He began this tuition on 13 July 1908, along with rehearsals for a contemplated production of Calderón's *Life's But a Dream* (which never took place).

To MOLLY ALLGOOD

[Silchester House, Glenageary]
Monday [13 July 1908]

My dearest Child

I got your poor little note this morning with my breakfast — it is hard to see so little of each other. I am getting better I suppose but it's very slow and I get very dull. I'm writing in the garden now on the back of a book so I cant make much of a letter — I stay out all day they say its good for me.

I wonder when we'll get another drive. I hope to hear particulars about your hours tonight or tomorrow morning. Then we'll see.

I am getting very anxious for a view of the world again, and of course of you.

F. Ross has come out this evening. She is going to Greystones in a day or two so she came to say goodbye. I wonder how you are getting on with Powell today. I am anxious to hear all about it. Goodnight my dear Heart.

Your O.T.

MS, TCD. *LM,* 253

To MOLLY ALLGOOD

Silchester [House, Glenageary]
14/July/08

Dearest Child

I got your little note as usual this [?morning]. Of course I cant fix anything about your coming down again till I know when you are free. Why do you say you have only a fortnight to get up the Dressmaker? I dont think [it] is on till the Horse Show and that is towards the end of August, so you have a long time.[1] You should get as much as possible out of Poel while you have him. I wonder what part he'll give you. I'll be interested to hear all about him when you come down again. I'm waiting to have another drive till I can have you with me. I walked out at the back gate today and round by the church and in at the front. I am getting on well I suppose but I have pains and aches that alarm and annoy me. I hope your mother is better, you ought to get a doctor if she is really ill.

This is a wet tedious day, and I feel very dull. Perhaps I'll hear from you again this evening. I heard from Lady G. this morning just to say she was glad I was out. Goodbye dear Heart

Your O.T.

MS, TCD. *LM*, 253

1 The theatre did reopen for Bank Holiday Monday, 3 Aug 1908, with performances of *Riders to the Sea* and Fitzmaurice's *The Country Dressmaker*.

To MOLLY ALLGOOD

[Silchester House, Glenageary]
15 July /08

Dearest Love

I am very glad to hear you have a good part. It is inconceivably small-minded of Sally to refuse Rosaura[1] — you would have done the same I'm afraid if you had been in her shoes all through — it is an attitude I cannot understand.

I hope everything is going smoothly. I have asked you FOUR TIMES to tell me what hours you are free so that I may ask you down, but you have never alluded to the matter.

I am glad to hear Dr Barry thinks well of you. Did Miss D[ickinson] go with you? Did you give him a fee?

I am not very well. It is hard to manage the wound without any skilled advise. In my efforts to keep it clean I have made the opening larger than it has been recently. Today I have asked my nephew to call on Sir Charles and ask him about it. It is cold and raw and wretched out here. I am all by myself this afternoon the others are out — as often happens. I have nothing cheerful to write, sitting here day after day is nearly intollerable. They have a tennis party here tomorrow to make things worse. They are all very kind but what can they do for me?

Your O.T.

How is your mother?

[*Enclosure*]

My dearest Love

My poor child, your second letter has come. I am ill with anxiety about you. For my sake do not have any unpleasantness, give what is necessary, and keep with Sally. Promise me this. For my sake have no rows, it would kill me. Do promise!

In great anxiety

Your O.T.

By the way, another matter, were you told to tell me to send on that play to Yeats?[2]

MSS, TCD. *LM*, 254

1 One of the female roles in Calderón's *Life's But a Dream*.

2 Perhaps *The Wonderful Wedding*, by John Guinan and George Fitzmaurice, submitted according to Holloway in April 1908 (*The Modern Irish Drama*, comp. Robert Hogan and J. Kilroy, vol. III [1978], 247), but not rejected by Yeats until August.

To MOLLY ALLGOOD

Silchester [House, Glenageary]
Friday [17 July 1908]

My dearest Love

I think you are treating me very badly — I suppose you are so busy, you have no time to think of me now. I am very lonely and very wretched and not very well.

On *Wednesday* at 7 o'clock I got your note about your troubles, and your promise that you would write again that same day. Then *all day yesterday* I got no news of [you] till I was perfectly sick and ill with anxiety and had a very bad night. *Then this morning* I hear from you and you promise to come down and tell *me for the first time what* hours you are free. Then *at 2.30* — after I have been out to meet the train I get a line from you to say you are not coming down at all. I am to be alone to day for six hours and I feel most wretched and broken down. — ——— — — — ——— If I write anymore I will say things that I do not wish to say. I am profoundly wounded that you have prevented me asking you down this week and left me so long in such great anxiety. I see you are busy tomorrow afternoon by your list of hours so we cannot meet till next week.

Your O.T.

Why do you tell me nothing of what has happened in your home, God knows it would not be much to spare ten minutes to write to me.

MS, TCD. *LM*, 255

To MOLLY ALLGOOD

Kingstown
18 July 1908 | 11.47 A.M.

M. Allgood   Abbey Theatre   Dublin   Yes tell Henderson you are coming   Synge

Telegram, Texas. *LM*, 256

To MOLLY ALLGOOD

Silchester [House, Glenageary]
Monday [20 July 1908]

Dearest Child

I wasn't able to write to you yesterday — when I came in to do a letter in the evening I found my brother-in-law hard at work in the little study so there was no place for me to go. I got your little note this morning — you dont say a word about going to Poel — yesterday I wonder if you went or what happened.

I am much as usual but I feel rather flat as I didn't got properly to sleep till 5 o'clock this morning my nights are nearly always bad now.

I'm half thinking of going to Bray this afternoon to get out of this perpetual garden — it is baking out there today. This is a foolish note but what can I do — I'm red hot and I've a pain in my b— stomach I mean. I've just got a hankering to go up and stay a couple of weeks at Lough Bray I dont see why I shouldn't.

Your old T

I'll write better the next time.

MS, TCD. *LM*, 256

To MOLLY ALLGOOD

[Silchester House, Glenageary]
Tuesday [21 July 1908]

Dearest Love

I got your letter about 2 o'clock today. It was taken to Glendalough House and the old woman brought it up to me. It is better to put c/o Mrs Stephens on the envelopes or else the postmen think they know more about it than you do.

You and Sally are a clever pair not to know where you were to see Poel — that sort of thing is a mistake; if it can be helped. (It puts people against you I mean.) I got a qualm when I read of your visit to the green — remember if what she told you is true the *danger* goes on *for years* no matter how well she may look. It is a terrible matter.[1]

I went to Bray today and sat on the esplanade for an hour and then came home again. I was very bored but I suppose it was good for me. I suppose Saturday would be the best day for us to meet again. They are having a tennis party here so I will want to be out of the way. We might go to Bray and have a drive and tea, and sit on the Esplanade. Nish! I suppose you will be free on Saturday. I haven't gone to Ball yet I'm going tomorrow or Thursday — I thought I told you I was going.

Your O.T.

MS, TCD. *LM*, 256

---

1 Molly's oldest sister Peggy, Mrs Tom Callender (1879–1959; see I. 192), who apparently was still living at 13 Stephens Green, had quarrelled with Molly over *The Playboy of the Western World*; see I. 319–21. Yeats recorded in his journal that JMS

> knew how to hate, as witness this: 'To a Sister of an Enemy of the Author's, who disapproved of *The Playboy*' [*Poems*, 49] . . . . When he showed me this, he said with mirthful eyes that since he had written it her husband had got drunk, gone with a harlot, got syphilis, and given it to his wife . . . . I do not know how he learned the facts about the husband and wife, but he was very truthful and ever matter-of-fact, being in every way very simple.
>
> W. B. Yeats, *Memoirs*, ed. D. Donoghue (1972), 201–2

To MOLLY ALLGOOD

[Silchester House, Glenageary]
Wednesday [22 July 1908]

Dearest Child

I got your little note — one of the *charming* ones — this morning. You mustn't mind my notes being so short I haven't anything to tell you. I wont write to you tomorrow till after my visit to Ball so that I may tell you what he says. My nights are bad now and they make me uneasy but I hope it is nothing. It is very hot today and I feel exhausted and wretched enough. You poor child you must be nearly dead with such long rehearsals. It is well you have only four days more. Find out if you are free on Saturday so that you may come to me if we can manage it. It will depend a little on how I am. Oh —— —— —— —— —— I'm so —— —— —— —— hot.

Take care of yourself and be good

Your O.T.

MS, TCD. *LM*, 257

To MOLLY ALLGOOD

[Silchester House, Glenageary]
July ? Thursday [23 July 1908]

My Dearest Child

I got your little note with its huffy beginning this morning, — the idea*r*! I was in with Ball today. He seems to think I am all right now, and says I may do what I like — only I am not to go to the Blaskets! He told me about the operation but I'm not much the wiser. I'll tell you what he said when I see you. I am glad Peggy's matter is well over — remember — if you have to go there — all I have said to you.

Dont forget to tell me in your next if you are free on Saturday — as usual I have asked you two or three times and you have taken no notise. Now you must write and tell me early tomorrow or I'll hardly have time to arrange. Nish!

I'm not very well with all Ball's talk and I had a worse night than ever last night. I think I'll go and see Parsons on Monday   I suppose you'll get this tomorrow before you're up.

Your O.T.

MS, TCD. *LM*, 257

To MOLLY ALLGOOD

[Silchester House, Glenageary]
Friday July [24][1] 1908

Dearest Child

Thanks for note. I was in town again today with Sir Charles as my wound was in a new stage — the skin closed too soon — that I did not know how to deal with.

I haven't heard yet for certain if you will be free tomorrow — I suppose you dont know yet yourself. If you are free my plan is that we go to Bray by the *quarter to Three* (I'll meet that train, if its fine), and if it's not fine we'll go down to Glendalough House and look through my books and *our* furniture[2] and get tea from Mary Tyndall and have a good time. Nish! It will be my sister's At Home day so I dont want to be here. Now is that all quite clear? You come down by the *quarter to three* and if I meet the train we go on, and if not you come to the "little gate" and we go to Glendalough. Dont miss the train — if you are coming — as I would have to go on to Bray by that train if I was there. Of course if you are not free I'll be all forlorn, trying to get along by my poor unfortunate self — I think you all deserve the afternoon's rest but of course you'll have to do what Poel says. I've no news   I'll wait now and see if there's a letter by this post it is due in 20 minutes.

No letter, well I heard this morning so I cant copy you and say ——.

If you can let me know before *eleven* tomorrow if you are coming, and come by the quarter to three that will give you time for your dinner

Your old T.

MS, TCD. *LM*, 258

1 Misdated 23 July.
2 Molly had packed up the furniture and belongings at 47 York Road and vacated the rooms on 25 May 1908.

To MOLLY ALLGOOD

[Silchester House, Glenageary]
Monday July 2? [27] 1908

My dearest Child

When I got your charming little letter this morning I felt very guilty for not having written to you yesterday. Somehow it isn't easy to write here on Sunday. My brother-in-law was in the little study all the evening and I had no place to collect my thoughts. It was well you wrote so particularly nicely as I'd have given a great scolding about your bicycle. As it is I feel a hurt that you let them knock about my present to you, the way you do — a fall does a bicycle more harm than six months riding. I hope you will make quite sure that the brake is quite secure. It is a *fatal* mistake to let anyone mend a bicycle except the makers or someone you know and can rely on a clumsy workman can do an extraordinary amount of harm in five minutes. I have had axles split and screws stripped and nuts twisted so I speak from sad experience. Nish! I wont scold you any more, you poor child. I'm very lonely and very low and not very well yet. I may go to Bray after lunch but I'm not sure. I have been reading your Chaucer all the morning, its a pity the print is so small. By the way, if your brothers[1] take your bicycle without leave it is easy to get a chain and padlock (*at a cycle shop*) for about 1/0 and then you can put the chain through the wheel and head and lock it and then you are safe, and no one can ride it. If you are in any doubt about the brake being all right take it to the maker I will pay if you like. You had better show it to O'Rourke or someone.

I was dreaming of Wright last night but nothing very sensational. This is dull external letter to send in answer to your nice one, my God if we could only be well again and out in the hills for one long summer day and evening what Heaven it would be. I feel ready to cry I am getting better so very slowly.

Good bye dear Heart
Your old T.

This is a beastly letter but forgive it and me I've a pain.

MS, TCD. *LM*, 259

---

1 Molly had two older brothers, George and Harry, both killed in the First World War, and two younger brothers: Tom, who became a Trappist monk, and Willie, who became a civil servant.

To MOLLY ALLGOOD

[Silchester House, Glenageary]
Tuesday July 2? [28 July 1908]

My dearest Child

I got your nice little note with my breakfast this morning, and it made me very gay. You will not get this till tomorrow morning, as I went to Bray today and have missed the post. I took paper and envelope with me and I meant to write to you in the train, but at the last moment I forgot my pencil. I have turned over fifty plans for meeting you tomorrow but I haven't hit on anything satisfactory so I suppose it'll have to be Friday or Saturday. I think you said you are going to Miss D[ickinson] tomorrow so I dare say that will be enough for you. It was very hot at Bray today and I felt quite 'done up' with the glare on the esplanade and now I have a pain as usual, God help me! — I nearly wrote God with a small 'g'!

How do you get on with Swift? He was over 40 I think when he wrote those letters.[1] Have you sent Lady Mary to Miss Grierson, Elpis?[2] I hope you've got your bicycle settled properly.

I heard from my mother today. She is only middling it seems. My nephew and brother-in-law have gone out to Aran again[3] so we are a small party.

Your old T.

MS, TCD. *LM,* 260

[1] Jonathan Swift's letters to Esther Johnson, written from 1710 to 1713 when he was in his mid-forties, were first published as his *Journal to Stella* in 1766 and 1768; a modern annotated edition was published by G. A. Aitken in 1901.
[2] On 21 July 1908 Esther Grierson wrote (TCD) from Elpis thanking JMS for the loan of books, including an edition of Swift's letters; the novel *Lady Mary* by Ann Sophia Stephens (1813–86), a well-known American author and editor, was not published until 1892, then reissued in 1902.
[3] Harry Stephens and his son Frank were responsible for negotiating the sale of land, under the Land Purchase Act of 1903, by Lord Ardilaun to the Congested Districts Board for division among the Aran Islanders, and had already made one trip to the islands in June 1908, which Harry described to Molly when he met her at Elpis on 20 June 1908 (David H. Greene and Edward M. Stephens, *J. M. Synge 1871–1909* [New York, 1959], 286).

To MOLLY ALLGOOD

[Silchester House, Glenageary]
Wednesday | July 29th [1908]

Dearest Child

Your letter came this evening at 7 I was looking out for it all day. Well we'll meet on Saturday I'll write you what train tomorrow I was very lonely and miserable in Bray yesterday by myself, and today I went to Blackrock and sat in the park and was lonelier again. Dr Parsons has gone away and Ball too so I'll have to get on as best I can till they come back. I had a wretched sort of night again last night. Still I hope it may be only the effects of the operation, and general indigestion. I am very lonely too, we must try and meet oftener after this once a week is far too seldom.

I am writting this in a hurry to catch the post tonight so that you may have this tomorrow morning. Have you got your brake settled yet? My second nephew[1] came home today he has been up with my mother for a month

Now be good and cheerful Dear Heart

Your Old T.

MS, TCD. *LM,* 260

[1] Edward M. Stephens.

To LADY GREGORY
          c/o Mrs. Stephens | Silchester House | Glenageary | Kingstown
                                                          July 30th/08
Dear Lady Gregory
     Many thanks for your letter and invitation to go down,[1] but I fear
I couldn't get so far at present, and when I do go it will have to be
to some very bracing place. I am staying on here waiting for my
wound to heal up, but it closes one day and breaks out again the
next so I am not making much way.
     I send you at last the little play you left with me. I doubt very
much that the 'dream scene' could be made anything of and there
are other obvious faults, still I think there is a play in it, if he would
pull it together.[2]
     I hope you and your party are well.
                                                   Yours sincerely
                                                      J. M. Synge

MS, Berg. *TB*, 287

     1 Lady Gregory wrote from Burren on the coast of Co. Clare on 13 July
1908, inviting JMS to join her, Yeats, Robert Gregory and his wife in the 'little
house' she had taken till the end of the month (*TB*, 286).
     2 The 'little play' may have been John Guinan's *The Cuckoo's Nest* (not
published until 1933), or *The Wonderful Wedding* (Guinan and Fitzmaurice;
see p. 168), both rejected by the Abbey.

To MOLLY ALLGOOD
                              Silchester [House, Glenageary]
                              Thursday July 30th [1908]
Dearest Child
     Your note came this morning. What is the splint? Is it to make
both sides of your face what, *Eh?* That['s] a nice way you keep me
informed of your doings! Nish. I'm beginning not to wonder that
you sometimes find it hard to write — these last days as you see I'm
not up to much. I've been in Bray again today from 5 till 7, it was
less hateful than it is earlier in the afternoon. I suppose the quarter
to three train would be the best for you to come by on Saturday.
If its fine we'll go to Bray and if not to Glendalough I suppose.
I've been invited to go and stay at my brother's house while he is
away, his daughter and F. Ross are to be there. I suppose I'll have to
go as they'll be getting this place ready for the wedding soon so I'd
be in the way.[1] My wound is just the same and I still have the bad

nights. Now good night dear Heart I'm very lonely and wretched without you.

Your o T.

MS, TCD. *LM*, 261

1 JMS's brother Edward, as a land agent, was frequently away on brief visits to the west of Ireland; his house was at Sandycove. Harry Stephens's sister Elizabeth was to be married on 18 Aug 1908 to Thomas Franks of St. Brigid's, Clonskeagh.

To MOLLY ALLGOOD

[Silchester House, Glenageary]
Friday | July 31st/08

Dearest Child

Well the week is gone by at last and I am to see you tomorrow. Come down by the quarter to *three* — dont miss it for Heaven's sake and we'll go to Bray or Glendalough House. I got your little card this morning — it doesn't seem to be weather for letter-writting somehow.

I sent off the little play to Lady Gregory today at last. It might possibly do [if] it was altered a good deal. I certainly agree with you that it is most mean and unfair of Sally to put you out of Scapin   She wouldn't do it if I was about.[1] It is a pity with all her fine qualities that she is so queer.

I hope we'll have a good time tomorrow. You had better be early enough to get a seat next the window so that I may see you in the train tomorrow — and dont go too far up the train. If I'm not there come on here.

Till then goodbye dear Heart

Your old T.

MS, TCD. *LM*, 262

1 With all the directors absent or otherwise engaged, Sara Allgood was in charge of the company as stage manager in preparation of the productions for Horse Show week (24 to 29 Aug 1908): *The Rising of the Moon*, *The Rogueries of Scapin*, and *Kathleen ni Houlihan*, alternating evenings with *The Gaol Gate*, *The Man Who Missed the Tide*, and *The Jackdaw*. Since Molly continued to play Zerbinette in *Scapin*, evidently she persuaded her sister to change her mind.

To MOLLY ALLGOOD

[Silchester House, Glenageary]
August 3rd [1908]

My dearest Child

I forgot somehow that there would be only one post today[1] or

I'd have written to you yesterday — now I'm afraid you'll be two days without a letter. I got your little note this morning   yes Saturday was *good*   Eh?

I had a pretty good night too and wasn't tired. However to make up I was very bad last night and I feel shaken and wretched today. There is no news. It is too hot and too crowded to go out so I am loitering about trying to pass the day, and to forget my miseries, God help me.

I'm too flat to write nicely it is impossible, so believe how much I love you and how I long to see you again

Your O.T.

MS, TCD. *LM*, 262

1 August Bank Holiday.

To MOLLY ALLGOOD

Silchester [House, Glenageary]
Tuesday Aug 4/08

My dearest Child

There are several pieces of news to tell you today. My mother is so unwell that she is coming home on Friday or next Tuesday, so I shall go down there instead of going to my brothers. We are anxious about her. Next I am very unwell myself so I am going in tomorrow I think to see young Ball[1] and have a talk with him. I cannot let things go on like this. I dont know what is going to become of me, I wouldn't be surprised if they send me back to Elpis for a while. You need not say anything about this to Henderson or the others they are too much given to gossiping. Anyhow I hope I'm not very bad as I was so well on Saturday. I meant to ask you down tomorrow but that is off now, and I dont know what time I'll be in town so I cant ask you to meet me. Then on Thursday afternoon I suppose you rehearse — what time do you finish? Please thank Henderson for his letter[2] and tell him I'll write and fix a day but that I'm going to the doctor tomorrow. Dont be downcast my little Heart there are bound to be ups and downs I suppose in my recovery.

Your O.T.

MS, TCD. *LM*, 263

1 Charles Arthur Kinahan Ball (1877–1945), son of Sir Charles Ball; a surgeon at Sir Patrick Dun's Hospital, he succeeded to the baronetcy at his father's death in 1916.

2 Henderson's letter of 1 Aug 1908 concerned bank deposits and a report on the directors' continuing campaign to persuade William Boyle (see I. 86) to return his plays, withdrawn over *The Playboy*, to the Abbey Theatre. 'I grossly insulted Mr Boyle by offering him 5/0 a performance for his plays,' wrote Henderson (TCD); the directors recieved nothing in royalties.

To MOLLY ALLGOOD

Silchester House [Glenageary]
Wednesday | August 5th/08

My dearest Child

I got your poor little note last night and your card this morning. I am not going to the doctor today so I am sending a line to Yeats to ask him to be sure and come. I had a very much better night last night, and other ways I am better so I want to wait a day or two to see how things go before I go to the doctor. In any case going to young Ball is not very much good, unless it is absolutely necessary. I hope you are not very unwell let me know how you are as soon as you can.

I dont know what day I'll go down to my mothers yet, it seems strange going back there after so long when I thought I had left it forever. My nephew heard from his 'fancy'[1] by the same post that I heard from you last night. He had three big sheets closely written on both sides so I felt that I had only come off second best. However of course she is in Wales so that they have to live on correspondence God help them.

"Oh, Johnny Gibbon
You're over the say!"[2]   (the splash is an extra dont mind it)
Nish amn't I better. If I get a good night today I'll be "grand".
Amen

Your O.T.

MS, TCD. *LM*, 263

1 Frank Stephens was engaged to Maud Gaussen, whose family came from Bournemouth.
2 The folksong is unidentified.

To MOLLY ALLGOOD

[Silchester House, Glenageary]
Thursday | August 6th [1908]

Dearest Child

I was delighted with your little note this morning. I am not so well today however and I'd bad pain in the night so we must[n't] hollow too much till we're out of the wood. I was very glad to see Yeats yesterday and talk over things with him[1] it seemed like getting back into the current of life again. I suppose Saturday will be the best day for us to meet again we can go to Bray or Glendalough House according to the weather. My mother is not coming home till Tuesday next so I suppose I'll stay on here till then. If you were rich you could come down on Sunday too and have tea with me in Glendalough but I suppose two days together would be a bad division. I have been in Bray today but I did not enjoy myself a bit.

Your O.T.

MS, TCD. *LM*, 264

---

[1] Yeats had come to Dublin from Coole to begin the rehearsals of Mac-Donagh's play *When the Dawn Is Come* (see *TB*, 287-8).

To MOLLY ALLGOOD

[Silchester House, Glenageary]
Friday [7 August 1908]

My dearest Child

I've had no news of you today. How's that, Eh?

Come down tomorrow by the quarter to three — unless you get a wire to put you off — and I'll either meet you at the station and go on to Bray, or else on the road and we'll go to Glendalough *Dont be late*. I had a very good night last night and thought I was 'grand' but I've not been quite so well today. I'm afraid I must go to young Ball on Monday. If I should have a *very* bad night tonight I might have to go to him tomorrow, so you need not be distressed if I wire to you; as we would meet on Sunday instead. But that's not likely I hope.

My mother comes on Tuesday — did I tell you that before I think I did. I have been to Bray again today for the good of my health, it's rather a fagging job going there alone. The regatta was on there again and rather a crowd in the train so it was hot. I hope I'll hear from you tonight

Your old
T.

MS, TCD. *LM*, 264

To MOLLY ALLGOOD

[Silchester House, Glenageary]
Monday 1 P. M. | August 10th | 1908

My dearest Child

I couldn't manage to write to you yesterday so I am writing early today. I am sorry to hear about Peggy for *my* sake, my dear child, be careful about these matters and make Sally be careful. I am going in to Dr Ball today at a quarter past two to see what he says to me. I was a good deal worse yesterday I am afraid than I have been yet, but I had a good night and I was better this morning, though the pains are beginning again now all up my back.

Florence Ross and Ada Synge were here all day yesterday, but I didn't see very much of them. When I am not feeling very well I find the large party here rather trying.

Yes I am not seeing you half often enough you must come much oftener now. I dont think I shall go down to Glendalough till Wednesday — as my mother does not get in till pretty late tomorrow, so that the house will be upset. Goodbye there is lunch now. Remember what I have asked you

Your O.T.

Tell Sally I'll be very glad to see her some day I'll let her know.

MS, TCD. *LM*, 265

To MOLLY ALLGOOD

Silchester [House, Glenageary]
11th August/ 08

Dearest Child

I was in with Dr Ball yesterday but he did not find much that was very definite. He found, he thinks the cause of the discharge — an *un*important one if he is right — but he does not really know what my severe pains are from   I liked him very much and I am to go back to him in a few days if I am not better. He takes more trouble and is much gentler than the old man.

I got your post card this morning I suppose it was better than nothing. Write me a better letter tonight. I move down to Glendalough tomorrow and then we must arrange to meet oftener. I had a line from MacKenna last night asking if I was still in the land of the living — I never answered his last letter.[1]

I hope my mother will have it fine for her drive down this evening — she is two hours drive from the railway in Wicklow town, and she is to have a two horsed landau to bring her down.

This is one of the days when I am not able to write. With ten thousand blessings — some how I can always bless you — your

O.T.

MS, TCD. *LM*, 266

1 On 8 July 1908 JMS received a letter from MacKenna telling him that he had tried twice, unsuccessfully, to visit him in Elpis and that his wife was to arrive from Paris that week, when they would take up residence at 5 Sea View Terrace, Donnybrook. On 16 July he wrote again, apparently acknowledging a letter now missing in which JMS had told him of his sister's garden at Silchester, and asking JMS to set a date when a visit would be convenient (both TCD). MacKenna's letter of early August is missing.

To MOLLY ALLGOOD

Silchester [House, Glenageary]
Wednesday [12 August 1908]

Dearest Child

I'm here still. My mother came home yesterday but is so unwell that she has to stay in bed so they thought it better for me to stay on here another day. There is a lady staying with my mother[1] so now I suppose I'll have to entertain while my mother is ill. That will be a job.

Your little line came this morning — poor Maire — that woman passes anything. I'm only very middling still. I went for a little walk today for half an hour but it makes me tired very soon when I have to walk without sitting down.

What did you see at the Gaiety?[2] I'm afraid I cant fix a day for us to meet till I get down to Glendalough and see how things are. I lay — or rather wriggled — awake last night till four o'clock so I do not feel very bright.

Good luck dear Heart

Your O T

MS, TCD. *LM*, 266

1 Miss Massey, who had been one of Mrs Synge's summer visitors in Wicklow as early as 1902 (Stephens, *My Uncle John*, 153).

2 During the week of 10 Aug 1908 Eugene C. Stafford's company was at the Gaiety Theatre, Dublin, performing in 'the world-renowned comedy' *The Private Secretary*, by Charles H. Hawtrey, with *The Wild Man from Borneo* as a curtain-raiser.

To STEPHEN MacKENNA

Silchester House [Glenageary]
Wednesday [12 August 1908]

Dear MacKenna

I've been pining for the sight of your face all these weeks, but somehow from the uncertainty of my inside I've never had the decision necessary to say "tomorrow I'll have MacKenna," and then to write to you to fix a time. In fact I've not been very well and I've been sitting quaking in the garden like a sear and yellow leaf.[1] The doctors say I'm a very interesting case and generally patronise my belly — to think that I used once to write "Playboys," MacKenna, and now I'm a bunch of interesting bowels!

My mother has come home unwell from the country so I return to Glendalough House tomorrow. Then forthwith I'll write and beseech you to come and see me — I am a little in dread of your ten minutes walk just yet.[2]

My cordialities to Madame and you,

Yours
J. M. Synge

MS, TCD

1 Cf. *Macbeth*, V. iii:
> I have liv'd long enough. My way of life
> Is fall'n into the sear, the yellow leaf;
> And that which should accompany old age,
> As honour, love, obedience, troops of friends,
> I must not look to have.

2 MacKenna replied immediately: 'My dear friend, you must not think there will be no let-up from this state of interesting bowelhood. This is a rest, a living of another kind: you will write more Playboys out of yet another kind of set of experiences.' (Undated, TCD)

To MOLLY ALLGOOD

Glendalough [House, Glenageary]
Friday | 14/8/08

Dearest Child

I am sorry to have left you a day without a letter but it could not very well be helped. I came down here yesterday about 6 and found your letter waiting for me but I was too tired then to write to you and go to the post. Your second note has just been brought me now from Silchester — It was a nice one.

My poor mother is not at all well and is in bed still. This illness seems to have aged her in some way and she seems quite a little old woman with an old woman's voice. It makes me sad. It is sad also to see all *our* little furniture stowed away in those rooms. It is a sad queer time for us all, dear Heart, I sometimes feel inclined to sit down and wail. Come down to me tomorrow, say by the *quarter* PAST TWO from *West Row* — a Saturday train I will either meet you, or else you can come here. Dont miss it or I will be lost. I heard from MacKenna today I will show you his letter tomorrow. Oh Mother of Moses I wish I could get well. I have less pain at night I think than I had but I'm all queer inside still.

It is kind of Sally to want to give me more books[1] — I'll think of one. She is good-natured in her own way. I'd like to go and have tea in the Abbey some afternoon next week — wouldn't that be fun?

By the way *dont* bring the typewriter tomorrow as we may be going on to Bray. I wish I had you coming down today — I feel so flat and sad.

Goodby now and dont be late tomorrow a *quarter* PAST *two*

Your O T

MS, TCD. *LM*, 267

1 Among JMS's possessions was a copy of A. E. Housman's *Poems* (London: Grant Richards, 1907), with the inscription 'J. M. Synge from Sara Allgood June 5th, 1908'.

To MAX MEYERFELD[1]

Glendalough House | Kingstown Co. Dublin
August 17th 1908

My dear Dr. Meyerfeld

I was very much pleased to hear from you again the other day — I have long meant to write to you but this last year my health has not been good, I have had to undergo two operations and to spend some three months in a private hospital, so I am sure you will excuse my long silence. I am gradually recovering again now and they say I shall soon be quite well again.

I am pleased to hear that my "Well of the Saints" has been produced in Munich. I would be interested to hear any further particulars. We revived it in the Abbey Theatre last spring, and I re-wrote and improved a portion of the third act.[2] Unfortunately I got ill during the rehearsals so I was unable to see the performances.

I am sending you a copy of my "Tinker's Wedding," slightly different from the version you saw in Manuscript. At present I am in treaty for the publication of my plays in America. During last winter, when well enough, I was working at a prose play on the story of Deirdre — I hope to finish it for our next season at the Abbey. I shall be much obliged if you will send the money to this address as before, and believe me with best wishes

your sincerely
J. M. Synge

MS copy (Meyerfeld), NLI

1 Dr Max Meyerfeld (1875–1952; see I. 111), translator into German of *The Well of the Saints.* When offered *The Tinker's Wedding* by JMS in MS, he refused it on the grounds of it being too parochial for a German audience; evidently he rejected *The Playboy* on the same grounds after seeing a performance and meeting JMS in London in June 1907.
2 In a letter of 13 Aug 1908 (TCD), Meyerfeld informed JMS that *The Well of the Saints* had been performed three times in Munich. JMS's marked copy of the play with revisions to the third act is in TCD; the emendations are annotated in *Plays,* Book I, 126–50.

To KAREL MUŠEK

Glendalough House | Kingstown | Co. Dublin
August 17th [1908][1]

My dear Mr. Musek,

I have wished to write to you for a long time, but as I dare say you have heard from Mr. Kelly[2] I have been very seriously ill for some time. I am much better again now, and I am beginning to do a little writing again. How have you been getting on with your theatre? I have just heard that my "Well of the Saints" has been produced in Munich.[3] What are its chances in Prague? Have you thought anything more about translating the Playboy, you remember I refused to let another gentleman translate it in order to keep it for you.[4] We had a good season at the Abbey last Spring. We did a translation of Moliere's Scapin, and my "Well of the Saints" was received with great success. I hope you will have time to let me have some news of you. We often speak of your visit to the Abbey. I hope you and your family are in good health. Please make my compliments to Madame Musek, and believe me

Sincerely yours,
J. M. Synge

MS copy (Mušek), TCD

1 Misdated by Mušek 1918.
2 Richard J. Kelly (1886–1931), barrister and editor of the *Tuam Herald,* who had introduced JMS's plays to Mušek; see I. 159.
3 See preceding letter.
4 See I. 337–40. On 9 Sept 1908 Mušek replied that he had translated *The*

Well of the Saints two years before and sent it to the Vinohrady Theatre, with
no word as to its chances of performance; he had postponed translating *The
Playboy* because both theatres in Prague were occupied with national plays and
produced no English-language plays 'with the exception of Shaw and Wilde'
(TCD).

To MOLLY ALLGOOD

Glendalough House | Kingstown
Monday [17 August 1908]

Dearest

I got your note this morning. I wish it was Wednesday I feel very
dull and wretched, it is very hot and my mother is still very poorly
and Miss Massey — the guest — is lying down with a head-ache.

I went to Merrion yesterday on top of the tram and walked along
a bit and came back again. It was very hot and I hated it. Today
I am going to Bray God help me.

I got a card from Lebeau this morning he is going to Canada in
three weeks for good. He has got a post there to teach French
literature in Montreal — in the university.[1] I sat down this morning
after breakfast and wrote to him and Musek and Meyerfeld — the
German 'Well of the Saints' man and then I got fagged. I think I'll
go in and see young Ball again tomorrow and then God send Wednesday.

They are in a great fuss at Silchester today getting ready for the
Wedding tomorrow. I'm glad you had a spin yesterday. Where did
you go.

Oh me God I'm as flat as a mangled pancake. Write me a nice
letter. I found Gullivers Travels today I'll bring them to you on
Wednesday

Your O T

MS, TCD. *LM*, 267

1 The McGill University archives record Henri Lebeau's appointment from
1908 to 1910 as Professor Extraordinarius of French; there is no record of him
after the notice that his re-engagement in 1910 would cover work in July of that
year.

To MOLLY ALLGOOD

[Glendalough House, Glenageary]
Tuesday [18 August 1908]

Dearest

I haven't gone to Ball today after all. I am going to him because

he said I was to go back and because the worries in my inside aren't
by any means gone. I'll go on Thursday perhaps.

Florence Ross and Ada were in here a little while ago in white
dresses on their way to the Wedding. They looked very nice, and for
the first time I felt a little qualm of regret that you would not have
a nice white brilliant wedding too. However any colour would do
us. If you only knew how much I am longing for our day to come.
I am afraid to think about it, God help me. I am going to try writing
crooked the way you do to see if you admire it as — oh damn where
shall I go now. Do you follow this joke   I'm not drunk but your
letters have been getting skewier and skewier and I'm beginning to
get hypnotised into doing the same. It's rather fun when you try it.

My mother is a little better today, she is beginning to come round
I think. I am sorry to hear that the men of the Company are giving
trouble. Sally had better report them to the Directors if they get
too bad.[1]

I had a wretched time in Bray yesterday all by myself. Come
down tomorrow (Wednesday) by the quarter to *three*. I'll join you
at Glenageary as usual. If not come here. Of course if it is a *wet* day
dont come. It wont be wet please God

Your O T

MS, TCD. *LM*, 268

1 'I notice some slackness in Miss Allgood's rehearsals. I noticed the same in
Fay's . . . . Miss Allgood . . . cannot distinguish between necessary reproof to
some actor and anger against him; this injures her authority.' (Yeats, journal,
March 1909, *Memoirs*, 182)

To MOLLY ALLGOOD

[Glendalough House, Glenageary]
[21 August 1908]

Dearest.

This is the only bit of paper I can find. I was 'a bit' disappointed
not to hear from you this morning, and I suppose you were the same
not to hear from me. Serves you right. I didn't got to Ball yesterday
it was so wet so I'm going today instead, to see what he says. Tomorrow is Saturday I believe, God be thanked, so come down if
it is fine by *the quarter* PAST TWO, we'll go to Bray or perhaps
Dalkey — but you'd better not come if its wet.

Miss Massey — the visitor is going away on Monday, so you can
come here more easily after that. My mother is getting a little better
by slow degrees. I am much the same. It's funny how a little piece
of paper makes me write little sentences — I feel as if I'd no room

is here a little while so in white Dresses on their way to the Wedding. They looked very nice, and for the first time I felt a little pride of regret that you could not have a nicer toilette, not be a ... a brilliant wedding too —

However any colour would do so so. If you as know how much I am longing for our day to come, I am afraid to think about it, (and ...)

help me, I am sorry to th—

writing crooked the way you admire it as ... way you do & see all
Oh damn where it if

I go now. Do you follow this ... I'm not drunk but your letters have been getting skewier and skewier and I'm beginning to get hypnotised into doing the same ... rather fun when ... it. ...

To Molly Allgood, 18 August 1908

for big ones. — This is a longer letter than usual, I am writting so small, so dont turn up your nose at it.

My mother will have to get a nurse I think after Miss Massey goes — it's a pity you aren't trained, and you could come. I feel, as you see, perfectly incapable of writing today I wish I was going to meet you in town today.

Your O.T.

MS, TCD. *LM*, 269

To MAX MEYERFELD

Glendalough House | Kingstown
August 22nd [1908]

Dear Dr Meyerfeld

I am much obliged for your order for £3.10.0 which I have just received.[1]

Yours sincerely
J. M. Synge

P.S. I am posting the Tinkers Wedding with this.

MS, NLI

1 Royalties from the Munich performances; see p. 184.

To MOLLY ALLGOOD

[Glendalough House, Glenageary]
Monday August 24th [1908]

Dearest Child

I wasn't at all the worse I think for our great little walk on Saturday. Henderson came in the evening and I talked business as spry as possible till ten and then I went to bed and slept very well. If it was[n't] for that bloody blood I'd be damn fine now Eh?

Magee[1] came to see me yesterday afternoon — I like him — and then afterwards I went for a little walk and met the red-headed Abbey enthusiast I've told you about, and he walked with me out and back again.

My eldest brother came back from America this morning I am very glad as Miss Masey has gone away and I felt anxious here alone with my mother. I think he will stay here till we get someone to look after her. The pretty young nurse cant come you'll be sorry to hear.

I've been working at Deirdre this morning — Nish — I've decided to cut off the second act, (you remember Jesus Christ says if thy second act offend thee pluck it out, but I forgot you're a heathen and theres no use quoting Holy Scripture to you,) so that I can take the one good scene in the II and run it into the third when D and Naisi are together. It will be useful there as Naisi part was so weak in the last Act. Now what do you say to me.

You must come down soon with my type-writer I'll tell you when soon. By the way do you rehearse tomorrow afternoon? I suppose not I think I'll go and see MacKenna this afternoon. Goodbye Dear Heart.

O.T.

MS, TCD. *LM*, 269

   1 W. K. Magee ('John Eglinton'); see below, p. 202.

To MOLLY ALLGOOD

[Glendalough House, Glenageary]
August 25th 08

Dearest

I got your letter at half past one so that wasn't too bad. I'm glad to hear the House was so good. What is wrong with Morgan?[1] at the other show he was quite good — even very good in places. What's happened to him.

You had better come down tomorrow (unless I wire to put you off — to the Abbey) by the quarter to three or the quarter to two if it suits you and bring me my type-writer. Then if its fine we can go somewhere.

Is the British Association *next* week? I thought it was further off.[2]

I had a letter from Jack Yeats this morning,[3] not a very interesting one. He is at Coole, but leaves tomorrow. I heard from Lady Gregory also. This is flatish kind of note because I'm to see you tomorrow I suppose so I'm too lazy to put energy into my letter —

I found our pictures today and I've put myself up in our parlour over the chimney-piece. I wish you hadn't that cigarette it makes your picture a little common. I found the mug also so nearly everything has turned up now, so till tomorrow good bye and goodluck

O.T.

MS, TCD. *LM*, 270

   1 Sydney J. Morgan (1885–1931) had joined the company early in 1908 and remained for almost twenty years, afterwards moving to London where he acted in many of Sean O'Casey's plays; he played Argante, father of Zerbinette, in *The Rogueries of Scapin.*

2 The company was to perform 3 to 9 Sept, presenting two special matinées
for delegates attending the meetings of the British Association for the Advance-
ment of Science, held in Dublin for a week from 2 Sept.

3 Jack Yeats wrote on 23 Aug 1908 (TCD) enclosing no. 3 of his *Broadside*
publications, describing his visit to Kinvara, and hoping to see JMS on his way
to Arklow.

To MOLLY ALLGOOD

[Glendalough House, Glenageary]
August 28th/08

Dearest Child

I got your nice little note last night at six — I am delighted that
the Abbey is going so well. I am going to Sir Charles today, so I
will have news for you the next time, let me know if you are coming
out tomorrow or on Sunday. I heard from Nurse Mullen[1] putting
off our party till the weather is more settled. My mother is getting
on well, but I've a pain today — my dinner wasn't a success yesterday
and I've been the worse for it ever since.

I've just had a wire from Roberts to say that he is coming out
today.

I'm very glad you like Gulliver there's great stuff in him. You see
I cant write today

Your old T.

MS, TCD. *LM,* 271

1 One of the nurses from Elpis Nursing Home; see p. 163.

To LADY GREGORY

Glendalough House | Kingstown
August 28th/08

My dear Lady Gregory

Thanks for your letter — I sent on the enclosure to Scott M.
Guardian.[1] I think it would be as well to say nothing about it over
here, to Henderson or any of them.

I have just been with Sir C. Ball. He seems to think I am going
on very well and says I may ride my bicycle and do what I like!
All the same I am not good for much yet I get tired out very easily.
I am half inclined to go to the Brit. Ass. matinee on Friday next,
I would like to hear Yeats speech,[2] and I dont think it could do me
any harm. In any case I will be able to go up and see you when you
are up.

I am thinking of going away to Germany or somewhere before very long. I am not quite well enough for the West of Ireland in this broken weather, and I think the complete change abroad would do me most good, I have old friends on the Rhine[3] I could stay with if I decide to go there.

I hear great accounts of the Abbey this week, it almost looks as if Dublin was beginning to know we are there.

I have been fiddling with my Deirdre a little — I think I'll have to cut it down to two longish Acts. The middle Act in Scotland is impossible. You will let me know when you come up please.

Yours sincerely
J. M. Synge

P.S. They have been playing the 'Well of the Saints' in Munich, I have just got £3.10. royalties.

It was a one-act version I have just heard this minute, compressed from my text![4]

MS, Berg. *TB*, 290

1 Apparently a letter of protest to the editor of the *Manchester Guardian*, eliciting a vaguely worded apology to JMS on 29 Aug 1908: 'Vigilance is at times relaxed or wired copy may come very late and escape the usual revision' (TCD). The reference may have been to a *Guardian* review of a performance of Lady Gregory's *The Rising of the Moon*, at the Theatre Royal, Manchester, on 18 Aug 1908, which alluded to 'the theatre Irish of the Abbey Theatre' (*TB*, 290).

2 The special British Association matinée on 4 Sept 1908, including *The Hour Glass, Spreading the News*, and *Riders to the Sea*, featured an address by Yeats, 'The Abbey Theatre — its Aims and Work'. Souvenir programmes were printed for both matinées.

3 The von Eicken family, Koblenz.

4 None of the extant letters from Meyerfeld to JMS (TCD) mention a one-act version of *The Well of the Saints*.

To MOLLY ALLGOOD

Glendalough Ho. [Glenageary]
August 28th [1908]

Dearest

I've been with Sir Charles, he says I'm not to mind my inside and that I may go away and ride my bicycle and do what I like — Nish!

I had Roberts out here today we have very complicated business to do over this American Edition. I hate this haggling over money. I wonder what you'll write to me about tomorrow, and if you'll

have had the good sense and forethought to make definite arrangements — I'm sure you will you're *so good at that!* Nish!

Your old T.

I walked up from Merrion Square today round through College
Green and back to the Station by Brunswick Street. If I'd known
where to find you I'd have got you for tea somewhere.

NISH

MS, TCD. *LM*, 271

To MOLLY ALLGOOD

Glendalough [House, Glenageary]
August 31st [1908]

Dearest

I am very glad to hear that you are better thought it gave me a
sorry qualm to hear of your expedition[1] — especialy as you let him
pay for you. I had a very pleasant afternoon at the MacKennas —
they have a charming old house full of excellent things that they
have picked up, among other a little bronze statuette by Rodin —
you have seen his work at Harcourt — which he gave to Mrs MacK.
I envy them — there is no one else in Ireland probably who possesses
such a thing. They have admirable furniture also and a lovely view
of the mountains. They want me to bring you to see them as soon
as I can shall we say next Sunday or when?[2]

I didn't got out with my nurse of course today — she wired to
say she was too busy and of course with this weather it wouldn't
have been possible. I hope you are feeling as well today, I've been
playing round and round my verses this morning — I cannot do any
work as I have no paper — isn't [it] too bad I asked you to get it
on Wednesday and I have lost nearly a whole week — I might have
written an act of Deirdre. However you haven't been well so I'll
forgive you this time. I'm a bit *bellysome* today — isn't that a fine
word — as I ate a whole dish of cabbage yesterday. When I'm by
myself I gobble up everything without thinking. I suppose you'll
come to me on Wednesday Eh. Write again

O.T.

MS, AS. *LM*, 272

    1 The company frequently arranged expeditions into the country, some-
times holding open-air rehearsals in Phoenix Park.
    2 Auguste Rodin (1840–1917), French sculptor considered, especially in
the early part of the twentieth century, one of the greatest portraitists in sculp-
ture; his worldwide success did not prevent national outcry when his statues of
Balzac and Victor Hugo were unveiled to the nation. The new Municipal Gallery

of Modern Art in Harcourt Street possessed five pieces by Rodin. Apparently Molly did not visit the MacKennas with JMS until just before he went to Germany in October 1908.

To MOLLY ALLGOOD

[Glendalough House, Glenageary]
Sept 1st 1908

Dearest

I have had no news of you today so far. I got impatient this morning so I troted off into town and bought my paper and a book and went to the bank. Then I came home on top of the tram in time for my dinner.

Will you come down tomorrow by the quarter to three? We'll go to Bray if its fine I rather think there is a travelling circus there which would be fun.

Roberts is coming out here tonight for me to read him my poems — it gives me a big 'D', as you call it. I dont know how I'll ever face showing them to Yeats, but it'll have to be done. God help me.

I felt nearly quite myself dodging about in town. Will you write tomorrow before 11 or tonight to say if you'll come tomorrow.

I'll leave this now to see if I hear from you at six.

No letter so good-bye Dear Heart till tomorrow. If it is wet you can come here.

O.T.

MS, Texas. *LM*, 273

To MOLLY ALLGOOD

[Glendalough House, Glenageary]
Sept 4th/08

Dearest Heart

You little —— not to write me a nice long letter yesterday! I am getting on very well indeed getting rid of my —— symptoms I think. But I'm so well I'm afraid to go to the Abbey for fear of bringing things on again. It's not worth the risk. Isn't that so? I am writting to Lady Gregory to ask if I can see her tomorrow. If she says I'm to go, I wont be able to see you till Sunday. I'm beginning to think in that case we wont go to the MacKennas till another day, so that we can go out on Sunday to Bray or somewhere.

What did you do yesterday. It was too wet for my expedition[1] that is the third time it has failed. Did you see about the woman who shot herself in Rathmines.[2] I used to know the man a little and his brother quite well. Do you see what comes of flirting, Eh?

I am going out now as I was at home all day yesterday

Your old Tramp

MS, TCD. *LM*, 273

1 Among JMS's papers (TCD) is a letter of 13 Sept 1908 from 'Dot' (Nurse Mollie Mullen, called 'the little black dot'), Elpis, saying it is too wet to go to Dalkey.

2 The *Evening Mail*, 1 Sept 1908, reported the suicide of a solicitor's wife in Moyne Road, Rathmines, after she had separated from her husband and been jilted by her lover, a horse trainer.

To LADY GREGORY

Glendalough House | Kingstown
Sept 4th/08

Dear Lady Gregory

I got your letter thanks the other day.

I am getting on very well, but now it comes to the point I dont feel equal to facing the crowded Abbey today. Will you be in Dublin tomorrow and shall I call and see you, the afternoon about 3 would do me best if that suits you.

Yours sincerely
J. M. Synge

MS, Berg. *TB*, 291

To MOLLY ALLGOOD

[Glendalough House, Glenageary]
Sept 5.08

Dearest

For three days I have heard nothing of you — I do not know when you left me so long before — I need not tell you that I am troubled and uneasy. You could find time to write me a line no matter how busy you are.

I have just come back from seeing Lady Gregory and Yeats. They seem very well. I am not quite so well today I have a pain under my wound. Will you come down by the quarter to three tomorrow. I will join you at Glenageary if it is fine and I am well enough. If I do not, then you come down here. A post is due now I wonder shall I hear from you. I am beginning to worry myself sick.

The post has passed I dont think ever since I knew you you have left me so long. Why do you do it? You seemed as usual when I saw you on Wednesday

Your O.T.

MS, TCD. *LM*, 274

To W. B. YEATS

Glendalough House | Kingstown
Sept. 7.th.1908.

Dear Yeats

Roberts wants me to give him the enoclosed verses for publication — I read them to him the other day, and he seemed taken with them — and I would be very grateful if you would let me know what you think about it. I do not feel very sure of them, yet enough of myself has gone into them to make me sorry to destroy them, and I feel at times it would be better to print them while I am alive than to leave them after me to go God knows where.[1]

If I bring them out I would possibly wrhite a short preface to say that as there has been a false 'poetic diction,' so there has been and is a false 'poetic material,' that if verse[2] is to remain a living thing it must be occupied, when it likes, with the whole of [a] poet's life and experience as it was with Villon and Herrick and Burns,[3] for although exalted verse may be the highest it cannot keep its power unless there is more essentially vital verse — not necessarily written by the same man — at the side of it.[4]

You will gather that I am most interested now in my grimer verses, and the ballads, (which are from actual life.)

There is a funny coincidence about the Curse[5] you will find among them;- the lady in question has since been overtaken with unnamable disasters. That is between ourselves.

Excuse this disjointed production — I cant write letters with a typewriter — and please let me know your opinion as soon as you can. If I print them I might put some of my Petrarch translations into the book also, to make it a little less thin.

Yours ever
J. M. Synge

TS (MS closing and signature), Berg. *TB*, 291

1 The MS draft JMS preserved (TCD; published in *Poems*, xv–xvi) differs considerably from the typed letter sent to Yeats. At this point JMS added ⟨and some of them I would not like to destroy⟩ There are a few of them at least that I would not like to destroy.'

2 MS draft adds 'even lyrical verse'.

3 MS draft reads 'with Villon, and Shakespears songs, and with Herrick and Burns'.

4 MS draft adds: 'as ecclesiastical architecture cannot remain fine, when domestic archicture is debased. Victor Hugo and Browning tried in a way to get life into verse but they were without humour — which is the essentialy poetic quality in what I call vital verse'.

5 Cf. p. 170, n. 1.

To MOLLY ALLGOOD

[Glendalough House, Glenageary]
Wednesday Sept 9th/08

Dearest

Your letter came last night, just in time to save you from another scolding! Nish. I got a letter from Yeats yesterday morning to say that some of the poems were *very fine*, (no less) and ask me to go in today to talk about them[1] so, I am going in after dinner. I may write to you a line tonight to fix something for tomorrow — no I think I wont the weather is so bad. Perhaps Friday will be better.

I was very much tickled by your story about Sally and the curse. I was sure it would 'fetch' Yeats. I wonder what he will advise. I would not be surprized if he still wants to put me off publishing them for the present. We'll see.

My mother goes into our little room now for a while in the afternoon, and she seems a little better   Still she is so unwell we are getting another doctor down from Dublin for a consultation tomorrow or next day I think.

I was in Dalkey Park[2] the last two evenings from 5 to 6 and it was so bright and wild and magnificent over the sea it almost reminded me of the West. You must come there some evening. I have decided to put my Wicklow and Kerry stuff into one book and publish it as soon as I can, though there is a good deal of work to do on it still. I have typed three pages this morning and I feel rather tired. It is another Wicklow for the Manchester Guardian and then for the book afterwards.[3] I wish I could get you down to type for me we'd have the book done in no time. You say no more about your head so I suppose it is all right. Isn't this what you call a stupid letter?

Your old T.

MS, TCD. *LM,* 275

1 Yeats's note of 'Monday' (7 Sept 1908) is at TCD; see *TB*, 292.

2 Sorrento Park, Dalkey.

3 'In Wicklow. On the Road', *Manchester Guardian*, 10 Dec 1908 (*Prose,* 213-15).

To MOLLY ALLGOOD

Glendalough House [Glenageary]
Sept ? [10] 1908

Dearest Pigeen

I hugged myself with delight when I got your offended card this morning, Nish! Miss Changlingette Miss Changlingeen, how do you like being neglected the way you neglected me last week? You used to write to me every day and I used to do the same but now you've taken to writing twice a week and Begob if you dont write to me I'll not write to you Nish Nish, *N I S H !*

I'm going up to see Parsons tomorrow and I'll be in Westland Row at 25 *to* three. Will you meet me there and walk up? I dont suppose he'll keep me very long if you like to wait for me in the Museum and then we could have tea. I was with Yeats yesterday after-noon and we had a long talk about the Poems. He is thinking of putting them with Dun Emer after all.[1]

Your O.T.

P.S. My dearest. You have given me a lot of misery, but perhaps what you did was mere carlessness, and if so I suppose my letter hurt you in turn. In that case I am sorry but when you do not write to me how can I know what to say to you.

However in a few days with the help of God we'll be out in the glens again and then we wont be in danger of getting at cross purposes as we are in these accursed letters. Remember always it is because I am so wound up in you that I am so sensitive about all that you do. That is a good symptom isn't it?

Your old T.

MS, TCD. *LM*, 274

1 Yeats apparently persuaded Roberts to allow his sisters' press (see p. 147) to publish JMS's poems first, in a limited edition, before the Maunsel trade edition.

To MOLLY ALLGOOD

[Glendalough House, Glenageary]
Sept 14th 08

Dearest Been

I dont know whether this will get to you tonight or tomorrow, but I must do it now. I am on the edge of a *bad cough* today, and my chest is very sore, but it may not come to much — if I have luck. You'd better take some warm things with you to Galway[1] as its likely your home journey in the night will be very cold. Look round in Galway for lustre jugs or Irish curios — *that are cheap.* When you're going away any where I always feel like God almighty dictating the ten commandments to Moses. However you ought to know my commandments by heart — why do we say by heart and not by liver or kidney? — before this so I'm D/ed if I'll repeat them — N I S H —

I got my poem right last night about midnight when I suppose you were snoring —

every There's snow in ⟨all the⟩ street⟨s⟩ Where I go up and down And there's no man or dog that knows My footstep in the town. I know the shops and men French Jews and Russian Poles For I go walking night and noon To spare my sack of coals.[2] (!)	I wonder if it is right after all? Anyhow its better. Be careful of this MS. and maybe you'll be able to sell it to an American collector for £20 when I'm rotten.

This would be a nice sheet to put up in the Museum over our skulls, bye and bye when we go up to keep Swift and Stella in countinance. Begob I think I'm feverish I'm writing such bosh — and I've no thermometer.

    Didn't we have a good day yesterday. Think of it, Little Heart, and be very wise — Think of me, sweet Kidney, and dont be frivol — How the deuce do you spell it? — lous.

Your O.T.

MS, TCD. *LM,* 276

    1 The company performed in Galway from 16 to 19 Sept 1908 during the Galway Agricultural Exhibition; see *TB,* 288.

    2 See *Poems,* 63 for the final version of this poem as published in the Cuala edition in 1909.

To MOLLY ALLGOOD

[Glendalough House, Glenageary]
Thursday [17] Sept. 08

Dearest

    I was very glad to get your letter this morning — I thought the post had passed and I was getting very cranky, but when I came down there was your letter. My brother-in-law is in Galway today I wonder if you will meet him. I'm sorry to hear of your discomfort, but that was almost to be expected in Exhibition time in a small town in the country. It's not for long anyhow. It is very fine here this morning so I hope it may be the same with you. I've had a bad enough sort of turn but I might have been worse. I haven't been out yet, and I dont think I'll get out today. It is a very great nuisance as it will put off my trip to Germany for a week and so run me in for the cold weather there. I'm afraid you'll never learn to take care of me, little scatter brain; it was folly for me to go and sit by the sea so late on Sunday when I was so bad. This is the first cough I have had since the operation on my neck last year — but now I've started I'll have them all the winter, unless Germany does wonders.

I have a headache still, little Heart, so I cant write you a very nice letter. I mean well as always, and I think about you a great deal. I hope your cold isn't bad, take care of yourself whatever you do. I'm afraid you'll be disappointed at not hearing from me sooner but as usual you gave me no address so I could not write sooner. My mother is still very poorly. I have been working at my Kerry book yesterday and today — it gives me a headache but I must do something. Goodbye and be very good indeed. I'll write to you again tomorrow, to reach you on Saturday, that will be my last to you there. By the way I had a long friendly letter from *Musek* last night![1] He must have heard us in Bray! I think you had better *not* ask Lady G. and W.B.Y. to sign the card, they might think it below their dignity. I can sign with the Co. or send one by myself.

———— ———— ———— ———— ————

———— ———— ————   Your O.T.

MS, TCD. *LM*, 277

1 Mušek's reply of 14 Sept (see p. 184, n. 4) to JMS's letter of 17 Aug 1908 is at TCD.

To MOLLY ALLGOOD

              [Glendalough House, Glenageary]
                     Friday Sept ? [18] 08
Dearest

I got your letter this morning. What a catasrophe about the scenery! I wonder whose fault it was, I can imagine Yeats delight in making his announcements.[1] Which arm of Daussy's did the dog bite? If it was the arm he gave you in London I'll say good dog and God speed you![2]

I haven't been out yet, I'd go today, but it is too wet. I've made my inside sore with the shaking of the coughs, and I feel very wretched. I'm not happy about your poor little nose, you'll have to show it to a doctor at once when you come back.

I dont know whether to laugh or cry over you for expecting me to write to you when you knew you had not given me an address. Did you think that half an hour after you posted your letter a little angel with an air-ship would sail in to Glendalough House to give it to me, and then sail back with my answer?

I'm very lonely and miserable, I've been four long days — this is the fifth — sitting in this room seeing no one God help me! and I'm not really a bit better yet.

You dont tell me much about your doings. I wonder if my brother-in-law and nephew[3] got beds yesterday they went down in the after noon. Oh be — — I'm very flat. Take care of yourself and be very good on your return journey I wonder if you'll have my people in the same train. If I can I'll write you a little note to meet you in Dublin and then on Monday thank God I'll see you.

Your ol T.

MS, TCD. *LM*, 278

1 The stage of the makeshift theatre in Galway, converted from a store, was too small for the scenery, so had to be draped with hessian hangings at the last minute.

2 J. M. Kerrigan, in an unpublished memoir, recalls, 'for a man of his experience and literary attitude towards life [he was] *extraordinarily conventional.* He met me one day on the Dublin mountains linking a girl & was amazed to learn I was not engaged to her.' (University of Victoria) See I. 178–80, 332.

3 His younger nephew, E. M. Stephens, who records in his unpublished 'Life' (MS, TCD) attending the Galway performances with his father on 18 Sept 1908.

To STEPHEN MacKENNA

Glendalough Hous | Kingstown
Friday [18 September 1908]

Dear MacKenna

I dont know how it is I've never got to see you! ⟨since⟩ — first Yeats and Lady G. were up and I had to see them, then the weather was bad and finally I've got knocked up with a cold and I've been in the house all this week.

Miss O'Neill was pleased and obliged that you and Madame asked her to visit your domain and we hoped to go long ago, but we couldn't fit it in. She is in Galway this week I hope next week we'll look you up Whenever I am well enough from taking cold I go to *Germany* for a month and then I hope come back to work. My medical man put me off the Mediteranean as he says the boat is rather small with stuffy cabin, and a possibility of sea sickness which might rend my inwards.

What have you done with Bullen?[1] Since I saw you I laid my verses before Yeats with many qualms, he highly approves, however, and I'm to publish them forthwith.[2] I told him you were here and writing leaders for Freeman, 'Oh' says he "that accounts for the extraordinary improvement I have seen lately in their articles." My compliments to Madame

Yours J. M. Synge

MS, Lockwood

   [1] MacKenna was negotiating with A. H. Bullen to publish a 'sample Christmas card' from his translation of Plotinus on the Beautiful.

   [2] MacKenna replied, 'Well I was sure the poems would stand the test though why you should test 'em I know not: I shall be glad to see you doing all the round poetry drama impressions — you'll end up in a novel — and then will come the essays I want to see. I suppose the impressions have the essay touch too, but then I haven't read them since I knew their incubation in Paris: I will read them soon however to see.' (Undated, TCD)

To MOLLY ALLGOOD

[Glendalough House, Glenageary]
Saturday Sept ?[19]/08

Dearest

I'm afraid I cant wait till Monday, so if you feel quite rested come down by the quarter to three tomorrow (Sunday) and come to the house. If you'd rather stay quiet of course do so and come to me on Monday instead, by the same train. I wont expect you tomorrow unless you come by that train.

Your letter this morning was a very charming one — I laughed till I coughed at the sentence you over-heard it was *magnificent*.

I was out a little yesterday and a little this morning but I dont feel very much the better yet. It is very trying. I am glad the weather is mild so that you will not be frozen ⟨tomorrow⟩ tonight night coming home.

I dont seem to have much to say today, except that I'll be in great spirits and joy to see you again. I wish I was there to hear Mac's speech![1] It would be a treat. Did Henderson stay with you all the time?

Your O.T.

MS, TCD. *LM*, 281

   [1] At the closing performance in Galway on 19 Sept Sara Allgood and 'Arthur

Sinclair' (F. Q. McDonnell), as leading actress and actor of the company, were presented with gold medals by Mrs Shawe-Taylor on behalf of the Exhibition Executive.

To W. K. MAGEE[1]

Glendalough Ho[use, Glenageary]
Tuesday [22 September 1908]

Dear Magee

When I heard the rain on Sunday I didn't think you'd come. My cold hangs on so much that there is no chance of my getting away before Sunday so I'd be very charmed to see you and Best then if that evening would suit you.[2] I'm here every evening and would be always delighted if [you] could come.

Yours
J. M. Synge

MS, Kain

1 William Kirkpatrick Magee, 'John Eglinton' (1868–1961; see I. 85), essayist and assistant librarian of the National Library and editor with F. J. Ryan of *Dana* (1904–5). E. H. Synge was convinced, as he wrote in a letter to Magee (Kain), that JMS included the reference to 'Red Shawn Magee' in his poem 'Danny', in retaliation for his article on Anatole France being rejected for *Dana* (see I. 87).

2 Richard Irvine Best (1872–1959; see I. 85), Irish scholar and bibliographer, was at this time an assistant director of the National Library. Magee had written to JMS on 20 Sept 1908 (TCD) to put off his visit until Wednesday evening when he would try to get Best to go with him.

To MOLLY ALLGOOD

Glendalough House [Glenageary]
Sept 24/08

Dearest

I got your letter last night, and the telegram came all right. I dont know who the goodman is who is so anxious to see me. I'm getting better I think by degrees, so I need not go to Parsons. I got a thermometer and my temperature is all right so I needn't bother. I hope to get away to Germany about the first of Oct. Will you come down tomorrow (Friday) by *the quarter to three?* If you'll do some typing for me I'll pay half your train, Nish, isn't that generosity? Joking apart it is a pity not to see each other when I'm going away so soon. I had Jack Yeats with me all the afternoon yesterday — It was a very heavy day and we both seemed to find it rather hard to keep up a flow of conversation. It isn't easy when you're not very well to be suddenly confronted with a man you haven't seen for a year or so. Still I was very glad to see him, and I think he was glad too.

I have no other news, except that I have nearly finished an Article for the Manchester Guardian — It will go off today or tomorrow I hope.[1] If you can and will come tomorrow you needn't write, but if you *cant* please send me a line tonight or BEFORE[2] 11 in the morning. I hope you'll come. It is very bright and sunny here today I wish you were here

Your O.T.

MS, TCD. *LM*, 282

---

[1] 'In Wicklow. On the Road' (see p. 196) was not acknowledged by C. P. Scott until 6 Dec 1908 (TCD).
[2] Underlined four times.

To MOLLY ALLGOOD

Glendalough [House, Glenageary]
Saturday [26 September 1908]

Dearest

I got another wire from that wretched man this morning at 7.30 asking me to supper with him tonight at 11 in the Shelbourne.[1] I wrote to say that I could not go, but I would lunch with him tomorrow if he liked but that I was only free till *2.30*. So *if* I go (— I will not go unless I hear in the morning —) I may be in your train. If I should miss it — by any chance you had better come on and wait here, or would you rather come by the three to make sure. If I go to the beast I'll go down again as soon as ever I can you may be sure of that. If he sees me to the station you needn't be alarmed he wont be coming here I told him I couldn't have him as my mother is ill. D— D— D— him. I am much better today. How are you Isn't this a scragly note.

Your old
T.

MS, TCD. *LM*, 282

---

[1] Among JMS's papers is a telegram from 'Ambrent' (unidentified): 'Lunch off Please come supper eleven' (TCD)

To DUDLEY DIGGES[1]

Glendalough House | Kings town | Co Dublin
Sept 26th/08

DUPLICATE
Dudley Digges Esq
Dear Sir; — I am sorry for delay — which was unavoidable — in answering yours of the 8th Inst.[2]

I am much obliged for your suggestion about "Riders to the Sea", For a number of reasons, however, I do not wish to have it produced in America — in two or three years time it may be different.

I am glad to be able to tell you that I am nearly re[co]vored from my late illness, and hope soon to be at work again.

With best wishes

Yours sincerely
J. M. Synge

MS copy, TCD

1 J. Dudley Digges (1879–1947), who began his acting career with W. G. Fay's original Comedy Combination, resigned in 1903 from the Irish National Theatre Society over the production of *The Shadow of the Glen* (see I. 62). He went to the United States in April 1904 to perform at the St. Louis Exhibition, and remained to become one of the principal members of the Theatre Guild, from its foundation in 1919 performing more than 3,500 times; he served as vice president of Actors Equity, and in 1939 was awarded the gold medal of the American Irish Historical Society. His memories of the early theatre are published in Fay and Carswell, *The Fays of the Abbey Theatre*, 68–70.

2 Writing on 8 Sept 1908 from the Garrick Theatre, New York, Digges explained that he was performing under Charles Frohman's management, 'and would be glad to bring the play [*Riders*] to his notice if I see a good opening for it at any time' (TCD).

To MOLLY ALLGOOD

[Glendalough House, Glenageary]
2.X.08

Dearest
I am not going to the Abbey today[1] as I have been in town every day since Sunday and I think it is time to take a good day's rest — though I am feeling well enough. I have got all my bills in now £114. or thereabouts, God help me. Parsons £20. Elpis £37. and Sir Charles £57.

I handed over the MS. of my poems to Yeats yesterday so I hope that will go all right now. I did one new poem — that is partly *your* work — that he says is *Magnificent*

I asked if I got sick and died would you
With my black funeral go walking too,
If you'd stand close to hear them talk and pray
While I'm let down in that steep bank of clay.
And, No, you said, for if you saw a crew
Of living idiots, pressing round that new
Oak-Coffin — they alive, I dead beneath
That board — you'd rave and rend them with your teeth.[2]

By the way did you ask about Marine Lodge[3] and what did they tell you. I think they ought to give it to me for nothing, because after we have lived there and written verses about it, it will become so famous that they'll be able to sell it to an American for £50,000. Did you tell them that? I'll be in town tomorrow and I'll see you then if I can. In any case I'll see you on Sunday of course.

Write me a line today if you can.

Your O.T.

MS, AS. *LM*, 283

1 The new season began on 1 Oct 1908 with the first production of *The Suburban Groove* (W. F. Casey) and *The Piper* (Norreys Connell).
2 Yeats at first assumed that something he had said to JMS had suggested the poem, but later Molly told him, 'He used often to joke about death with me. One day he said, "Will you go to my funeral?" and I said, "No, for I could not bear to see you dead and others living on"' (Yeats, *Memoirs*, 202, 216). An earlier version in JMS's notebook (TCD) is dated 28.9.08; see *Poems*, 64 for the final version published in the Cuala edition, 1909.
3 Thom's 1907 Dublin directory lists a Marino Lodge in Killiney.

To MOLLY ALLGOOD

Glendalough [House, Glenageary]
[5][1] Oct [1908]

Dearest Child

This is a little line to bid you goodbye. It is ten o'clock and I'm very tired, with fussing and packing. I was in town this morning till the 1.30. train Then I got back here and did some packing. Then out comes Roberts — though I had just left him — over some business about the poems, then I do some more packing then at 6 out comes Colum[2] and settles down to talk, and stays till eight. Then I pack more — Isn't this a model of a sentimental lover's goodbye letter? I'm too tired to write. Thats what it is. I am writting with my new fountain pen. God help me I feel down and lonely going off this way. Good bye sweet Heart be very good.

T.

MS, TCD. *LM*, 284

1 Misdated 8th Oct.
2 Padraic Colum (1881–1972; see I. 70), poet, playwright, short-story writer and biographer, one-time member of W. G. Fay's company before joining the nationalist seceders in 1906.

To MOLLY ALLGOOD

CITY OF DUBLIN STEAM PACKET COMPANY
ROYAL MAIL STEAMER "LEINSTER"
[6 October 1908]

Dearest

Here I am on the boat. We are near Holy Head now so I've run down to write you a line. It is rolling "a bit" so I cant write very much. I feel very well — the sea has been clear and calm couldn't have been better.

Write me a letter with nothing *very* confident[ial] for fear of accidents to address on other page

c/o Fraulein von Eicken
Oberwerth
Coblence
Germany

I'm thinking of you a lot.

Your old T

MS, TCD. *LM,* 284

To MOLLY ALLGOOD

London. Wed[nesd]ay | evening. Oct 7th/08

Dearest

I am just beginning to pack up for my start to Germany at 8.35 tonight. I was very tired when I got here last night — I was turned away from three hotels — so I had to go to a sort of Boarding House. I have taken a very quiet day today however and I feel fairly fit again. I sat all the afternoon on a chair in Hyde Park and then had tea in the Express Tea Shop where I went with you last year. So I've been thinking of you a great deal. I hope this trip will set me up — I am only beginning to realize what a wreck this business has left me. However I wont be downcast — though it has been a depressing sort of day sitting about here by myself. I hope I shall find a letter from you when I get to Germany — I must stop now. I may have to post this letter without a stamp. Will you think it worth /2d?

Your old Wreck.

MS, TCD. *LM,* 285

To MOLLY ALLGOOD
c/o Fraulein von Eicken | Oberwerth | Coblence | Germany
Thursday | Oct 8th?/08

Dearest Child

I have got safely to my journey's end, and found the letter you wrote to Glendalough House waiting for me. You poor little animal to be making yourself unhappy because I did not run in to the Abbey in the Middle of a Rehearsal for an unsatisfactory half minute!!! When am I to have a letter from you to me here? I have been thinking about you to no end all this journey God bless your poor little soul. This place is a good deal changed but ⟨not⟩ very pleasant still

I have been out by the Rhine till six o'clock, — it was very clear and beautiful. I hope this will make a man of me again. As soon as ever I got into the train last night I felt better, and I got on as well as possible on the journey I got here a little after two this afternoon it was very hot the last part of the way and through a very uninteresting country

Oh how I hope I'll soon get back to you as well as ever my own little treasure of the world. Write me a really nice letter please.

Your J.M.S.

MS, Texas. *LM*, 285

To MOLLY ALLGOOD
[Oberwerth, Koblenz]
Friday [9 October 1908]

Dear Child

There is no letter for me this morning — it is very strange that you have not sent me [a] line — I gave you this address in time surely.

I'm sitting ⟨down⟩ by the Rhine now about ten o'clock. I wish I could make you see it ⟨all⟩. The river is so wide the people look quite small on the oposite bank, and big⟨ish⟩ steamers are going up and down.⟨Here⟩ It is often very foggy in the morning — it is so now — and then about 12 or 11 the sun comes out and it is a beautiful day. At the other side of the Rhine I can ⟨just⟩ see masses of trees, with bits of hilly vineyard behind them, and clumps of houses — ugly houses, yet quaint and German, in a way, — ⟨lower down⟩ —

Now ⟨I see⟩ a whole bevy of boats and steamers are coming up out of the fog on my left, and the sun is beginning to glitter in an extraordinary way on the water under the oposite ⟨bank⟩ side. The Rhine is ⟨usually⟩ a wide steady sweep of water, but when steamers pass waves begin curling ⟨and nestling under my feet⟩ up the bank.

A little steamer has just galloped by — Police boat No VII. on it. Now a big tug with two funnels is coming up & towing a string of ⟨big⟩ barges ⟨that following⟩ nearly a quarter of a mile long — two little fellows with mops are leaning over the edge of the tug washing her sides. The barges all have little houses on the lower end of the deck, and you can see the women smacking their children just as if they were on land. It is all ⟨?singularity⟩ interesting and unlike what we are accustomed to. Does this sort of stuff bore you Eh? If it does mind you tell me. I must wander on now I'm ⟨a⟩ getting a coldness where I'm sitting on the stones.

10.X.08 | Saturday

Dearest

Your little note of the 7th has reached me this morning — it was a wee bit long coming and I was getting uneasy; dont bother reading all the blather on the back of this[1]   I wanted to show you this place and I haven't brought it off. Its not easy; when I start describing anything I feel as if I was writting an article and then I get impersonal, and then its a ⟨bloody⟩ bad letter — ⟨That's personal anyhow. Nish!⟩

Evening

I've been knocking round here all day — it's wonderful autumn weather — and lying under the accasias. The last half hour I've been sitting out on the balcony in the dark wondering what you were at, and if you missed me ⟨much⟩ — I felt desolate enough.

Yesterday at dinner one of the von Eickens plumped out that Mrs Vanston[2] had told them that I was engaged to an actress — and then they popped out their eight heads to see what I'd say. So I told them the story and now they know all about you. Of course I'd have told them in any case. The married sister and her daughter have been here for the last couple of days and when they were going away the good lady made me a long speech of congratulations and good wishes for my marriage and so on, so on, so on! So you see you aren't forgotten.

All the von Eickens are very kind — by the way its Fräulein — not *Fraw* — but poor things they are most of them getting old. My friend is nice still[3] but you needn't be uneasy, I am beginning to count the days till I can get back to you. I am still a little knocked up from that journey. I wonder are you writting me long letters too get a little book like this and write in it whenever you've a little time. That will be good for both of us. Now I must wash my hands and get ready for supper. I wish you could have seen that German girl — not a bit pretty — she was something quite different from anything I've ever seen. Her mother had admirable gestures — I think you could learn a great deal here on the Continent. I'll never go abroad again without you. Nish!

Sunday

No letter today — one little hurried line only the six days I am out of Ireland   You must write to me better than that. I am dissappointed.

I suppose you'll get this on Tuesday — this is my 4th letter to you since I left Kingstown   I wonder if you have got them all, one on the boat, one in London and two here. I hope you are well and taking care of yourself.

Your old T.M.S.

MS, Texas. *LM*, 286

1 This and the following letter (12 Oct 1908) are written on the leaves of a small notebook similar to the one JMS had used the previous year in Kerry.
2 Perhaps the wife of John S. B. Vanston, solicitor and commissioner for oaths whose office was at 31 Abbey Street Lower, several doors down from the Abbey Theatre. A postcard from Emma von Eicken, 22 Aug 1908 (TCD) sent greetings in Irish from 'J. Vanston'.
3 Six von Eicken sisters (Emma, Claire Hedwig, Maria, Thekla, and Valeska; see I. 8) ran the guest house at Oberwerth. The married sister was Augusta, her daughter Ruth. Valeska von Eicken (1863–*c.* 1940), had been JMS's confidante during his years in Germany.

To MOLLY ALLGOOD

[Oberwerth, Koblenz]
Monday [12 October 1908]¹

My dearest Heart.

I got your little letter this morning and it nearly wrung my poor guts out with delight. I cant tell you how I liked it, you little blasted Changling!

I have come away in to the woods this morning by myself. It is inconceivably wonderful — so still my breath sounds like a fog-horn, and nothing but masses of trees everywhere. Towards the sun it is misty and silvery, and looking away from the sun it is all gold and green. I have been wandering on for an hour squating down on every seat I came to (every quarter of a mile or so) to rest my poor ripped belly. The weather couldn't be better. Now I've come out of the trees into the sun on a big cliff over the Rhine, and I'm sitting in front of a Restaurant with a bottle of beer. It is perfectly blue and sunny over head, but there is fog down on the river so that I can not see the steamers.

— I think this knocking about in the woods may help me with Deirdre in a way. I have written no more verses since I came here. I am not alone enough for one thing and for another the confusion of images one gets travelling about does not help one to write.[2] A friend of the von Eickens, that I used [to] know, is an actress now and has played some good parts — leading female in 'the Red Robe'[3] for instance. They tell me she only gets £6 a month and has to buy *all* her costumes out of her salary. How would you like that, you little Been!

How are your lessons with George[4] getting on, or was that *all talk*? I wonder if you are able to read this stuff that I scribbl down so from one minute to another? On Saturday night a friend of the von Es. sent in a present of a great dish of oysters. They wanted me to have some, but like a wise man I didn't, glory be to God, for the family began to pewk yesterday and nearly split themselves! N.B. *Dont eat oysters*!

Evening

I am down by the Rhine and the lights are coming out all along the banks. When I think of you and all the nice things you've written to me I get a ripple of delight all through me. I'm reading a play of Sudermann's — the author of Teja — now but it isn't very much good.[5]

⟨Wednesday⟩ Tuesday 13.X.08

I'm just going off to the town of Coblence — we are outside — to buy some books so good morning to you meanwhile. How are you getting on with the Galleries? It is a week today since I left Kingstown so a *quarter* of my time is over. The pewking ladies are better again today. It is funny when I'm down by the Rhine all the signs the people make to me from the barges going by. Yesterday there was a woman beating a cushion, and when she saw me lying on the stones she held it up and patted it as much as to say — Would you like that to put under yourself! Another girl waved her bowl of soup at me. So my own little heart good bye till the next time. By the way dont say by*e* the way.

Your old T.   J.M.S.

MS, Texas. *LM*, 288

---

1 Molly has written the date at the top of the letter.

2 'He was very anxious for impressions to sink in before they had become blurred by other later impressions. I once asked him to go for a walk with me and on his demurring reminded him that he had enjoyed this walk a few days previously. [He explained that] . . . he wished to make his impressions of the previous day more his own and that the aspect of the place might be different to-day and would hinder him.' (Nicholas Grene and Ann Saddlemyer, 'Stephen MacKenna on Synge: A Lost Memoir', *Irish University Review*, vol. 12, no. 2 [Autumn 1982], 149)

3 *La Robe Rouge* (1900), a satire on the law by Eugène Brieux.

4 Probably Molly's favourite brother, at this time an ardent nationalist; he was killed in the war, in 1915.

5 Hermann Sudermann (1857–1928) wrote six full-length plays in addition to his one-act plays, of which *Teja* had been produced by the Abbey in Lady Gregory's translation. *Die Heimat* (1893), translated as *Magda* and performed by Mrs Patrick Campbell among others, was the play of his best known in English.

To MOLLY ALLGOOD
c/o Fraulein von Eicken | Oberwerth | Coblence
Wednesday | 14/X.08

Dearest Herzchen (little heart)

I suppose I'll hear from you tomorrow — and of course you'll tell me all about the Galleries you've been to! I'm getting on well I think on the whole. Yesterday I went into Coblence and ordered books Walter von der Vogelweide, and Hans Sachs — two old German poets — I want to do some translations from them if it goes, like the ones I did of Petrarch and Villon.[1] Today I took a long walk into the woods to a bierhouse and drank my bottle of beer. I'm beginning to wish I was home again. Do you? Eh? I've just been down on the Rhine in the twilight, with a big bat gadding about me, and partridges making a great stir in the accasias. Do you know what accasias are? If you dont go to Glasnevin and look in the garden[2] one of the men would show them to you. I lie under them here half the day. I am more alone now as my novelty has worn off — they [are] still very good and kind. They are always enquiring about you. Now we'll see what tomorrow's post brings —

Thursday evening

No letter today, so I was a little dissappointed I went out this morning to a place called Rhens one of the oldest little town[s] on the Rhine, with little [houses] exactly as they were in the time of Aucassin and Nicolette — or a couple of centuries later. I'll try and get you some photos before I go back. I was too tired when I got there to do more than go into a Wirthhaus and drink a bottle of beer which cost /1½d. On my way out in the tram — the tram took me half way — they were gathering the grapes along the Rhine for the wine making   In one place there was a big barrel of grapes on the side of the road, so they stopped the electric tram, and the conductor and driver rushed over and came back with their hands full of grapes, and gave me a big bunch — I was [the] only passenger. We have jam here made of *our* little purple grapes — the frocauns — its great stuff. There are no heathy mountains here but they grow in the woods. I'm looking forward to hearing all about your gallery-visits. I suppose you play the 'Squeal' for the first time tonight.[3] I wonder how it'll go. I wish I was *home*. Nish! Nish.

Friday morning.

No letter! You wrote to me last Saturday the letter which I got on Monday. Now Sunday Monday, Tuesday, Wednesday you have not written — though I have been writing to you so much   I am profoundly hurt and uneasy. — I came skipping down the stairs today absolutely certain that you would have written, but instead I only had the news that my mother is not getting on well so my good spirits are gone —

Saturday.

Still no letter — It is a fortnight tomorrow since I saw you and, you have written me only one line before I started and then one letter? I cannot conceive what has happened. I am ill and giddy with anxiety. ⟨In the two years we have known each other you *never* did anything like that before.⟩ If you are ill *get Sally to write. If I do not hear by return of post* I will go home.

J.M.S.

c/o Fraulein von Eicken | Oberwerth | Coblence. Germany.
[*Scribbled at top of letter*]
Can you have made any mistake with. Great Christ I am sick with wretch[ed]ness.

MSS, ('I suppose I'll hear . . . and the conductor') AS; ('and driver . . . go home') TCD. *LM,* 289

---

1 The Cuala edition of JMS's *Poems and Translations* included two translations from the French of François Villon (b. 1431) and eight sonnets from the Italian of Petrarch (Francesco Petrarca, 1304–74); for the 1910 Maunsel edition Yeats selected four further sonnets from Petrarch, to which Robin Skelton added five more for the Dolmen edition of *Poems and Translations* (1961). Yeats also selected one translation from the German of Walther von der Vogelweide (*fl.* 1200) for the 1910 edition; the 'Judaslied' published in 1961 may be from the German of Hans Sachs (1494–1576), the shoemaker of Nuremberg.

2 The Botanic Gardens of the Royal Dublin Society, Glasnevin.

3 The first title for Thomas MacDonagh's *When the Dawn Is Come*, produced 15 Oct 1908, was 'The Sequel'.

To MOLLY ALLGOOD
c/o Fraulein von Eicken | Oberwerth | Coblence
20/X/08

My dearest Child

I was very much relieved to get your letter on Sunday — you shouldn't have left so long.

I am very sad tonight as I have just got very bad news of my poor old mother — she is much worse I am afraid — if she does not soon get better I shall have no one in the world but you, — one's brothers and sisters though mine could not be kinder — are never the same as one's mother or one's wife. I have a lump in my throat as I am writting — She is in bed again now too weak to read or write, Her life is little happiness to her now and yet one cannot bear the idea of not having her with us any more. If she gets worse I will go home, perhaps, very soon   I do not like to think of her all by herself in the house.

Oct 21st.

Your letter has just come. We wont quarrel about the number of your letters — at any rate you left me six days without news — and you said yourself in ⟨that⟩ your last that you were *"a beast"* to have left me so long. I dont think any of your letters have gone astray as you have acknowledged all mine date by date, — one from my brother however *has* gone astray. I think I had better send you this today as I want you to know what I tell you in it. You mustn't think I'm crusty because its so short, I'm not but its too cold to write in my room and I have to go out early. I sent you a card yesterday to acknowledge the Sunday letter. I cannot find any very interesting cards. Is Yeats back in Dublin yet? A thousand blessings, write soon again, and so will I. I had asthma the last two nights and I'm rather knocked up.

Your old T.M.S.[1]

MS, Texas. *LM*, 291

1 Molly has written at the top of this letter 'answered 24.X.08'.

To MOLLY ALLGOOD

[Oberwerth] Coblence etc.
23/X/08

Dearest Child

I have just got your letter of the 21st. It came very quickly, it is stamped Dublin 5 A.M. 22nd Coblence 4 P.M. 23rd and I have got it at 5. I am very sorry my card didn't please you. I thought that as I had scolded you, you would like to know I had got your letter and I thought the Irish would do as Tom[1] could read it. He cant know much Irish as there is quite a different word for the cold one gets. I wrote that it was cold here. I got the card in Coblence and wrote it on a seat by the Rhine and sent it off —

I hope you are quite well again. I am uneasy about you, so you must write again by return and tell me how you are. I wrote you a letter on Wednesday too, I suppose you have got it by this. I have had no further news of my mother I shall probably hear tomorrow morning before I post this. I feel lonely and sad here now and I am counting the days to get home. At the latest I go home, all being well, on Thursday week so I have only about 12 more days here. I think I am much better, and I can walk quite a good deal. The weather has been very cold, but with bright, sometimes magnificently bright, sunshine. Yesterday I went a bit up the Rhine to where another river the Lahn joins in, and I sat on a seat in the sunshine oposite a little hill with a big mediaeval castle on it, and read a modern German translation of the Tristram and Isold that you read the other day. The English version is very much cut down, and things the good lady[2] didn't approve of are left out. Today I went to Rhens — the little old town again — it is extraordinarily quaint. There are houses that were built in 1400, with ordinary peasant people living in them still. I wish I could get some photos of them, I'll try tomorrow.

Saturday 24th

I have heard from my sister this morning that my mother is a little better again, so I am in better spirits. Dont *you* get ill now, and be sure you write to me by return to say how you are.

It is still bright and cold here. This morning I am going into Coblence to get stamps and to see if I can find any interesting postcards for you. I hope you feel very penitent for having scolded me for sending you the picture p'card as a little joke for you, you little Been!

I got a post card from Lebeau this morning from Canada[3] — he is still very lonely and unhappy   I must write to him soon. Good God I'm freezing I'll die of cold if I dont go out soon and get warm. I'm writing in my room with the double window wide open and the frost coming in. There is a lovely view, by the way, from this window of a queer old German farm first, and then of the Rhine hills with woods on them. If you were here we'd have great times but by myself, it's no fun. I'm going to the Market in Coblence this morning to look at the peasants etc.

Now be sure you write a nice and a long letter, little Been, to cheer me up again. In twelve days — damn them — I'll be on my way back to you. So now take care of yourself goodby dearest

J.M.S.

MS, TCD. *LM,* 292

1 One of Molly's younger brothers; see p. 173.
2 Probably Jessie L. Weston, whose translation of von Strassburg's *The Story of Tristan and Iseult* JMS read in Elpis in June 1908; see p. 157.
3 Written 12 Oct 1908 (TCD).

To MOLLY ALLGOOD

[Oberwerth] Coblence
Monday [26 October 1908]

Dearest Heart

I wrote a long cheerful letter to you yesterday and this morning[1] but I do not care to send it to you tonight as I have just got the bad news that you have probably heard. When I came in from my walk today one of the von Eickens came up to my room to say that a telegram had just come to say that my poor mother had passed away.[2] I am hardly able to realise it. I wish I had you near me, now I have you to live for only. The von Eickens are exceedingly kind. Write to me here again when you get this — I cannot write much, I am very sad when I think of all my life and how endlessly kind and good she has been to me.

Yours, my own heart,
J.M.S.

MS, AS. *LM*, 294

1 i.e. the letter begun on Sunday, 25 Oct 1908, and continued the following morning; see pp. 215-16.

2 Robert Synge's telegram read, 'Mother has passed away funeral Thursday dont come unless strong enough for journey'; a second telegram the same day read 'You ought not to come in that case funeral Wednesday reply Summerville' (both TCD).

To MOLLY ALLGOOD

[Oberwerth] Coblence
SUNDAY 25/X/08

Dearest Child.

I am sitting up in my little room reading Walter von der Vogel-weide and waiting for supper. I wonder what you're at! This has been a *diabolical* day, cold raw and wet, with snow in the morning — the first bad day since I left home. It reminded me of the speech in the Well of the Saints about the Almighty God looking out on the world bad days etc etc.[1] I'm lonesome, it is absolutely silent up here except for an odd whiff of piano. The man who is playing is the landlord of Oberwerth — a baron — and lives in a big house stuck on to this one. He was married a long time ago and had one daughter, then he got tired of his wife, and when I was here last she was a faded poor creature who used to go streeling about by herself. The next thing was he fell in love with one of his farm girls and 'kept' her in Coblence. The wife heard of it and went off to Vienna and sent for the Baron. He went to her, and she asked him would he break off his connection. He said divel a bit, and came back here! The next day he got a telegram to say his wife had poisoned herself. He put the girl into a convent for six months and then married her. Now she is the lady baroness going about in furs and furbelows, and the men she used to make hay with are still working in the yard. The baron is cut by everyone and shuts himself up and plays the piano and composes all day. He is grey haired now, but a fine musician. They have three children — fine ones too.

Monday morning

I have just got your letter written on Saturday, and also a letter from my brother to say that my mother is still a little better. She is quite too ill to see anyone so she could not see you if you called, but you can call and enquire if you like. She is so ill I dont suppose they would even tell her you'd been there. So you have got a house with a nice view! I'm very glad you are leaving Mary Street but I hope you wont be very long in the new place.[2] How are you, I am nervous now when I hear of you getting unwell in yourside after all I have gone through myself. My asthma is gone again, but I'm a little queer inside still. What a bit of news about old Yeats![3]

I did *not* know about Sally — It must have happened since I left and I have not heard from the Directors — I forgot as a matter of fact to give them my address. I am sorry you think Sally a fool for doing what is honorable.[4] I can only hope you wrote that without thinking, I'd like to give you a good scolding but I'll let you off as you have been ill. Please tell Yeats that I am going home on Thursday week — the time is coming near at last thank God. I'm weary to death of being here though they are all very kind. It is very foggy again today but not so cold as it has been.

Wednesday evening

Dearest Child.

I have had two very sad days since I wrote to you, but I am trying to be cheerful again, and to think happily of my poor old mother as I know she would have wished. She was 73. or 74 I think and unless people are exceptionally robust — which she never was — life after that age is mere fatigue and suffering. She often said she would rather die with all her faculties still clear than drag on into real old age. I wonder how you are. I am a little uneasy as I wrote on Saturday and asked you to write by return but you haven't. Do take good care of yourself — remember you are the whole world to me now. I wonder if you heard the sad news before my letter came to you. It must have been in the Irish Times on Tuesday and I should think some of you must have heard of it. My going home now will be very sad — I can hardly bear to think of going to Glendalough

House she was always so delighted to see me when I came back from a journey — I cant go on.

Thursday morning

I expected a letter from you this morning — perhaps you think I am on my way home. I shall get a letter from my brother tomorrow, and then I will let you know what day I go home. I may stay on here for the week my health is now all important. Do be careful of yourself

Your J.M.S.
Thursday

N.B. This is the letter I had written to you before I got the bad news when I thought all was going so well.

MS, TCD. *LM*, 294

---

1 'I do be thinking it should be a hard thing for the Almighty God to be looking on the world bad days, and on men the like of yourself walking around on it, and they slipping each way in the muck' (*The Well of the Saints*, Act II, Martin Doul to Timmy the Smith; *Plays*, Book I, 105).

2 Sara Allgood had taken a house at 2 Vincent Terrace, Glasnevin, according to a letter from her to Joseph Holloway, 22 Oct 1908 (NLI); presumably the whole family moved with her.

3 Rumours reached Dublin that J. B. Yeats was planning to marry 'a rich American widow' (Murphy, *Prodigal Father*, 344).

4 Apparently Sally had asked permission of the directors before negotiating a contract with Mrs Pat Campbell to perform in two of her productions at the New Theatre in London; see below, p. 222, n. 1.

To MOLLY ALLGOOD

[Oberwerth, Koblenz]
Friday [30 October 1908]

My dearest Treasure

I must just write you a line to thank you for your little letter and to tell you what an inexpressible comfort it is to me. You could not have written anything more tender or beautiful.

I am going to stay on here till Thursday so please write to me again. I do not know whether I shall go back to Glendalough House or to Silchester. My poor sister has not written to me yet. I had a kind letter from my brother this morning.

I am doing my best to be cheerful, and to pick up my health for your sake and mine.

Yours forever
J.M.S.

MS, TCD. *LM*, 296

To HENRI LEBEAU[1]

[Oberwerth, Koblenz]
[2 November 1908]

. . . The day before I came away I signed the agreement with my publishers for an edition of my poems, but they are not likely to be available just yet as they are to come out first I believe in the Dun Emer Press. You remember Dun Emer? I do not know how you will like my verses — I wrote most of them different time[s] — during the last 18 years — when I was ill and unable to do any other work. Yeats thinks highly of them . . . .[2]

MS copy (H. Lebeau) (fragment), TCD

1 Henri (or Henry) Lebeau (see I. 110), who met JMS when travelling in Ireland with the Breton writer Anatole LeBraz from February to May 1905, became a close correspondent of JMS although the two never met again. His article on *The Well of the Saints* in *Revue de l'art dramatique*, 15 Apr 1905 (reprinted in *Dana*, April 1905), prompted Max Meyerfeld to translate the play. Other publications include travel articles and a book, *Otahiti: Au Pays d'éternel Été* (Paris, 1911); a volume of essays on literary figures he had known, mentioned as forthcoming in Bourgeois, *J. M. Synge and the Irish Theatre*, 268, does not appear to have been published. Despite repeated efforts to trace him, nothing further has been discovered about Lebeau; the last record is a letter from him to Molly from London, 17 June [?1910], asking for an interview 'to speak with you of the great friend and artist whose loss has been so severe a shock to me' (AS).

2 Lebeau replied from Montreal on 23 Dec 1908, 'excuse me for having not answered sooner your letter from Coblenz telling me of the unexpected death of your mother . . . . I was gratified to hear that there was (at least last month) a much better prospect for the improvement in your health, since you were at that time again thinking of getting married in a not very remote future' (TCD). The passage printed here has been copied by E. H. Synge on the back of a page of a letter from Agnes Tobin to JMS and headed, 'From a letter of J. M. Synge to Henri Lebeau, written from Coblenz (Germany) on Nov. 2nd, 1908'. According to E. M. Stephens (Stephens MS), Lebeau had sent a copy of the letter to Molly, some time after JMS's death.

To MOLLY ALLGOOD

Coblence
Tuesday Nov 3rd/08

Dearest Heart

I was glad to get your note last night — the one you wrote on Saturday. This is a line merely to tell you that I leave here on Thursday — the day after tomorrow — and stay Friday night in London, so that I get to Kingstown at five o'clock on Saturday. Please write to me to Glendalough House.

I shall write to you on Saturday evening to arrange where to see you on Sunday. I suppose it will be at Glendalough House.

This last week here has been interminable I can hardly sit quiet I am so anxious to be off. It will be very sad going to Glendalough House, still I shall have the great joy of seeing you again.

So — you will not hear again till Sunday morning.

Yours ever and always

J.M.S.

MS, TCD. *LM*, 297

To MOLLY ALLGOOD

MONTAGUE HOTEL,

2 & 3, MONTAGUE STREET, | RUSSELL SQUARE,

LONDON, W.C. Nov 6th 1908

Dearest

I have got as far as London on my way back — and my journey has been satisfactory so far. I have just had breakfast and now I have to loll about and rest myself all day. I left Coblenz at 4 P.M., got to the boat at 11 last night, and reached England at six this morning. The sun rose over low bogey tracts and arms of sea just after the train started. It was indescribably wonderful. We must often get up early and see the sun rise.

I am infinitely glad to be on my way home — though at times a wave of sorrow comes over me that nearly breaks me down. You will get this I suppose on Saturday morning, please write then to say if you can get your dinner early enough on Sunday to come down by the quarter to two! The days are so short now the quarter to three would leave us little time. I think this first day we will be happier out walking than in Glendalough House. I hope I shall find a nice letter to cheer me when I arrive. I can hardly realize how empty the house will seem

Your old T.

MS, TCD. *LM*, 297

To MOLLY ALLGOOD

[Glendalough House, Glenageary]

[7 November 1908]

Dearest

I am home at last. I am inexpressibly sad in this empty house. You had better come by the quarter to *three* tomorrow (Sunday) otherwise you could not dine. I will meet you at Glenageary and we can go to Bray for a while. It is too sad here. I hope you were not hurt by your fall. I am sorry to hear you are not feeling well again.

Till tomorrow — I am too unhappy to write you anything that is not gloomy.

Your O.T.

MS, TCD. *LM*, 298

To MOLLY ALLGOOD

Glendalough House | Kingstown
Nov 9th /08 | five o'clock

Dearest

I have just been in town and ordered my black suit. I have to try it on tomorrow so you will not be able to come and see me here. Will you meet me at *Tara Street* at twenty minutes to three. I am to try on at four so we could take a little turn and then have tea.

It is very dreary coming back to this empty house. Last night when I came home I found I was locked out. The little donkey of a servant had gone out and left both the latch and lock on. She had the lock key and I had the latch key so she couldn't get in either. I found her and got in about half past seven. I wasn't very well last night. I woke up feeling very queer and I thought I was going to get very sea sick, but it didn't come to anything.

My sister told me all about the money affairs today. I am to have £1500 share (at 5%) out of the property, that with what I have will make £110 a year, so — if only my health holds we will be able to get on now. My sister says that apart from my share of the things — I can have all the little things I need for a house if I take one carpets, saucepans linen etc etc. I will not get any money for six months. You need not repeat these particulars. The £1500 is I think really mine, not for my life only, so I will have that to leave you. Otherwise I should have had to save closely. If the Abbey breaks now we will have enough to live quite comfortably in Dundrum or somewhere in the country.

Your old T.

If you're not at Tara St. I'll understand you cant come. I hope you'll take care of yourself tonight.

MS, TCD. *LM*, 298

To MOLLY ALLGOOD

[Glendalough House, Glenageary]
Monday night. [9 November 1908]

Dearest Child

I have just been out and posted a letter to you and then walked up and down in the dark. As you are not here I feel as if I ought to keep writting to you all the time though tonight I cannot write all that I am feeling. People like Yeats who sneer at old fashioned goodness and steadiness in women seem to want to rob the world of what is most sacred in it. I cannot tell you how unspeakably sacred her memory seems to me There is nothing in the world better or nobler than a single-hearted wife and mother. I wish you had known her better, I hope you'll be as good to me as she was — I think you will — I used to be uneasy about you sometimes but now I trust you utterly, and unspeakably. I am afraid to think how terrible my loneliness would be tonight if I had not found you. It makes me rage when I think of the people who go on as if art and literature and writing were the first thing in the world. There is nothing so great and sacred as what is most simple in life.

MS (fragment), TCD. *LM*, 299

To MOLLY ALLGOOD

Glendalough [House, Glenageary]
Saturday [14 November 1908]

Dearest

I may see you tonight at the theatre[1] but I'm writing this in case I dont. Come down tomorrow by the quarter to three — I suppose it's the best — and come here. We may go for a little walk but not to Bray. I'm getting on pretty well, but I'm very lonely. Yesterday was the first day I've had here all by myself.

I did a good [deal] of work on Deirdre not on the MS. but just notes for a new scene in it. I'm going in to Lady G today at five. I didn't ask you to meet me earlier as you should not walk and I should not sit, and there's no good knocking ourselves up. Excuse this hasty line — I was going to write to you an hour ago but my sister came in and I couldn't

Yours ever only
J.M.S.

MS, TCD. *LM*, 300

1 There was a special performance on 14 Nov 1908 of *The Clancy Name*

(Lennox Robinson), *The Shadow of the Glen*, *Dervorgilla*, and *The Scheming Lieutenant* (Sheridan), after performances from 9 to 11 Nov of Yeats's *Deirdre* with Mrs Pat Campbell.

To MOLLY ALLGOOD

[Glendalough House, Glenageary]
Monday [16 November 1908]

Dearest Love

I haven't much to say since yesterday except that its mighty cold and I've got into my warm garments. Air yours tonight and put them on, it is far more comfortable, I believe all my inside misery has come from cold.

Come down by the quarter to eleven tomorrow if its fine and if it isn't come by the quarter to two — and come to the house. If there's any change of plans I'll wire to you at cock-crow I hope you're warm and good and happy.

Your old
Tramp

I enclose the cutting for Sally bring it back to me

MS, TCD. *LM*, 300

To MOLLY ALLGOOD

Glendalough [House, Glenageary]
Nov 17th 1908

Liebes Kind

Ich habe belly-ache. How are you getting on and why do you never write to me now?

Will you come and see me tomorrow by the quarter to three? I think I've got a good scene now for the begining of Act II, Deirdre, altogether between Lavarcham and Deirdre.

Heave you heard from Sally?[1] I have reuhmatism in my back and neck today and I'm not at all happy.

So I cant write still I have written a whole sheet Eh?[2]

J.M.S.

MS, TCD. *LM*, 301

[1] Sara Allgood had now gone to London to act with Mrs Pat Campbell in a series of matinées at the New Theatre: in Hofmannsthal's *Electra*, translated by Arthur Symons, and in Yeats's *Deirdre*, 27 Nov, 1, 8, 10, and 11 Dec 1908.

[2] Scrawled in large writing across the second side of the page.

To MOLLY ALLGOOD

[Glendalough House, Glenageary]
[21 November 1908]

Dearest

I'm just off to the Abbey. This is to say you're to come down tomorrow Sunday by the quarter to *three*. If it's fine I'll meet you and we'll go on to Bray, if not come here.

I was very glad to get your letter this morning — I was just thinking last night of the time you used to write to me every day — when we were young.

I'm better inside I think

Your old T   J. M. Synge

MS, TCD. *LM*, 301

To MOLLY ALLGOOD

Glendalough [House, Glenageary]
Nov 24th/08

Dearest Child

Will you come down to me on *Thursday* by the quarter to three? I am going to MacKenna tomorrow and he forgot to ask you — I told him what you'd said about them but he took it (from the way I put it) to refer to his wife only — you remember you said what a lovely world it would it would be if there were many like them.

He writes — "It was really good of you to tell me that pleasant remark
J.M.S.
upon my Lady, of course it is true (!) but also it was pleasant to hear. My wife too was greatly pleased with Miss O'Neill, greatly attracted (no less! J.M.S.) to her, and greatly enjoyed pleasant talk in the garden and over the house. We both hope to have many such pleasant talks round the friendly table."[1] Nish! He probably feels that after all that has happened here I might like to go there alone the first time and sit with him quietly in his book room. I am really delighted that you've 'captured' Madame. Why wouldn't you, but still women are strange beasts, and she's capricious in her likes — the same as your own self. I suppose you're very hard at work this week.

I strained my knee getting in to the tram yesterday — the fellow started full tilt before I got up and then my foot slipped off the step as it was slippery with the mud. So my knee is stiff and queer. I have very nearly got a full version now of the second Act of Deirdre. I wish I could see a show of the Well of the Saints. The third Act used to go so well, and I thought I had improved it, but now you say it drags.² At Cambridge Fay got round after round of applause during the last half of the third Act.

I suppose you'll be at the Theatre of Ireland this afternoon.³ Write me a nice letter to say you'll come on Thursday.

Your O.T.   J.M.S.

I wrote another poem on you last night.
Did you find the House? in Glasnevin.⁴

MS, TCD. *LM*, 302

1 JMS's letter is missing; MacKenna's acknowledgement of 23 Nov 1908 is at TCD. Marie MacKenna née Bray (1878–1923; see I. 57), an American pianist, married Stephen MacKenna in 1902.

2 JMS's revised third act to *The Well of the Saints* was printed in the 1932 edition of the plays.

3 The Theatre of Ireland rented the Abbey Theatre 23 and 24 Nov 1908 for productions of plays by 'Rutherford Mayne' (Samuel Waddell) and Seumas O'Kelly.

4 Presumably Molly was looking for a house for them near the one taken by her sister.

To ELIZABETH CORBET YEATS

Glendalough House | Kings town
Nov 24th 08

Dear Miss Yeats

I am sorry you have had bother over my book of verses. I talked over the matter with your brother on Saturday and he agreed that you should leave out the Curse, the Ballad about 'Danny' and the couplet that I understand you object to, in the poem about the Queens. I am not quite sure now if we can retain the tittle for the division "Ballads and Outrages," as the outrages are left out. What do you think?¹

You may think it queer that I did not authorise you to leave out these poems without consulting your brother — but he had given me so much help in making this selection, and I had left the matter of arranging with you so entirely in his hands — I meant ⟨them⟩ to give the poems to Roberts originaly — that I didn't like to do so. When do you think you will want the preface — I will do quite a short one?

Do you send me proofs?

I wish it was easier to get from this to Church town, so that I might look in and see you.

Please remember me to your sister² and beleive me

Sincerely yours
J. M. Synge

MS, Berg

¹ Lolly Yeats replied on 25 Nov 1908, 'The only two that I would like left out are "The Curse" and "Danny" I hope you don't think it silly of me to want them taken out?' and offering a royalty of 15 per cent (TCD). When the volume was finally published, there were six division headings: 'Two Love Lyrics', 'Ballads and Wanderings', 'In Desolate Humour', 'In Youth', 'In Poverty', and 'With Petrarch'.

² Lily Yeats was in charge of the embroidery aspect of Dun Emer/Cuala Industries; see I. 139.

To EDWARD SYNGE[1]

⟨Glendalough Ho⟩ [Glenageary]
⟨Nov 26th⟩ [1908]

⟨Dear Ned
I understand that I am to hand²⟩

MS fragment (draft), TCD

¹ Edward Synge (1859-1939; see I. 66) whose own financial worries made him less sympathetic to his brother's way of life and plans for marriage.

² This draft fragment is struck out and the other side of the paper used for the letter to Molly of 28 Nov 1908 (see below, p. 226).

To LADY GREGORY

Glendalough Ho[use, Glenageary]
Nov 27 [1908]

Dear Lady Gregory

I hope to go up for Cockade tomorrow afternoon¹ — Do you think there will be time enough to talk over Miser cast² — and whatever else may be necessary after the show? Or shall I go to you in the forenoon — ?

I suppose you go away on Sunday.

Yours sincerely
J. M. Synge

MS, Berg. *TB*, 293

¹ The regular season at the Abbey ended with performances of two plays by Lady Gregory, *The White Cockade* (1905) and *The Workhouse Ward* (1908), 26 to 28 Nov 1908.

² Molly played Marianne in *The Miser*, Lady Gregory's adaptation of Molière's *L'Avare*, which received its first production in January 1909.

To MOLLY ALLGOOD

> Glendalough [House, Glenageary]
> Saturday Nov 28th/08

Dearest Child

I feel very lonely this wet day thinking that I'll have no more of you for ten days.[1] I wrote to Lady Gregory yesterday to ask if I should have my talk with her after the matinée or this morning, and she has replied 'after the matinée', so I will not be able to be with you. This weather I am quite sure it would be foolish to bring you down here tomorrow before your long journey, so there is no chance of seeing you. Be sure to send me your address when you get to Belfast and to tell me how you have got on. You must write very often — a post knock even is a relief in this empty silent House. I got letter from my aunt in Greystones[2] asking me to bring *you* down there to lunch some day — I have answered that you are very shy (!) (little brassy!) but that I would do my best. So we can do whatever we like. It is very kind of her. There is a sentence in her letter I will quote to you the next time I have not got her letter with me now. My poems have come back from the Nation as "not quite suitable"   I'm not much surprised.

I wrote to a houseagent yesterday and got a list of a lot of little houses in Rathgar — all in Red Terraces I am afraid — from £34 to £45 a year.

excuse the paper I am getting very economical.[3] I am sad. Be *very good* on your tour, and take care of yourself

> Your old Waif,
> J.M.S.

Am I to address you as Miss O'Neill on tour?

MS, TCD. *LM,* 303

1 The company was playing at the Theatre Royal, Belfast, for the week of 30 Nov to 5 Dec 1908.

2 Mrs Harriet Traill Dobbs, Mrs Synge's sister, had written from Knockdolian, Greystones, on 26 Nov 1908, inviting JMS and his 'friend': 'Your dear mother was glad to have her out to see her, and you, and for her sake, and for your sake, I would like to be friendly with her' (TCD).

3 The letter is written on the draft of JMS's letter to Edward Synge of 26 Nov 1908.

To LOUIS UNTERMEYER[1]

Glendalough House | Kingstown | Dublin
Nov.29th 08

My dear Mr Untermeyer

I must thank you for your letter and your article, and for your kindness in sending me the Magazine that contained it. You will easily believe that I am pleased to see people cropping up here and there who like what I have done, particularly when as in your case ⟨you⟩ they manage to say one or two things — I wont say which they are — that I am specially glad to have said about me. There is another play "The Tinkers' Wedding" which you may not have seen — it was written before W. of Saints or PlayB, — but only recently published — I'll tell Maunsel to send it to you,[2] — it is slight but may interest you. I am at work on a Saga play — after the Play boy I wanted a change from Peasant Comedy — or thought I did — on the Deirdre story that Yeats and so many other have treated here in one way or other. I have been at it for a long time, but last spring I got some — how do you spell it? — in the — inside — (you'll find the right phrase in Burns' Death and Dr Hornbook)[3] and the doctors cut me open and had me on the verge of Limbo for five weeks, so much time was lost.

Yours cordially
J. M. Synge

address as before

c/o Maunsel and Co
96 Mid Abbey Street
Dublin

MS, Lilly

---

1 Louis Untermeyer (1885–1977), major anthologist and minor poet, contributing editor to *The Liberator* and *The Masses*, later poetry editor for *the seven arts* (1916) and during the 1930s, for the *American Mercury*. The twenty-three-year-old American wrote from New York on 28 Oct 1908 (TCD) as 'one of your most ardent followers' and enclosing 'an appreciation', very likely Untermeyer's article 'J. M. Synge and the Playboy of the Western World', *Poet Lore; a Magazine of Letters*, IX, 3 (Autumn 1908), 364–67.

2 *The Tinker's Wedding* was acknowledged by Untermeyer on 31 Jan 1909, but JMS's letter did not arrive until 6 Feb 1909; Untermeyer acknowledged it in a lengthy letter the next day, and quoted it in part in an obituary letter of 17 Apr 1909 in the *New York Times Saturday Review of Books*, 247.

3 'A Country Laird had ta'en the batts, / Or some curmurring in his guts', from 'Death and Doctor Hornbook. A True Story' (1785), by Robert Burns.

To MOLLY ALLGOOD

Glendalough Ho[use, Glenageary]
Nov 30th/08

Dearest Child

You are very good — I have had two letters from you today — I laughed over Mac and the four porters, I wish I had seen it. I think I am a little better I took a hard quick longish walk with my nephew yesterday and I think the exercise did me good.[1] After that I came home here and had tea and then wrote a lot of letters that I have had lying over for a long time.

Today I went to town after my dinner, and went to the National Gallery — I'M not an old stick in the mud — and saw a new picture that's there lent by Hugh Lane a Titian a wonderful thing that filled me with deligt.[2] I also saw portraits of Swift and Stella, and I wondered how *we'll* look when we're stuck up there!

So you saw a Turner sunset![3] That was very clever of you. Nish. After the N.G. I went to Roberts on business and had a long talk with him. Then I had a D.B.C.*T.*[4] — (isn't that smart) — down stairs, and on my way to the train I met Miss Garvey.[5] She says she hears that Frank Fay is to get the sack after Christmas. I dont know who she heard it from it evidently wasn't from Frank.

I wonder how you are doing tonight. Hone saw Mrs P[at]'s Deirdre in London. He says it was not so well done as ⟨it⟩ in the Abbey, but that it was very well put on and the men were tall and fine-looking.

I think I have got the first scene in A.II right now — so the Act may be nearly finished when you come back. Yes I'll go to Parsons this week, God help us.

I've been working at the Preface to my poems tonight   Be very good and write very often

Your old T.   J.M.S.

MS, Texas. *LM,* 304

1 The nephew was perhaps Edward Hutchinson Synge ('Hutchie', 1890–1957; see I. 66), whose diary is quoted by his younger brother, J. L. Synge, in 'My Uncle Johnnie' (*Irish Times,* 16 Apr 1971, 8): 'I used to meet him on the roads near Glenageary out for a stroll fairly often during the end months of 1908 and in January 1909. I went to see him at Glendalough House, Glenageary. I only met him once again on the road after that visit, as he got rapidly worse towards the end of January and returned to hospital.'

2 Titian's portrait of Baldassare Castiglione, later bequeathed by Hugh Lane to the National Gallery of Ireland.

3 The land- and seascapes of Joseph Mallord William Turner (1775–1851) contain strikingly coloured skies.

4 The Dublin Bread Company tea room at No. 7 Lower Sackville Street (see

p. 106), was just round the corner from Middle Abbey Street where Maunsel had its offices.

⁵ Mary Garvey (Maire ni Garbhaigh, d. 1946; see I. 91) joined Fay's Irish National Dramatic Society in January 1904 and resigned with the other seceders in 1905, returning to perform occasionally later; she became engaged to George Roberts in April of this year.

To MOLLY ALLGOOD

Glen[dalough House, Glenageary]
Dec 2nd/08

Dearest Child

Your little note came today by the second post I am sorry your business is so bad — I am not so sure that it is all Scapin's fault. Why didn't you send me a cutting or two? I am not surprised that the 'Shadow of the Glen' wasn't a great success — Kerrigan does not suit the tramp and without the tramp there is no play. I suppose Sally is with you today. Perhaps the end of your week will be better.

I haven't been to Parsons yet, but *I'll go*. Yesterday I went to Bray and walked up as far as the 'little woodland path' as you used to call it, and back by that road. It was a most wonderful evening. Today I took a walk from here round the golf-links and round a road you've never been. The only excitement I had — it was a vile muggy day — was that I saw a squirrel fall out of a tree!! He was high up skying along from one tree to another and he missed his poor little shot and down he came head over tail with a thud behind the wall. I ran across and looked over, but he was gone, so he was killed out-and-out.

I feel pretty wretched, and very lonely tonight. Any how you've only three days more. I'm glad you are dull as you'll be all the gladder to come back. Did you see the letters in today's Irish Times from Miss Horniman and Conolly?[1] She's not going to give them the theatre any more and they are naturally raging! If any one talks to you about it up there — the Ulster people I mean — you'd best say that it is Miss Horniman's affair — it is her theatre and she can do what she likes.

I haven't anything to make this letter interesting. — I am always over-joyed to hear from you.

My brother was in for a few minutes this morning except for him I've seen no one all day — it isn't very cheerful.

Deirdre's going well I think D— her.

Your old T——!

MS, TCD. *LM*, 305

1 While the Theatre of Ireland was renting the Abbey Theatre on 23 and 24 Nov 1908 for its revival of Rutherford Mayne's *The Turn of the Road* and a production of Seumas O'Kelly's new play, *The Flame on the Hearth* (see p. 224), William Mollison, in whose company Mayne was acting, invited the Theatre of Ireland to appear with his own company which was playing during the week at the Gaiety Theatre; in his newspaper advertisement of 25 Nov 1908 he stated that *The Turn of the Road* would be performed by members of the Abbey Theatre Company. Miss Horniman's letter in the *Irish Times* of 2 Dec 1908 objected to the use of the name and announced that henceforth neither 'The Abbey Theatre Company' nor 'The Theatre of Ireland' would be permitted to hire her theatre. On the same day James H. Cousins and Seumas O'Connolly, secretary of the Theatre of Ireland, replied denying any responsibility for the confusion of names. (*Modern Irish Drama*, III, 253–6)

To MOLLY ALLGOOD

Glendalough Ho[use, Glenageary]
Dec 4th/08

Dearest Child

Your little note came today — it was very short and hurried and scrappy with very little to cheer me up in my solitude.

I have just come from Dr Parsons. I will tell you all he said when I see you. Is it you and Sally or you and Dossy who are stopping at the Wrights? in Balbriggan? You can do what you like.

Henderson has sent me one paper each day. It is silly stuff they write even when they praise. Hendersons booming of Sally has not had a good effect. I am glad you are to be home so soon. I am very lonely.

I hope you will enjoy the supper tomorrow night.

I seem to be unable to write, this evening. Blessings on you. Come home safe

Your old T.   J.M.S.y.

You'll not hear from me again of course till you get home.

MS, TCD. *LM*, 306

To MOLLY ALLGOOD

Glendalough House [Glenageary]
Saturday Dec 5/08

Dearest Child

I'm afraid my letter yesterday wasn't very agreeable — I was discouraged and sad and lonesome, and your proposal to stop at Balbriggan with the Wright and his people of course hurt me. What would you think if I was travelling with company and I got out at a station with Miss Gildea[1] to stay with her and her relations. I can imagine the sneers and jokes there'd have been at *me* among the company if you had done it. I didn't mean to allude to it all, in this letter but I've done it surely.

I am glad to see by the papers today — that Henderson sent — how well things have gone after all. It is very unfair how the booming of Sally has influenced the papers. For instance Mac in the Sergeant — or you in Nora Burke are certainly better than she is in The Man who Missed.[2] Yet look at the papers!

Will you come down here on Monday! I believe there is a fire rehearsal at the Abbey — I dont know what time. You can come here any time you like, but send me a line to say.

I was at the Municipal Gallery today but it [was] too dark to see anything with comfort. God help me I'm afraid I'm not very well.

I met Roberts and Miss Garvey in Grafton Street. They looked very beaming.

So till Monday I hope

                                  Your O.T.

MS, TCD. *LM*, 306

1 Miss Ida Gildea (later Mrs Hargreaves Heap; see I. 352), an Irish friend of Miss Horniman, who had assisted with publicity during the May–June 1907 tour. A letter from her to JMS from Ingleside, Croyde, Devon on 14 May 1908 (TCD) expresses regret at his illness, invites him to visit her, and speaks of having had a letter from one of his admirers.
2 F. Q. McDonnell ('Arthur Sinclair') played the Sergeant in Lady Gregory's *The Rising of the Moon*; Sara Allgood played the doctor's wife, Mrs Gerald Quinn, in Casey's *The Man Who Missed the Tide*.

To ELIZABETH CORBET YEATS

                     Glendalough House | Kingstown
                                    Dec 6th/08

Dear Miss Yeats

I send you a short Preface as I promised. — You can use it or not as you think best. If you dont use it let me have the MS. back please. I dont much fancy it myself but that is no test for the moment.[1]

I hope you got the Poems all right I posted them to you yesterday, registered

                                 Yours sincerely
                                    J. M. Synge

MS, Ray

¹ The brief Preface, dated 'Glenageary, December 1908', was published in the Cuala edition.

To M. J. NOLAN¹

Glendalough House | Glenageary
Dec 7th/08

M. J. Nolan Esq
Dear Sir

I have just read your little play — so I will answer you at once. I laughed at the apendicitus Ode and rather liked your beggar — and I thought one speech the, top one of p 16, excellent comedy growing out of the situation of the two characters — but I am afraid as a whole ⟨it⟩ the play is quite too slight for performance — and *too* without *shape.* For one thing it is not possible to have changes of scene in a Curtain Raiser — a moment's thought will show you that the final change (for a scene where nothing is really said or done) could not be effective. Also one has to enterlace one's characters — a first Act all A + B., with a second Act all A + C is not satisfactory. I think your language is a little too medical!

I trust you will not mind my frank criticism.²

Yours faithfully
J. M. Synge

P.S. If you haven't read Molière's "Malade Imaginaire" you ought to do so.

MS, TCD

1 M. J. Nolan, a fruit salesman (see I. 297), first wrote to JMS in February 1907 sending a critique of *The Playboy*; little else is known of him.
2 Nolan acknowledged the letter on 13 Dec 1908 (TCD), thanking JMS for his comments on 'The Dyspeptic'.

To T. P. GILL¹

Glendalough House | Glenageary
Dec 9th/08

Dear Mr Gill

I would be peculiarly pleased to meet Monsieur René Bazin and his daughter² but, alas, I am not well enough yet — you may have heard how ill I was in the early summer — to be out at night and enjoy a dinner and talk.

— They say it will be a year or near it before I am quite comfortable again. So I must thank you very cordially for your kind invitation, which, to my infinite regret, I cannot accept.

Yours sincerely
J. M. Synge

MS, TCD

1 Thomas Patrick Gill (1858-1931), formerly editor of the *Catholic World* magazine and associate editor of the *North American Review*, before returning to Ireland to enter Parliament as a Parnellite (1885-92). Associated with Sir Horace Plunkett in founding the Department of Agriculture and Technical Institution for Ireland, he served as its secretary from 1900 to 1923, and became editor of the Dublin *Daily Express* when it was purchased by Plunkett.

2 Gill had written on 8 Dec 1908, inviting JMS to meet M. René Bazin (1853-1932), law professor at the Catholic University of Angers and prolific novelist, dramatist, and travel writer, and his daughter Mme Antoine Sainte-Marie Perrin, née Elisabeth Bazin (1879-1926), 'who wishes to write an article on "Irish idealists" for *Revue des Deux Mondes*' (TCD). Mme Perrin, also a novelist, was the author of an introduction to the works of Paul Claudel.

To MOLLY ALLGOOD

Glendalough House [Glenageary]
Dec 11th/08

Dearest Child

Why didn't you come down today — or at least send me a line to say you couldn't come.

I am not at all well and I feel deserted and wretched. A week of holidays is over now and you've only come to me once. Will you come tomorrow? Please write by return.

The servant is just going out so I will send this by her.

Your old T
J.M.S.

I met the train today fully certain that you'd be in it.

MS, TCD. *LM*, 307

To STEPHEN MacKENNA

[Glendalough House, Glenageary]
[?15 December 1908][1]

MacKenna
I take my pen a
Word to tell you

That if I'm well, you
(Damn rhyme)   Will see us tomorrow
afternoon.   D.V.[2]

MS, TCD

1 MacKenna's postcard of 15 Dec 1908 seems to be a reply to this announcement; 'Come 'searly as you can since yez'll not stay for supper . . . . Good luck my boy we're delighted to have the visit of yourself and Miss O'Neill' (TCD).

2 *Deo volente.*

To W. A. HENDERSON

Glendalough House [Glenageary]
Dec 18th/08

Dear Henderson

Will you please come down to me on Monday afternoon about 3 — There is a quarter to three from West. Row that would be your quickest way.

I'll be delighted to see you.[1]

Yours
J. M. Synge

MS, NLI

1 Evidently an earlier exchange of letters is missing, for on 17 Dec 1908 Henderson acknowledged a letter which enclosed signed cheques he had requested earlier. 'There is just this difficulty about the latter,' he explained, 'that the majority would be required to be made payable to myself as I get £10 at a time to pay staff salaries, small accounts etc. The cheques cannot be crossed as the bank would not give me the money if they were. In future however I will try and run down myself with them . . . . I will come down any afternoon that suits you, Saturday or Monday or any day about three o'clock.' (TCD) With Lady Gregory at Coole and Yeats in Paris, JMS was the only Abbey director at hand.

To MOLLY ALLGOOD

[Glendalough House, Glenageary]
Friday Dec 18th/08

Dearest

Will you come down tomorrow (Saturday) by the quarter to three for a good long afternoon. If you cant come let me know and if you can write and say so.

I've spoken to no one since I left you except Brigit — and a beggar man. How did you get on last night? I wonder will you *have had* the grace to write to me about your adventures, before this reaches you.

I heard from Agnes Tobin today.[1] She had seen Sally and Mrs P[at]. She [says] Mrs P had lovely moments but was spoiled by a bad company and a poor mise-en-scène. I dont take her criticism very seriously. That's all that's happened I think — I've done the usual amount of Deirdre, and had the usual belly-aches and taken my usual little walks, — bad cess to the lot of them.

Be sure and come tomorrow. I feel like a watch that wants to be wound when you dont come. Henderson is coming on Monday

Your O T
J.M.S.

When is Sally coming back?

MS, TCD. *LM*, 307

1 Her letter of 17 Dec 1908 is at TCD.

To MOLLY ALLGOOD

Glendalough House [Glenageary]
Dec 21st/08

Dearest

Brigit wants to go into town for a day's shopping tomorrow so I'm afraid you'd better *not* come for lunch. She'll be in a great fuss all the morning. Come by the quarter to three, of course, and make my tea for me here.

I've had Henderson here for two hours, and I've told him my mind, or some of it. I'll tell you more tomorrow.

So good night Dear Heart
Your O.T.

I hope you enjoyed the Municipal Gallery!!

MS, TCD. *LM*, 308

To MOLLY ALLGOOD

[Glendalough House, Glenageary]
22nd/XII/08

Dearest

I remembered your pupil[1] last night (after I had written) and wondered if you'd come. Will you come to lunch tomorrow — you do not say what day you rehearse — if you will come let me have a line by *return* or there'll be nothing to eat. If you are rehearsing in the morning come in the afternoon will you? Anyhow let me know. I dine with my brother in the evening, but that wont interfer.

It is frightfuly damp out here now   I dare say it's dryer in Glasnevin. I wish I was out of this house.[2] I've nothing much to tell you. I've pretty nearly gone on to the end of Deirdre and cut it down a little. It is delicate work a scene is so easily spoiled. I am anxious to hear you read it to me.

You ask *me* to write you letters and then what is it I ask you, that you write yourself? I dont see any notice of the Carols this year I wonder if they are coming off. If they do I suppose we should go.

Your ——
——
——
——

J.M.S.

Give my love to Sally.

MS, TCD. *LM*, 308

1 Both Sally Allgood and Molly took private voice pupils.
2 A letter of 6 Nov 1908 from JMS's brother Edward to Robert Synge describes the financial settlement in Mrs Synge's will and reports his discussion with Annie Stephens: 'Annie thinks the best plan will be for Bridget to housekeep for John under her supervision while he is there and to get the things at the old shops and at the end of the present month if J. has no funds I can pay the pass books out of the balance of the £50 you sent home — I think this will be most satisfactory. I suppose he will tell you something of his intentions as soon as he rests and has time to look round.' (TCD)

To MOLLY ALLGOOD

[Glendalough House, Glenageary]
Dec 24th/08

Dearest

I feel humiliated that I showed you so much of my weakness and emotion yesterday. I will not ⟨be⟩ trouble you any more with complaints about my health — you have taught me that I should not — but I think I owe it to myself to to let you know that if I am so 'selfpitiful' I have some reason to be so ⟨and⟩ as Dr Parsons report of my health, though uncertain, was much more unsatisfactory than I thought it well to tell you. I only tell you now because I am unable to bare the thought that you should think of me with the contempt I saw in your face yesterday.

Your O T

MS, Texas. *LM*, 309

To MOLLY ALLGOOD

[Glendalough House, Glenageary]
Dec 25th/08

Dearest Child

Your letter reached me today and was a great relief to me. I am not sure if I will be at the Abbey tomorrow. I haven't been very well the last couple of days, and I will not be able to go in unless I am better. You needn't be uneasy it is nothing new, only the same troubles inside somewhat worse than they were.

I am here alone all this afternoon, Brigit is gone to Lucan for the day.

Your present hasn't come yet or if it came the house was empty so I hope I'll get it tomorrow. I got *one* Xmas card — from Martin Harvey of all people in the world!

I heard also from Florence Ross she says she will be very glad if you'll go out to see her.

Will you come to me as usual on Sunday — come here if I do not meet you —

Your old T.

MS, TCD. *LM*, 309

PART THREE

January–March

1909

*

The Slow Business of Dying

To MOLLY ALLGOOD

[Glendalough House, Glenageary]
Jan 1st 1909

Dearest Child

A Happy New Year to you and many of them! I was very pleased
to get your nice little note today, — it was a nicer one than I've had
for some time. I was in bed by that hour though I could just hear
the steam whistles roaring through my sleep. I dont think you
would find Saturday a good day to go to the Miss Yeats' — *unless*
they said so — as they are likely to give their girls a halfholiday
and shut up their work rooms — which you are going to see. If you
do go tomorrow you'll have to go by train — it is too long a walk
for you from the tram.

If you dont go then you'd better come here, and if you do send
me a line before 11. G.P.O. to say you're coming. If you cant come
tomorrow come on Sunday of course. Have you acknowledged Miss
White's cheque?[1] You should do so at once if you haven't.

I have been trying to keep myself busy the last couple of days
to see how that will work. I went to MacKenna yesterday. He was
out when I went and I'd a long talk with Madame — then in came
Master Stephen with his hair on end and a mass of mud down from
his ear to his heel — you never never saw such a sight. He'd fallen
in a tram-line and nearly been decapitated by a motor. Then we
chatted till 6.30 and he walked down to the tram with me. They
renewed their invitation for you to go as often as possible.

Today I took a long walk in the morning, and then I went in on
top of the tram and saw Roberts on business, and came home. I
couldn't have arranged to meet you as I was quite uncertain if I'd
go. Nish!

A thousand blessings and come soon — *Dont kill* yourself trying
to write in the morning if it [is] not easy I'll be about here in any
case if you come.

[*Unsigned*]

MS, TCD. *LM*, 313

1 Miss Henrietta Margaret White, principal of Alexandra College from 1890
to 1932, had engaged Molly to assist with the girls' Christmas entertainment;
among JMS's papers (TCD) is her letter of 2 Dec 1908 asking for Molly's charges
and on the back a draft in JMS's hand of Molly's reply: 2/0 an hour for fourteen
hours.

To MOLLY ALLGOOD

Glendalough House [Glenageary]
Saturday Night [2 January 1909]

Dearest Child

Hell and Confusion and Brimstone! I have just got a post card from Magee[1] to say that he and Best are coming out to see me tomorrow afternoon at 4 o'clock

```
————————B ————————————G.
           ——————Ch ——————
  H ————————————————————
           ————————————————Y
```

That means I am afraid that you cant come tomorrow. What a pity. I have tried to think of some alternative plan but there is none so you must come on Monday or Tuesday instead. What a great evening we had today and tomorrow we'll be lonesome O be C Oh ——— B Oh

Write to me a long letter instead

Your old T.

MS, TCD. *LM*, 313

1 The postcard, dated 2 Jan 1909, is at TCD.

To LADY GREGORY

Glendalough House | Kingstown
Jan. 3rd/09

Dear Lady Gregory

Many thanks for your letter the other day — and the one you wrote to me the day you were leaving Dublin which I meant to answer but never did — I was delighted to hear in it that there is some hope of a good play from Norreys Connell.[1] Nothing would serve us better at present. I have done a great deal to Deirdre since I saw you, — chiefly in the way of strengthening motives and recasting the general scenario — but there is still a good deal to be done with the dialogue, and soon scenes in the first Act must be re-written to make them fit in with the new parts I have added.[2] I only work a little every day as I suffer more than I like with indigetion and general uneasiness inside — I hope it is only because I haven't quite got over the shock of the operation — the doctors are vague and dont say much that is definite.

Things seem to be going well and quietly in the Theatre — though

Miss Allgood came home rather unhappy as Mrs Campbell offered to get her £50 a week to sing Irish songs in the Coliseum, — and made some further mischief, but all is forgotten now I think. I have at last got Henderson to fill up his cheques before sending them down to sign — and I have spoken very strongly to him about the exagerated starring of Miss Allgood. He is quite infatuated. He says Scapin did not go in Belfast — "because Scalpin is *nothing* without Miss All-good"![3]

They are working at the Miser now, and are all very pleased with it and themselves as far as I hear.[4] I have not been in to see a rehearsal yet, as I keep out in the country as much as I can.

I hope soon to hear further good news from you. I suppose it is likely to be some time before you are up again in Dublin.[5] Please remember me cordially to your son and believe me

Yours sincerely
J. M. Synge

MS, Berg. *TB*, 296

1 Lady Gregory's brief New Year's note of 30 Dec 1908 (*TB*, 295) was her first since a lengthy letter from the Nassau Hotel on 29 Nov reporting on Yeats's assessment of Norreys Connell's new play and giving a cheerful overview of the Abbey company and box office (*TB*, 293).

2 After a visit to JMS on 5 Mar 1909 Yeats wrote in his journal, 'He said the third Act was right, that he had put an extra character in second Act and intended to weave him into Act one. He was to come in with Conchubar, carrying some of his belongings, and afterwards at end of Act to return for forgotten knife — just enough to make it possible to use him in Act Two' (*Memoirs*, 177); the new character was Owen.

3 Sara Allgood played a minor role in *The Rogueries of Scapin*, while Molly had the leading female part.

4 Like Yeats, JMS was impressed by Lady Gregory's adaptations of Molière, commenting to Henderson that 'it puts life into the dead bones of the plays' (Joseph Holloway, diary, 17 Dec 1908, NLI). *The Miser* was first performed on 21 Jan 1909.

5 Robert Gregory's wife gave birth to a son, Richard, on 6 Jan 1909.

To MOLLY ALLGOOD

[Glendalough House, Glenageary]
[5 January 1909]

Dearest Child

I went to Parsons today but he was running off to the country to somebody and could not see me so I am to see him tomorrow. Then I went up the Quays and looked at the book shops for a while and came home by the quarter to four. I met Starkey[1] — and he seemed amazed to see me; he said he had heard that I was ill again. Remember if any one asks you how I am you are to say I'm all right I dont want to have people condoling with me.

I suppose you'll go to the Miss Yeats tomorrow and then I think you had better come down to supper on Thursday however I'll write to you tomorrow and fix up.

I am better than I was yesterday and I have done a good deal of Deirdre today

Your old T——

Excuse this shabby line I'm in a hurry for the post — I only wrote because I thought you might be on the look out for news of Parsons.

MS, TCD. *LM*, 314

1 James Sullivan Starkey ('Seumas O'Sullivan', 1879–1958; see I. 95), poet and editor, was a member of the early nationalist group which founded the Theatre of Ireland. Years later Starkey recalled (TS, TCD) sending JMS a copy of Palgrave's *Golden Treasury* with poems by Herrick when 'Synge lay dying' in Elpis.

To STEPHEN MACKENNA
[Glendalough House, Glenageary]
5. I. 09

Dear [*deleted*]¹

I have read your article on W.B.Y.² and I think it is excellent. I have only read it once through hastily — [*deleted*]³ — but I seemed to feel a sureness of touch and an entirely successful vehemence that delighted me. All you say is wise and the way you say it has a certain authority. Yeats, unless he is a fool, will be pleased with it. I wish you'd lift the pledge from my tongue and leave it to my discretion and the chances of talk whether I reveal your authorship to him or not. The matter is of little consequence either way, but I feel it a sort of folly that you should ask your friends to hold a bushel over your head.

Yours
J.M.S.

I think [*deleted*]⁴ is a scandal — in spite of the tenderness of my belly I feel I could swallow [*deleted*] for the sake of spewing him out of my mouth!

Note. I wonder are my Scriptural allusions⁵ all lost to you, you blighted Papist

MS, TCD

1 Throughout the letter, MacKenna has erased or scribbled over passages he considered injudicious, including JMS' salutation to him.

2 'An Argument and an Appreciation', a review of Yeats's *Collected Works*, (1908) signed 'A. O'L', appeared in the *Freeman's Journal*, 2 Jan 1909; in his undated letter enclosing a TS of the essay MacKenna pledged JMS to secrecy, probably knowing that the *Freeman* editor, William Brayden, hoped for a hostile review.

3 'here, an irrelevant jocose reference to a third person' (MacKenna's insertion).

4 'a certain matter unrelated to the main theme of the letter' (MacKenna's insertion).

5 Cf. Luke 11:33: 'No man, when he hath lighted a candle, putteth it in a secret place, neither under a bushel, but on a candlestick, that they which come in may see the light.'

To MOLLY ALLGOOD

Glendalough House [Glenageary]
Jan 6th/08

Dearest

I saw Parsons today — there were 17 people waiting in his room but he took me first as I had an appointment. He does not think I am worse than I was a month ago, and he has given me some medicine and he says he thinks I'd better look in and see Ball and see what he thinks of me.

What about tomorrow evening? Do you feel you would be fresh enough and energetic enough to come down so late and for so short a time? I'll be delighted if you'll come but try and let me know by the early post if you are coming — That is to say dont ride under a tram or do anything rash in order to get to the G.P.O. on time — but write if you can.

Parsons says I may cycle a little if I like   I think I'll begin soon I've been working at Deirdre at [*for* a] lot but I'm not satisfied at all.

Your old T

If you come tomorrow it would have to be by the quarter to five — later trains would be too late — if it was as fine as tonight we might go and walk on the pier by moonlight after supper.

J.M.

MS, TCD. *LM*, 315

To ELIZABETH CORBET YEATS

Glendalough House | Kingstown
Jan 7th/09

Dear Miss Yeats

Many thanks for the proofs and your letter.[1] I hope you will not be alarmed at the number of changes I propose — I know so little of printing that I do not know whether changing the pages about causes great trouble or not.

If not too troublesome I would like the "On a Birthday", transfered to the 'In Youth' section, as it is not strong enough for its present place. Then I would like the 'Passing of the Shee' moved also to the place I indicate in proof, as it does not make a good opening to the section — The "Curse" which we have suppressed was the original opening.

On page 22 two poems have got into one page and will have to be separated. I have written in headings to *all* the poems for capitals, and I think that will improve their appearance. I ⟨didn't⟩ dont like the look of page 34 so I have marked it for two paragraphs only or more if you like but there are too many at present. I am doubtful about last paragraph of page 39. What do you think? You have far more authority in this matter than I have. The other Petrarchs I do not object to — and I leave them in your hands to alter the setting up if you think fit. I have no views on printing.

How innocent all my little poems look! I almost regret that we have left out the 'Curse' and 'Danny' as the poems now seem to want strength a little.[2] However it doesn't really matter. I suppose you'll let me see a revise when you are ready. I think the red — as you suggest — would look well, I am not sure about repeating title over Preface[3] — I do not see the page in my mind's eye. I am getting on pretty well, and working slowly at Deirdre

Yours very sincerely
J. M. Synge

MS, TCD

1 Lolly Yeats wrote from Cuala Industries, Churchtown, Dundrum on 6 Jan 1909 enclosing proofs of the volume and inviting JMS to 'make any alteration you want' (TCD).

2 See p. 224. In her acknowledgement of 8 Jan 1909 Miss Yeats replied, 'I wish I knew whether it was wise (from a business point of view) to include "The Curse" and "Danny" but I don't really know' (TCD). In his Preface to the Cuala edition, Yeats quoted 'The Curse', but 'Danny' was not published until the 1910 Maunsel edition.

3 Her letter of 6 Jan had suggested putting subtitles in red and repeating the title of the book above the word 'Preface'.

To ELKIN MATHEWS

Glendalough House | Kingstown | Dublin
Jan 8th/09

Dear Mr Mathews

May I ask you to be kind enough to let me have an account of the sales of the second edition of my little volume of plays, and whatever royalties are now due to me. You have heard I think that we propose to issue my plays in America in one volume, — the plays you have published for me will of course make a very small portion of the volume so it [will] be fair I think if we allow you a royalty of one per cent. — while your agreement with me is still in force. The terms offered by the American publisher do not admit I need hardly say, of our allowing you a larger royalty.

With best wishes.

Yours faithfully
J. M. Synge

MS, Gilvarry

To C. P. SCOTT[1]

Glendalough House | Kingstown | Dublin
Jan 8th/09

Dear Mr Scott

I was glad to get your letter of the   of December,[2] and to hear that you were pleased with my Article — the delay I had hardly notised as I had been away for some time in Germany. I do not quite gather if you have used my article so far, and I would be glad to know if you done so[3] — or when you do — as I have a couple of articles on Kerry that I would like to send you when the other is out of the way. I am working at a new play at present but when that is off my hands I hope to do you the article on the Types that we have been talking of for so long. It will depend a little however on my health which is not yet all that I could wish.

With best greetings for the season

Yours sincerely
J. M. Synge

MS (draft), TCD

1 Charles Prestwick Scott (1846–1932; see I. 110), editor of the *Manchester Guardian* from 1872 to 1929.

2 Scott had written on 6 Dec 1908 (TCD), apologizing for not answering an earlier letter from JMS, and reminding him of the article on 'Types' he was to do with Jack Yeats; see p. 42.

3 Scott replied on 10 Jan 1909, 'the last article you kindly sent appeared on Dec 10, so please do not let that stand in the way of sending another' (TCD).

To F. R. SIDGWICK

Glendalough House | Kingstown
Dublin Jan 8/09

Dear Mr Sidgewick

I am much obliged for your letter which came to me some weeks ago.[1] Our project for a collected edition of my plays in one volume has come to nothing for the present — in this country at least — chiefly owing to impossibity of coming to what we thought a satisfactory arrangement with Mr Matthews. That being so I am interested to know how long your stock of the "Well of the Saints" is likely to last. I think it better to tell you frankly that I am convinced — with my limited public — that it will be much to my advantage to have all my stuff in the hands of one publisher — and that that publisher will be Maunsel, for many and obvious reasons which I need not point out to you. My agreement with Mr Bullen expires — I think next year and then I think it will be best to get Maunsel to republish the Well of the Saints.[2] Perhaps at some future time I and Maunsel may be stoned out Ireland and I may be only to glad to come back to you — if you will have me! As to the little sum that is due to me for royalties if it is too disgracefully small let me know it and I'll take it out in books from your list many of which interest me greatly![3] I am fairly well now — thank you — though rather shaken by what I've been through this last year

Yours cordially
J. M. Synge

MS, Langmuir

1 Sidwick & Jackson wrote to JMS on 19 Dec 1908 (Synge estate) stating that they had taken over the publication of *The Well of the Saints* from A. H. Bullen and suggesting that the rights held by Elkin Mathews for *Riders to the Sea* and *In the Shadow of the Glen* be recovered so that they could then publish, with Maunsel, a collected edition of JMS's works.

2 Actually, the royalty agreement between JMS and Bullen, dated 19 Jan 1906 (Synge estate), was for five years; Maunsel was not free of obligation to Sidgwick & Jackson until the publication of the *Collected Works* in 1910. On 14 Jan 1909 Sidgwick & Jackson wrote (Synge estate) that they had refused Maunsel's offer for the remaining stock of *The Well of the Saints* because it was not good enough.

3 Royalties due JMS, according to Sidgwick & Jackson's statement of 31 Dec 1908 (TCD), were 19/1.

To MOLLY ALLGOOD

[Glendalough House, Glenageary]
Jan 11th/09

Dearest

I am writting this in a hurry — merely to tell you that I've seen Ball ⟨but⟩ and that he is hopeful, and has ordered me a big dose of Castor oil to clear me out. I forgot that my cousin will probably be here *tomorrow* so do not come down unless I wire for you.

This must go now so god bless us.

I met Columb today in town, he's a queer looking little creature now.

Your O.T.

MS, Texas. *LM*, 315

To MOLLY ALLGOOD

Glendalough House [Glenageary]
Tuesday Jan 12th [1909]

Dearest Heart

This is another mere line to tell you I am getting on well I think — though for the time being I'm more wretched than ever. Sir C.B. was evidently right in what he thought — or part of it — but I'm not cured yet, so I'll have to give myself more doses, God help me. However if that will set me right then may Heaven's eternal fragrance fall on Castor Oil. I wonder if you can follow all this. I've been thinking about you a great deal with your little socks for me, and all your little attentions and I'm ready to go down on knees to your shadow — if I met it in a dry place. — I think I'm drunk with Castor Oil!

My cousin[1] was out with me today for a long time and he's coming again — tomorrow Wednesday afternoon, so I wont see you I fear till Thursday. Write me a nice letter — there's a bit of hope for us still Glory be to God.

Your old Tramp.[2]

MS, AS. *LM*, 316

1 Probably Edward M. Synge, the etcher.
2 Molly mistakenly wrote on the envelope, 'my dear ones last letter to me'.

To ELIZABETH CORBET YEATS

Glendalough House | Kingstown
Jan 13/09

Dear Miss Yeats

Thanks for the revise, the changes in arrangement etc. are a great improvement I think. I have been uneasy ⟨but⟩ about the look of the Petrarch Sonnets at the end they seemed so bare at the corner of the page with no heading, so I now send you headings — to be in italics like page 36.

Do you think it would be an improvement? There are little headings like them in my Italian edition so we are justified in putting them in, if you think they are desirable. I am never sure whether I shall like a change till I see it done: for instance the hyphens I asked you to put in on page 19 are certainly a mistake and make the whole poem look like a Chinese puzzle. I think the proofs are now correct at least I can detect no mistakes. I fear we must put "Poems and Translations", by J. M. Synge as the title. It is clumsy, but when there is so much translation I dont like to call it 'Poems' only. Perhaps I may think of something better.

The Postage of the big packet you sent me last week was /5^d — it had two 2½ stamps and of course the registration docket, perhaps the packet is charged extra, but I think there must have been some mistake as it could hardly have been five pence without the registration —[1]

Yours sincerely
J. M. Synge

MS, Berg

[1] As a postscript to her letter of 11 Jan 1909 (TCD) accompanying the revised proofs, Miss Yeats asked for details of postage costs because of difficulties with the post office.

To MOLLY ALLGOOD

Glendalough House [Glenageary]
Saturday 16.I.09

Dearest

I've had such a take in. That wretched man[1] wrote that he was coming down this afternoon. Then at 20 to three he drove up on a car, left his car outside, came in for ten minutes, and then off again, leaving me here for a wretched lonely day. I took more Castor oil this morning but it is no use I'm afraid.

Of course you'll come down tomorrow by the quarter to three. I wonder if you are skating today — if you are happy and amusing yourself that's one good thing at any rate. I haven't been out at all today

Your old T.

I am watching every footfall in hopes that you may come still. It is only four thirty. How shall I get through the evening?

MS, TCD. *LM*, 316

1 Unidentified.

To ELKIN MATHEWS

Glendalough House | Kingstown | Co Dublin
Jan 20th/09

Dear Mr Mathews

Excuse my delay in acknowledging your letter, and thanking you for your cheque for £1 "8 "0. which I received some days ago.[1]

I referred in my letter — as you understood — to the American edition of my plays only — the proposed edition in this country will, I believe, have to be postponed for some time, or, rather, abandoned for the present.

The American edition is still a little uncertain as to date and other matters — I will let you know in due course when things are definitely settled.

With best wishes
Yours faithfully
J. M. Synge

MS, TCD

1 Elkin Mathews had written on 13 Jan 1909 (TCD) accepting the 1 per cent royalty on the American edition (see p. 246) and enclosing a royalty statement.

To M. J. NOLAN

Glendalough House | Kingstown
Jan 31st/09

Dear Mr Nolan

I am very unwell at the present time so I am unable to write to you as fully as I would wish about the poem you sent me the other day.

I think there IS something in it, and that you have certainly a capacity for verse-writ⟨t⟩ing. It is likely that plenty of men who afterwards made themselves a place, of one kind or other in letters began with work not unlike yours — ⟨and⟩ but also there are thousands who have begun with work like yours and got no further.

You say something in your letter about abandoning the "plough-share", and perhaps you will permit me to make a remark on it. I do *not* think it possible to be a fashionable doctor and a literary man at the same time,[1] but I think it should be — *and is* — perfectly possible to combine some other study with that of ⟨that⟩ letters, so that if a man finds, when he is thirty, that he cannot do any thing worth doing in literature, he may have something else to do that is worth doing, instead of becoming a mere wreck and waster.[2]

I meant to criticise 'Blumene' at length but that is beyond me. It is unequal, as you say, and all, of course, very uncertain in its note. One moment you are Spencerian, then say Byronic, and then Wordsworthian. Some of your lines are not quite gramat⟨t⟩ically or verbally accurate and do not quite say what they ought — at least that was my impression when I read you. I dont think your story is a very good one in itself, or very well told — there is too much desciption and your characters are not alive enough. All these faults are *inevitable* in inexperienced work.

When I am better again I will be always glad to give you any advice that I can

Yours faithfully
J. M. Synge

I do *not* mean this letter to discourage you

MS, TCD

---

1 Perhaps a reference to Oliver St. John Gogarty.
2 Nolan replied on 2 Feb 1909 (TCD) confessing that he was a salesman in the wholesale fruit market and was publishing a series of articles on fruit market-ing in the *Cork Examiner*.

To MOLLY ALLGOOD

[Glendalough House, Glenageary]
[1 February 1909]

Dearest

I am going in to Elpis tomorrow to get there about one. I'll be very tired and they'll probably put me to bed and keep me very quiet.

I am certainly a little *better* today so that is a great thing. Eh, Mister?

Will you please send me "The Mill on the Floss" — *or else* "Silas Marner", both by George Eliot both published by Nelson /6d — I

think — to Elpis some time any time tomorrow. I'll let you know
how I do. Now I must stop.

Your old Tramp

MS, TCD. *LM*, 317

To ELIZABETH CORBET YEATS

Elpis [Nursing Home, Dublin]
Feb 19th 1909

Dear Miss Yeats
      I think you[1] might put in your brother's picture certainly but I
suppose you would give it a title "Tinkers" to explain it.[2]
      The corrections look all right but I cannot go through them so
use your own discretion.
      They say I'm getting on well but I'm in bed still

Yours sincerely
J. M. Synge

MS (partly in another hand), Berg

1 Up to this point in someone else's hand.
2 JMS did not reply to Miss Yeats's earlier letter of 3 Feb 1909 asking for
more poems 'to make the book larger' (TCD); her letter of 18 Feb (also TCD) enclosed a drawing (now missing) by Jack Yeats as a possible frontispiece. The
published book contained no drawing by Jack Yeats, although Lady Gregory's
proof copy (TCD) included his *Two Tinkers* before the Preface. Printing was
completed on 8 Apr, fifteen days after JMS's death.

EPILOGUE

The last five weeks passed slowly and quietly, with Molly visiting him daily except for a week's tour to Manchester in February, and one or other of his relatives in almost constant attendance. On 6 March Yeats reported to Lady Gregory, who was ill at Coole, 'I saw Synge again, very pale and thin but not I thought gloomy. He gives me an impression of peaceful courage whenever I see him, yet I thought he was certainly doubtful of the result. There are various lumps in his side he says but the doctors tell him very little. He has asked them if they mean to operate again but they do not seem "anxious for an operation".' (Berg)

Two days later he saw Synge again, reporting on 8 March that he 'looked very very ill' (Berg). But when death finally came, at 5.30 in the morning of 24 March, Yeats was too late to answer the urgent summons brought to him by Molly, and so had not the comfort of farewell. 'You will have had the telegram Henderson sent,' he wrote that day to Lady Gregory. 'In the early morning Synge said to the nurse "It is no use fighting death any longer" and turned over and died. I have seen Mr Stephens, he says Synge wanted to see me to make some arrangements about his work. He says he wished that his shares in the Society should be divided between you and me.' (Berg)

Lady Gregory wrote to Yeats the next day, 'What a quiet end that was! No struggle or disturbance, just what he would have wished . . . . I feel very downhearted for it is such a break in our very very small group of understanding friends — which indeed has been little more than a triangle.' (Berg) Yeats suffered an even greater sense of loss; 'He feels it deeply and says he now has no near friend left,' Lily Yeats reported to her father (Murphy, *Prodigal Father*, 345). From that time on the Abbey Theatre became, for Yeats, Synge's legacy.

Synge's will left Molly the financial protection with which he had been unable to provide her in his lifetime. She remained with the company until her marriage in 1911 to G. H. Mair of the *Manchester Guardian*. She had two children by him but she returned to the theatre occasionally for limited engagements. After Mair died she married her fellow Abbey player Arthur Sinclair ('Mac'), and with her sister Sally they toured America in O'Casey's plays. But her final years were spent alone, mainly in London, at work on stage, film, and radio; and she preserved Synge's letters until pressed by E. M. Stephens to sell them to him for use in his monumental life of his uncle.

Apart from Molly's lifetime annuity of £80 (reduced to £52 if she married), Synge left his property and the income from his plays and books to his nephews Edward Stephens and Edward Hutchinson Synge.

After many delays, *Poems and Translations* was published by the Cuala Press in June 1909. *Deirdre of the Sorrows*, assembled from the manuscripts by Yeats and Lady Gregory with Molly's help, was finally produced on 13 January 1910 under Molly's and Lady Gregory's direction, with Molly playing Deirdre as Synge had wished. Yeats wrote to Miss Horniman on 15 January 1910, 'It is, as Synge left it, a rather loosely jointed rather monotonous play with some moments of magnificent tragedy' (NLI); it was published by Cuala in July 1910. Meanwhile, on 11 November 1909, *The Tinker's Wedding* received its first production, in London at His Majesty's Theatre, under the auspices of Beerbohm Tree's Afternoon Theatre Company; Synge would have enjoyed the irony of seeing Mona Limerick (Mrs Payne) performing the May-struck young tinker woman Sarah Casey.

But controversy continued to surround his work. In September 1910 Yeats wrote an angry letter (TCD) to Synge's brother Edward, withdrawing his introduction to the four-volume collected works being published by George Roberts of Maunsel, who insisted on including the *Manchester Guardian* essays against Synge's wishes. The introduction, 'a eulogy upon your brother's genius', was published finally by the Cuala Press. A year later, the company finally toured the United States, where *The Playboy of the Western World* landed them all in court, defended by John Quinn.

By then Synge had become part of Yeats's mythology; in a lecture to raise funds for the Abbey Theatre after Miss Horniman's withdrawal of her subsidy, he spoke eloquently of his colleague in words (published in the *Manchester Guardian*, 15 November 1910) which serve as fitting conclusion to the letters of this complex, proud man: 'Noble art was always passionate art, and in Synge's passion asceticism, stoicism and ecstasy all came together.'

CHRONOLOGY

EDMUND JOHN MILLINGTON SYNGE

1871–1909

1871	16 Apr	Born, youngest child of John Hatch and Kathleen (Traill) Synge, at 2 Newtown Villas, Rathfarnham, Dublin.
1872	13 Apr	John Hatch Synge dies of smallpox.
	Summer	Mrs Synge moves to 4 Orwell Park, Rathgar, Dublin, next door to her mother, Mrs Anne Traill.
c. 1881		Irregular attendance at Mr Harricks's Classical and English School, 4 Upper Leeson Street, Dublin.
c. 1884		Irregular attendance for one year at Aravon House, Bray School.
1884–8		Private tutoring at home three times a week; regular Bible classes at Zion Church, Rathgar, supplemented by Mrs Synge.
c. 1885		First reads Darwin, and begins to doubt his mother's Evangelical theology.
1885	December	Joins the newly established Dublin Naturalists' Field Club.
1887	13 Oct	First violin lesson with Patrick J. Griffith, Dublin.
1888	18 June	Passes entrance examinations for Trinity College, Dublin.
1889	February	Attends first lectures at Trinity College where his tutor is his mother's cousin, Anthony Traill.
	November	Enrols in Royal Irish Academy of Music for classes in violin, musical theory, and composition.
	December	Informs his mother that he will no longer attend church, except during summers in County Wicklow.
1890	October	Following the death of her mother, Mrs Synge rents 31 Crosthwaite Park, Kingstown, next door to her daughter, Mrs Annie Stephens.
	Autumn	Takes third class in Little Go examinations at Trinity College; is certified by Royal Irish Academy of Music for advanced study in counterpoint with Sir Robert Stewart.
1891	January–March	Joins student orchestra at Academy; plays in first concert at Antient Concert Rooms, Dublin.
	Summer	Begins to study German privately.
	Autumn	Studies Hebrew and Irish at Trinity College.

1891	December	His cousin Florence Ross joins Mrs Synge's household after her mother's death.
1892	16 Mar	Awarded scholarship and medal in counterpoint at Academy.
	June	Takes first place in examinations in Hebrew and Irish at Trinity College.
	20 July–15 Sept	With Mrs Synge at Castle Kevin, Co. Wicklow.
	15 Dec	Awarded second class B.A. from Trinity College.
1893	28 Feb	Canvasses for anti-Home Rule petition.
	17 Apr	Arranges and publicizes piano recital by his cousin Mary Synge at Antient Concert Rooms, Dublin.
	Spring	His sonnet 'Glencullen' published in *Kottabos*, Trinity College.
	7–30 June	Resumes study of German with Herr Wespendorf.
	1–24 July	With Mrs Synge at Avonmore, Co. Wicklow.
	26 July	Leaves for London.
	29 July–21 Jan 1894	Lodges with von Eickens, Oberwerth, near Koblenz, Germany, while studying music.
1894	22 Jan–1 June	Lodges with Frau Süsser, Hanger Ring 16, Würzburg, while studying violin and piano.
	20–27 Mar	Holiday with von Eickens in Koblenz, returning by way of Frankfurt.
	April–May	Begins to write his first play (uncompleted), and turns from study of music to literature.
	1–12 June	Visits von Eickens in Koblenz.
	14 June	Returns to Dublin.
	3 July–5 Sept	With Mrs Synge at Castle Kevin, Wicklow, where Cherrie Matheson spends two weeks from 28 July as sketching companion for Florence Ross.
	30 Oct	Returns to Koblenz by way of London.
	3 Nov–31 Dec	Lodges with von Eickens while studying German and French.
1895	2 Jan	Lodges with M. Arbeau, 94 rue Lafayette, Paris X^e. Joins the Société Fraternelle d'Étudiants Protestants.
	10 Feb	Death of his aunt Jane Synge who leaves him a legacy of £500.
	1 Apr	Lodges with M. Peter, 2 rue Léopold-Robert, Paris XIVe.
	25 Apr	Enrols at Sorbonne in courses in modern French literature with A. E. Faguet and medieval literature with Petit de Julleville; starts course in general and comparative phonetics with Paul Passy at the École Pratique des Hautes-Études.
	3 June	Begins exchange of language lessons with Thérèse Beydon.

1895	28 June	Leaves Paris for Dublin by way of London.
	6 July–5 Sept	With Mrs Synge in Wicklow (Lough Dan, 5–31 July; Castle Kevin, 31 July–5 Sept); refuses to attend church.
	11 Nov	First lesson in Italian with Signor Morosini, Dublin.
1896	2 Jan	Leaves Kingstown for Paris by way of London.
	3 Jan–3 Feb	At Hôtel Corneille, 5 rue Corneille, Paris VIe. Italian lessons with Dr Meli.
	5 Feb–30 Apr	Studies art and Italian in Rome (5–7 Feb, Hotel Continental; 7–17 Feb, Pension Hayden; 17 Feb–30 Apr, lodges with Signor Conte Polloni, 73 via Aureliana). Sends reports to *Irish Times*.
	1 May–1 June	Studies in Florence; meets Maria Zdanowska and Hope Rea.
	3–29 June	At Hôtel de l'Univers, 9 rue Gay-Lussac, Paris V^e.
	9 June	Writes to Cherrie Matheson proposing marriage; is rejected.
	30 June–14 Sept	With Mrs Synge at Castle Kevin, Wicklow.
	21 Oct	His brother Samuel Synge leaves for China.
	26 Oct	Leaves Dublin for Paris by way of London.
	29 Oct–29 Dec	At Hôtel Corneille, Paris VIe. Meets Stephen MacKenna. Takes courses at Sorbonne on Petrarch with Emile Gebhart, on La Fontaine with Faguet, and on French literature with Petit de Julleville. Studies socialism, and joins an English debating society.
	21 Dec	Meets William Butler Yeats.
	29 Dec	Lodges again with M. Peter, 2 rue Léopold-Robert, XIVe.
1897	1 Jan	Present with Yeats at inaugural committee meeting of the Association Irlandaise at Maud Gonne's.
	6 Apr	Resigns from Association Irlandaise; studies spiritualism.
	13 May	Leaves Paris for Dublin by way of London.
	25 June–31 Aug	With Mrs Synge in Wicklow (Castle Kevin, 25 June–31 July; Casino, Avondale, August).
	11 Dec	Undergoes operation to remove swollen gland in his neck; writes about experience, 'Under Ether'.
1898	19 Jan	Leaves Dublin for Paris by way of London.
	23 Jan–22 Apr	At Hôtel St Malo, 2 rue d'Odessa, XIVe. Begins novel on nurses (unfinished). Meets Richard Best.
	18 Feb	Enrols at Sorbonne in course by d'Arbois de Jubainville on Irish and Homeric civilizations.
	2 Apr	Meets Margaret Hardon.
	22 Apr	Leaves Paris for Dublin.

1898	10 May–25 June	Visits Aran Islands for first time (10–24 May, Atlantic Hotel, Kilronan, Aranmore; 24 May–9 June, with Patrick McDonagh, Inishmaan; 9–25 June, Kilronan).
	27–29 June	Guest of Lady Gregory at Coole, with Yeats; visits Edward Martyn.
	2 July–2 Sept	With Mrs Synge at Castle Kevin.
	November	'A Story from Inishmaan' in *New Ireland Review* (Dublin).
	14 Nov	Leaves Dublin for Paris by way of London.
	18 Nov	Takes over Richard Best's room at 90 rue d'Assas, VIe, his permanent address in Paris until 1903; begins studying Breton.
1899	28 Jan	'Anatole Le Braz. A Breton Writer' in *Daily Express* (Dublin).
	3–16 Apr	Visits Quimper, Brittany.
	7 May	Leaves Paris for Dublin by way of London.
	12 May	Attends Irish Literary Theatre production of Yeats's *The Countess Cathleen* in Antient Concert Rooms, Dublin.
	1 June–5 Sept	With Mrs Synge at Castle Kevin.
	9 Sept	To Galway on way to Aran; visits Martin McDonagh.
	12 Sept–7 Oct	On Inishmaan, except for few final days on Inishmore.
	3 Nov	Leaves Dublin for Paris.
1900	22 Mar	'A Celtic Theatre' in *Freeman's Journal* (Dublin).
	23 May	Leaves Paris for Dublin.
	1 June–30 Aug	With Mrs Synge at Castle Kevin, where Rosie Calthrop is her guest.
	15 Sept–14 Oct	On Inishmaan except for a few days on Inishere.
	17 Oct	Returns to Kingstown from Galway.
	1 Nov	Returns to Paris.
1901	April	'The Last Fortress of the Celt' in *The Gael* (New York).
	6 May	Returns to Dublin.
	4 June–6 Sept	With Mrs Synge at Castle Kevin.
	14–20 Sept	With Lady Gregory and Yeats at Coole.
	21 Sept–19 Oct	On Aran (Inishmaan 21–30 Sept; Inishere 1–19 Oct).
	21 Oct	Attends Irish Literary Theatre production of Yeats's and Moore's *Diarmuid and Grania* and Hyde's *Casadh an tSugáin* at Gaiety Theatre, Dublin.
	26 Nov	Leaves Dublin for Paris by way of London with MS of *The Aran Islands*.

1902	14 Feb	Enrols at Sorbonne in course in Old Irish by d'Arbois de Jubainville.
	15 Mar	'La Vieille Littérature irlandaise' in *L'Européen* (Paris).
	April	Begins writing verse plays.
	17 May	Returns to Dublin from Paris.
	31 May	'Le Mouvement intellectuel irlandais' in *L'Européen*.
	7 June	Review of Lady Gregory's *Cuchulain of Muirthemne* in *The Speaker* (London).
	21 July–6 Sept	With Mrs Synge at Tomrilands, Co. Wicklow.
	6 Sept	'The Old and New in Ireland' in *The Academy and Literature* (London).
	8–13 Oct	With Lady Gregory and Yeats at Coole; shows them *Riders to the Sea* and *In the Shadow of the Glen*.
	14 Oct–8 Nov	On Inishere.
	23 Nov	Cherrie Matheson marries Kenneth Houghton.
	? 4 Dec	Sees W. G. Fay's company for the first time performing *The Laying of the Foundations*, *The Pot of Broth*, *Eilís agus an Bhean Déirce*, and *The Racing Lug* at Camden Street Hall, Dublin.
1903	9 Jan	Leaves Dublin for London.
	12 Jan	Lodges at 4 Handel Street, Russell Square; is introduced by Yeats and Lady Gregory to John Masefield, G. K. Chesterton, Arthur Symons, Pamela Colman Smith, and others.
	6–13 Mar	Crosses to Paris to give up his room at 90 rue d'Assas; spends time with James Joyce.
	18 Mar	Leaves London for Dublin.
	April	'An Autumn Night in the Hills' in *The Gael*.
	23 May	Completes one-act play, *When the Moon Has Set*.
	? June	'A Dream of Inishmaan' in *The Green Sheaf* (London).
	28 Aug–19 Sept	Lodges with Philly Harris, Mountain Stage, Glenbeigh, Co. Kerry.
	October	*Riders to the Sea* published in *Samhain* (Dublin).
	8–10 Oct	*In the Shadow of the Glen* produced, with *The King's Threshold*, by W. G. Fay's Irish National Theatre Society at Molesworth Hall.
1904	25–27 Feb	*Riders to the Sea*, with AE's *Deirdre*, produced by Irish National Theatre Society at Molesworth Hall.
	26 Feb–8 Mar	Ill in bed.
	March	'A Dream of Inishmaan' in *The Gael*.
	24 Mar	Leaves for London with players; stays at 4 Handel Street.

1904	26 Mar	*The Shadow of the Glen* and *Riders to the Sea* performed at matinée, Royalty Theatre, London.
	2 Apr	Review of d'Arbois de Jubainville's *The Irish Mythological Cycle*, translated by Richard Best, in *The Speaker*.
	30 Apr	Leaves London for Dublin.
	16–31 July	At Coole helping Lady Gregory revise her *Kincora*.
	1 Aug–1 Sept	With Philly Harris at Mountain Stage, Co. Kerry.
	17 Sept–1 Oct	Bicycles through North Mayo instead of returning to Aran.
	10 Oct	Lodges with Mrs Stewart, 15 Maxwell Road, Rathgar.
	31 Oct	Present with John Quinn from New York at first rehearsal in new Abbey Theatre.
	December	*The Shadow of the Glen* published in *Samhain* and privately published by John Quinn in New York.
	27 Dec	Opening of the Abbey Theatre; revival of *The Shadow of the Glen* on the 28th.
905	24 Jan	'An Impression of Aran' in *Manchester Guardian*.
	4–11 Feb	*The Well of the Saints* produced; Molly Allgood has a walk-on part.
	7 Feb	John Quinn copyrights *The Well of the Saints* in New York simultaneously with publication of theatre edition by Maunsel & Co. (Dublin).
	11 Feb	Letter to *United Irishman* over renewed controversy concerning *The Shadow of the Glen*.
	13 Feb	George Moore writes to the *Irish Times* praising *The Well of the Saints*.
	15 Feb	Moves back to Crosthwaite Park; 'The Oppression of the Hills' in *Manchester Guardian*.
	8 May	*The Shadow of the Glen* and *Riders to the Sea* published in Vigo edition by Elkin Mathews, London.
	3 June–3 July	Tours the Congested Districts of west of Ireland with Jack B. Yeats for *Manchester Guardian*; publishes 12 articles.
	7 Aug–16 Sept	Visits West Kerry (William Long, Ballyferriter), the Blasket Islands (Shawn Keane, 13–?27 Aug), and Mountain Stage.
	16–20 Sept	Attends policy meeting at Coole with Yeats, Lady Gregory.
	22 Sept	Company votes to become a limited company with Yeats, Lady Gregory, and JMS as directors; JMS, George Russell, and Fred Ryan authorized to draw up rules.

1905	20 Nov–12 Dec	In England, staying first with Edward Synge at Byfleet, Surrey. Company on tour 23–30 Nov to Oxford, Cambridge, and London; JMS joins them at Cambridge. In London, stays at Kenilworth Hotel from 26 Nov; meets Charles Ricketts and Charles Shannon.
1906	12 Jan	Max Meyerfeld's translation of *The Well of the Saints* performed at Deutsches Theater in Berlin.
	6 Feb	Lodges at 57 Rathgar Road.
	7 Feb	Karel Mušek's translation of *The Shadow of the Glen* performed at the Inchover Theatre in Prague.
	26–27 Feb	Accompanies players to Wexford; first public indication of his attachment to Molly Allgood.
	17 Mar	Accompanies players to Dundalk.
	23–30 Apr	Accompanies players on tour to Manchester, Liverpool, and Leeds.
	15 May	Accompanies players to Dundalk.
	26 May–9 July	Accompanies players on extensive tour to Cardiff, Glasgow, Aberdeen, Newcastle, Edinburgh, and Hull.
	9 July	Moves with Mrs Synge to Glendalough House, Glenageary, Kingstown.
	17–18 July	Joins Yeats, Lady Gregory, and W. G. Fay for policy meeting at Coole.
	24 July–4 Aug	Entertains Karel Mušek in Dublin.
	25 Aug–12 Sept	With Philly Harris, Mountain Stage, Kerry.
	Autumn	'The Vagrants of Wicklow' in *The Shanachie* (Dublin).
	30 Nov–14 Dec	Visits cousin Edward Synge in Byfleet, Surrey.
1907	26 Jan	First performance of *The Playboy of the Western World*, to unruly audiences for a week; theatre edition published by Maunsel.
	4 Feb–11 Mar	Ill at mother's home; Molly visits regularly.
	6 Mar	*The Playboy* copyrighted by John Quinn in New York.
	March	'The People of the Glens' in *The Shanachie*.
	?28 April	*The Aran Islands* published by Maunsel and Elkin Mathews.
	9 May	'At a Wicklow Fair. The Place and the People' in *Manchester Guardian*.
	11 May–17 June	Company on tour to Glasgow, Cambridge, Birmingham, Oxford, and London, performing *The Playboy* in Cambridge, Oxford, and London.
	30 May	Leaves Dublin to visit Jack Yeats in Devon before joining company in London on 8 June; stays at 4 Handel Street.
	17 June	Returns to Dublin with players.

1907	Summer	'In West Kerry' in *The Shanachie*.
	28 June–28 July	In Glencree, Molly also except for 11–23 July.
	1 July	'A Landlord's Garden in County Wicklow' in *Manchester Guardian*.
	22 Aug	*The Shadow of the Glen* produced at National Theatre, Prague.
	13–26 Sept	In Elpis Nursing Home for removal of swollen glands in neck.
	Autumn	'In West Kerry. The Blasket Islands' in *The Shanachie*.
	12–16 Oct	Visits Kerry, asthma attack forces return to Kingstown.
	Winter	'In West Kerry. To Puck Fair' in *The Shanachie*.
	23 Dec	*The Tinker's Wedding* published by Maunsel.
1908	13 Jan	The Fays resign from company.
	24 Jan	'Good Pictures in Dublin. The New Municipal Gallery' in *Manchester Guardian*.
	2 Feb	Takes rooms at 47 York Road, Rathmines, in preparation for marriage to Molly.
	26 Feb	Directs Lady Gregory's translation of Sudermann's *Teja*.
	4 Apr	Directs Lady Gregory's translation of Molière, *The Rogueries of Scapin*.
	30 Apr–6 July	To Elpis Nursing Home for abdominal operation 5 May; inoperable tumour discovered.
	14 May	Revised version of *The Well of the Saints* performed, with costumes and setting designed by Charles Ricketts; Molly playing Molly Byrne.
	6 July–13 Aug	Convalesces at his sister's home, Silchester House, Kingstown.
	6 Oct	Leaves Dublin for Koblenz by way of London.
	8 Oct–5 Nov	With the von Eickens, Koblenz.
	26 Oct	Mrs Synge dies.
	10 Dec	'In Wicklow. On the Road' in *Manchester Guardian*.
1909	2 Feb	Enters Elpis Nursing Home.
	24 Mar	Dies.
	5 June	*Poems and Translations* published by Cuala Press, Dublin.
1910	13 Jan	*Deirdre of the Sorrows* at Abbey Theatre, with Molly as Deirdre.
	5 July	*Deirdre of the Sorrows* published by Cuala Press.
	22 Nov	*The Works of John M. Synge*, 4 vols., published by Maunsel.

INDEX OF RECIPIENTS

GENERAL INDEX

JMS = J.M. Synge